国际海关新视野

上 海 海 关◎编译

中国海关出版社

图书在版编目（CIP）数据

国际海关新视野/上海海关编译．—北京：中国海关出版社，2012.10
（“关务通·双语系列”丛书）
ISBN 978-7-80165-918-7

Ⅰ.①国… Ⅱ.①上… Ⅲ.①海关—研究—世界—汉、英 Ⅳ.①F745

中国版本图书馆 CIP 数据核字（2012）第 243285 号

国际海关新视野
GUOJI HAIGUAN XINSHIYE

编　　译：上海海关
总 策 划：谭宁
策划团队：刘倩　马超　冯楠　钟刘
责任编辑：刘倩
特约编辑：张幸天
责任监制：王岫岩
出版发行：中国海关出版社
社　　址：北京市朝阳区东四环南路甲 1 号　　邮政编码：100023
网　　址：www.hgcbs.com.cn；www.hgbookvip.com
编 辑 部：01065194242-7554（电话）　　01065194234（传真）
发 行 部：01065194221/4238/4246（电话）　　01065194233（传真）
社办书店：01065195616/5127（电话/传真）　　01065194262/63（邮购电话）
北京市建国门内大街 6 号海关总署东配楼一层
印　　刷：北京京都六环印刷厂　　经　　销：新华书店
开　　本：710mm×1000mm　1/16
印　　张：16.75　　字　　数：256 千字
版　　次：2012 年 12 月第 1 版
印　　次：2012 年 12 月第 1 次印刷
书　　号：ISBN 978-7-80165-918-7
定　　价：60.00 元

前　言

为适应海关国际合作形势的发展与深化，满足海关现代化改革发展对海关对外交往与合作的现实需求，努力落实“四好”总体要求，上海海关在外事工作的实践基础上，借助海关关际合作、与商界交流合作等平台，介绍和解析当前国际海关工作的热点与难点，呈现国际海关的全新视野，以期与广大读者共同探询国际合作与海关业务改革发展的契合点，更好地务实推进海关国际合作，为海关改革与现代化建设服务。

本书共分为“供应链管理”“海关三大技术支柱”“国际海关最佳实践”三大板块。全书采用中英文对照形式，内容上既涵盖了供应链安全方面的常见问题、主要项目和最新技术，也有对海关估价、归类和原产地三大技术领域的知识普及和难点探究，同时亦关注全球海关所日益面临的非传统职能的改革与挑战，分享国际性战略项目在各国海关的推广及其实施经验。

“合抱之木，生于毫末；九层之台，起于累土。”我们将一如既往地遵循求真、务实的宗旨，本着严谨、踏实的态度，不断收集、编译有关国际海关的先进经验和最佳做法，以适应海关改革发展与国际做法接轨的需求，开拓更加广阔的交流平台。

本书由上海海关关员翻译。由于时间仓促，水平有限，书中不足之处，还望各位读者批评指正。

Preface

This book is published to adapt to the development and enhancement of the international cooperation between Customs and to fulfill the demand of China Customs' modernization reform for customs international exchange and cooperation, as well as making great efforts to achieve Four Goals of safeguarding national gateway, providing quality service, preventing potential risks and building qualified forces. On the practical basis of foreign affairs of Shanghai Customs, taking advantage of the Customs – to – Customs and Customs – to – Business cooperation platforms, the book introduces and analyses the international hot points and difficulties for Customs work currently, presenting a new vision from the international Customs community. With this book, we hope to discuss with the readers about the corresponding point between Customs international cooperation and the development and reform of Customs business, to carry forward Customs international cooperation in a better and pragmatic way, and to serve Customs reform and modernization.

This book includes 3 parts, Supply Chain Management, Three Technical Pillars of Customs and International Customs Best Practices, presenting bilingually. This book covers frequently asked questions, major programmes and cutting edge technologies involving supply chain security, general knowledge and difficult points of Customs valuation, classification and rules of origin, and it focuses on the non – traditional challenges and reform for Customs globally as well, sharing practical experience of Customs worldwide in implementing international strategic programs.

Just as the saying goes, "A huge tree must grow from a tiny sprout, and a nine – storied terrace must be built upon its lowly base. " We will always follow the truth – seeking and pragmatic purpose, bearing a rigorous, pragmatic attitude, and constantly collect and translate, cutting edge experience and best practices of foreign Customs in order to meet demands of China Customs development and reform for getting connections with international standards, as well as to broaden the communication platform.

All the translations are done by officers of Shanghai Customs. Owing to the limitation of time and our abilities, please correct us on some inappropriate parts in this book.

目　录

第一编　供应链管理

第二编　海关三大技术支柱

第三编　国际海关最佳实践

第一编

供应链管理

供应链管理常见问题

（原文摘自《供应链安全指南》，世界银行编写）

（办公室外事办　庄硕　冯赟　译）

一、供应链安全是什么？

“供应链安全”可以被定义为用于解决针对供应链的威胁，以及针对公民和有序社会经济、社会和身体健康方面的相关威胁的包含项目、制度、程序、技术和解决方案的一个概念。

供应链中有许多风险，其中大部分属于犯罪活动和恐怖主义威胁。本文对自然灾害和“天灾”的讨论将是有限的，但必须指出的是，本文提到的许多预防、减轻和恢复措施对这些问题也是最有效的。

目前在国际贸易和运输方面最重要的问题是犯罪活动。犯罪威胁包括以下方面：一是货物盗窃；二是运输工具盗窃；三是走私和偷渡；四是逃税；五是攻击某一运输节点。

供应链安全方面的恐怖主义威胁可分为以下几类：一是将货物用作武器；二是将集装箱用作武器；三是将集装箱用作运输武器、炸药、生化或放射污染物及其前体的工具；四是将运输工具用作武器；五是利用运输工具进行传递；六是产业间谍或破坏。

恐怖活动的目标包括：一是破坏、摧毁或利用供应链、物流系统、基础设施与信息管理系统；二是造成人员伤亡；三是造成经济危害和损失；四是导致人们的自由遭到限制并且失去安康感。

为有效应对这些威胁及其后果，供应链安全有如下五大支柱：

意识：识别/理解威胁，评估薄弱点，确定潜在的影响和后果；

预防：侦测、阻止和减轻威胁；

保护：保护人民和关键基础设施，使财产免受犯罪侵害；

回应：管理和协调对犯罪行为或其他紧急情况的应对措施；

恢复：犯罪行为或其他紧急情况发生后，组织力量恢复运营。

二、供应链安全中的主要成员是谁？

表1－1描述了供应链安全的主要成员在供应链当中的角色：

表1－1　供应链安全的主要成员及其担当的角色

角色	供应链参与者
	第三方物流提供商
	买方（收货方、进口商）
便利交易	买方代理
	货运代理或无船公共承运人
	报关公司
	船运代理
运输任务（对货物或集装箱的物理移动）	集装箱空箱站经营者
	仓库/集装箱货运站经营者
	多式联运经营者（如公路—铁路，公路—驳船，铁路—驳船）
	卡车司机与多式联运（短途，长途）
	铁路承运人
	驳船经营者
	海运承运人
	港口码头经营者
	其他港口服务经营者
授权/管理	海关与移民管理局
	进口/出口许可证管理局
	农业、卫生、兽医管理部门
	港口管理部门
	进出口统计部门
	其他（商会，领事馆等）

续表

经费筹措	银行（卖方通知银行，买方或开证银行）
	保险提供商（运输保险）

三、了解供应链安全为何重要？

许多国家的政府和企业可能会提出这样一个问题："供应链安全与我有关吗？"不同群体对此有不同的答案。

对各国政府来说，绝大多数已签署了《世界海关组织（WCO）全球贸易安全与便利标准框架》（以下简称《标准框架》）。该框架要求各国政府实施国家供应链安全计划，其中包括技术、认证、相互承认认证、风险管理和提前货物信息（ACI）。这意味着大多数国家的政府都致力于发展自己的国家计划。因此，作为世界海关组织的缔约国政府，理解《标准框架》的支柱和要求，并着手制订切实计划、实施国家供应链安全计划，非常重要。

世界海关组织为此提供了多项工具，本文将提到这些工具作为参考。

在实施国家供应链安全计划后，相互承认其他现有的计划是下一个"热点"问题。这就需要相关国家从政治上作出努力，往往事关时间，特别是国家间的互信。由于只有少数几个国家签订了相互承认国家供应链安全认证协议，相互承认在本文中作为一个尚待解决的问题进行讨论。尽管存在这些问题，但没有必要再搞创造发明，这是因为，诸如《标准框架》所建议的工具提供了一个在国际上多边的公认平台，如果得到充分执行，将有助于顺利推动彼此兼容与承认。

企业方面，则另有动因。竞争力，行业需求，以及越来越多的发生在外包地点的意外事故，如盗窃、盗版和自然灾害都引发了安全意识的提升。尤其是在风险管理方面。今天，商业领域对于安全的投资集中于两个方面：一是在发生灾难或其他破坏性事件时，造成了商业运作中断时须保持业务连续性；二是减少盗窃/犯罪。同样重要的是，企业会对参加各种国家或国际项目的成本和利益二者之间进行权衡。

对企业来说，越来越多的是“如果你不参与其中，你就出局了”，意思是说，虽然大多数情况下供应链安全计划是自愿参加的，但如果没有参加，该公司就有可能被排除在国际贸易与货运之外，或是可能会发现自己与参与计划的竞争者相比处于不利的位置。

四、什么是供应链安全管理？

根据海提萨2009年的看法，供应链安全管理涉及首尾相接地系统地打击供应链犯罪的所有流程、技术和利用的资源。每一项供应链安全管理措施的首要目标不是防止、侦查犯罪，就是犯罪事件发生后尽快复原。单一的供应链安全管理措施通常分为五类：货物、设施、人力资源、信息技术和管理系统。典型的供应链犯罪包括盗窃、走私、伪造、破坏、获取经济利益、恐怖主义破坏以及任何形式的欺诈和腐败行为（具体犯罪定义要参照国家和国际规定）。

供应链安全管理可以定义为运用政策、程序和技术来保护供应链资产免受盗窃、损坏或恐怖主义侵害，并防止未经授权的走私货物、人员或大规模杀伤性武器进入供应链（克劳斯与麦盖瑞，2004年）。

五、什么是风险管理？

风险管理的重点是确定和实施措施来限制风险暴露或发生负面或不良结果的事件的可能性。在贸易方面，风险管理的重点是系统地确定最有可能违反海关法律法规的进出口和对国家安全造成的最大风险。海关当局凭借多层次方法，使用多种风险管理战略，能够识别和定位风险最集中的领域，并据此相应地分配资源。各类货物安全项目一般通过以下措施实施类似的风险管理战略：一是从各种渠道收集数据内容和详细货物信息；二是利用基于规则的计算机程序和海关布控团队分析和评估风险；三是授权行动，如进行非侵入式/人工查验或扣押；四是跟踪和监测风险管理过程和结果（拉杜巴，2005年）。

六、什么是多层次方法?

供应链安全多层次方法背后的假设是，以同样数额的资金仅投入两个或两个以上的安全层，相比一个安全层能够实现“更好的安全结果”。任何节点或运输环节的不安全因素会损害整个供应链。因此，确保供应链安全的努力依赖于多层次安全的概念。这种方法在系统内建立了有余量的和额外的保护措施，因此某一层次的安全问题可以在下一层次得到解决。例如，在实际情况下，多层次方法可以由以下组合构成：一是提前出示货物信息的监管要求；二是实施风险管理；三是倾向于使用非侵入式查验设备；四是经认证的经营者计划（“被信赖的经营者”认证计划）。在多层次供应链安全中，每一层都能应对其他执行层的潜在漏洞，从而使彼此的结合比任意单一层更能确保安全。

七、什么是相互承认?

相互承认是指各个国家接受通用安全参数与彼此认证。目前，美国海关商界反恐伙伴项目实现了与约旦、新西兰和加拿大的互认。美国海关和边境保护局与欧盟已经制定了相互承认的路线图，计划到2009年年底实现相互承认海关商界反恐伙伴项目与欧盟经认证的经营者项目。

八、港口/货运界的作用是什么?

港口/货运界是供应链安全中最重要的参与者之一。这基于两方面的事实，一是它们代表供应链中的节点，二是它们使用专用系统捕捉并传播相关的货物数据。《国际船舶和港口设施保安规则》（ISPS码）早于其他全球性计划得到通过并实施，这证实了它们的重要性。

与此相关的是，港口/货运界通常是较早采纳各种计划的参与者之一，因为在这样一个竞争很激烈的领域，它们要实施新措施以获得竞争优势，在经济环境困难的时候尤为如此。

尽管这些参与者非常重要，但所有国际贸易成员在供应链安全中照例都是重要的，因为链条的强度取决于最薄弱的一环。

九、供应链安全现状如何?

供应链犯罪与供应链安全并非是新现象。犯罪和安全都有很长的历史。海盗、土匪和走私一直影响我们的贸易路线，而企业和政府一直在争论采取何种安全措施，需要安全到何种程度，以及最重要的，谁来承担安保费用。

政府的传统职能更关注于税收征集与保护，主要是海关在跨境流通上的任务；调查重大盗窃案，主要是警察的任务；处置盗版产品，海关和警察的共同任务。而且一般国家只有少部分约束性法规，且主要针对危险货物运输和储存，以及航空运输。如今，各个部门执行的供应链安全项目或计划为数众多，往往缺乏协作。政府与企业之间、不同的政府机构之间、不同的国家以及不同的大洲之间都存在计划和目标差异，需要国际社会参与以拼凑出一个协同的标准。其中的一个例子是《标准框架》。

十、供应链安全管理经历了怎样的发展?

诸如海盗之类的供应链犯罪可以追溯到3000多年前。最早记载的海盗行径始于一个称为“海洋人”的组织。这些海上袭击者生活在公元前1200年左右，他们驶往地中海东岸，造成政治动乱，并中断了所有贸易。在非洲东海岸，我们可以看到，这种状况至今没有多少改变。

“9·11”恐怖主义袭击已成为供应链安全管理的标志性时刻。在此之前，政府的重点是贸易便利化、依法纳税以及京都公约推行的大环境所要求的协调贸易规则和实践。“9·11”事件后，全球贸易经历了极端的变化，注重点从贸易便利与协调转变为安全和反恐措施。这一急剧变化从整体上修改了供应链安全规则。

2001年9月11日前，货物运输安全讨论的重点是控制盗窃，减少毒品等违禁品、非法移民、出口被窃车辆与建筑设备。9月11日后，货物运

输安全的最高定义由防盗转变为防止供应链破坏。（李和沃尔夫，2003 年）

新焦点的部分要素包括：一是防止生化物质侵入产品；二是防止非法商品混入货物；三是防止非法货物或人员与货物掉包；四是防止货物被利用为武器。（赖斯和卡尼亚托，2003 年）

这一新的以安全为导向的反恐机制也向供应链管理提出了新的要求。过去，安全仅限于"企业内部"，现在安全的观念已扩大到整个供应链。由于相互依存的世界贸易，一个国家或区域的特定重点方式已经扩大为全球重点方式。

"9·11"恐怖袭击说明了供应链中的相互依存不仅存在于贸易伙伴之间，还存在于涉及货物流通和运输基础设施的政府机构。今天的贸易运行环境也要求有新的组织能力。具体来说公司需要与致力于使供应链更安全的政府机构建立新的关系。同样地，供应商与客户应建立更深层次的关系，以共同创造一个更加安全的网络。来自内部的最大组织挑战可能是使个人切实理解目前存在的相互依存关系和业务需要。（赖斯和卡尼亚托，2003 年）

由于这些新的安全要求和政府与企业间相互依存的需要，各国政府、国际组织和一些协会发起了各种安全倡议，包括：一是 24 小时舱单规则；二是海关—商界反恐伙伴关系；三是美国的集装箱安全倡议；四是拉丁美洲的安全商务伙伴计划；五是经认证的经营者项目；六是《标准框架》；七是运输资产保护协会；八是全球性的《国际船舶和港口设施保安规则》。

所有这些倡议的共同目标是在便利全球贸易无缝流动的同时，把供应链遭破坏的风险降到最低。

十一、目前有哪些强制要求？

目前世界上共有 8 个强制性供应链安全项目，包括：一是 2003 年美国的提前货物信息计划，即 24 小时舱单规则；二是 2007 年日本、加拿大和墨西哥采用的提前货物信息计划；三是 2009 年到 2010 年美国采取的"10 + 2"提前货物信息计划；四是 2009 年到 2011 年欧盟采取的到达前/离境前提前货物信息规则；五是 2009 年中国采取的提前货物信息规则；

六是2004年的《国际船舶和港口设施保安规则》。

100%扫描规则将根据美国法律在2012年实施。

十二、提前货物信息计划的作用是什么?

除了《国际船舶和港口设施保安规则》，唯一的强制性供应链安全计划就是提前货物信息计划。该信息是由所有供应链的参与方提供，使海关当局能够作出有情报根据的布控与干预决定，将资源应用于高风险的问题和货物。提前货物信息计划是所有供应链安全计划的基石之一，最相关的例子是美国24小时舱单规则、美国的“10+2”要求，以及欧盟、中国和墨西哥的计划。

十三、供应链安全倡议强制实行后有哪些要求?

首先，许多港口已经实施《国际船舶和港口设施保安规则》，这一规则详尽地解释了供应链安全的基本知识。一般情况下，供应链安全计划是自愿的，不是强制性的，但随着越来越多的港口和物流运营商参与这些计划和倡议，因此，越来越少的“外人”将受到更严格的监控和处理。因此，如果某机构没有经过供应链安全认证而其他竞争对手都获得了认证，该组织将受到系统性的监控。此外，贸易合作伙伴将“不选择”未经认证的伙伴。这意味着，如果一个企业希望保有国际贸易供应链中的一席之地，自愿遵守的计划最终会成为一种标准做法和必要条件。

一个很好例子是如今为了与某些客户做生意，许多合同要求公司获得ISO9001认证。事实上，美国和欧洲的许多零售商已要求其贸易与物流伙伴提供供应链安全认证作为继续与他们做生意的必要条件。

十四、从监管的角度看，供应链安全处于何种位置?

全球范围内，许多国家实施了供应链安全项目，最著名的两个是美国的海关商界反恐伙伴项目和欧盟的经认证的经营者项目。此外，最引人注目并最具有争议的法律是《美国安全港口法案》，该法案要求到 2012 年，所有输美货物在出发前 100% 经过集装箱扫描。

一个最重要的“监管”（这里的“监管”不是严格意义的监管）模式工具是《标准框架》。由于绝对多数的世界海关组织的成员已签署，事实上，这一框架是全球供应链安全方法的最佳共识基础。

Frequently Asked Questions About Supply Chain Management

(Obtained from "*Supply Chain Security Guide*", The World Bank)

(Translated by Zhuang Shuo and Feng Yun, Foreign Affairs Office of General Office)

1. WHAT IS SCS?

The term "supply chain security" can be defined as a concept which encompasses the programs, systems, procedures, technology and solutions applied to address threats to the supply chain and the related threats to the economic, social and physical well – being of citizens and organized society.

There are many different threats to the supply chain which fall primarily into the categories of criminal activities and terrorist threats. The discussion of natural disasters and "acts of God" will be limited in this document, however it must be noted that many of the preventative, mitigating and recovery measures noted here are most relevant for those issues as well.

Criminal activities are by far the most important problem in international trade and transport. The criminal threats cover a wide range of aspects:

- Cargo theft
- Conveyance vehicle theft
- Goods and human smuggling
- Tax and duty evasion
- Attack on a transportation node.

The terrorist threats to SCS can be categorized as follows:

- Use of the cargo as a weapon
- Use of the container as a weapon
- Use of the container as a delivery mechanism or to move weapons, explosive, biological and radiological contaminants and their precursors
- Use of the conveyance vehicle as a weapon
- Use of the conveyance vehicle as a delivery mechanism
- Industrial espionage, sabotage.

With the goal of the terrorist activities being:

- Damage, destroy, or exploit the supply chain, logistics systems, infrastructure and information management systems
- Cause victims and casualties
- Cause economic harm and cost
- Results of reduced freedoms and loss of the feeling of well – being.

In order to effectively counter these threats and their consequences there are 5 key pillars to SCS, these are:

- Awareness: identify / understand threats, assess vulnerabilities, determine potential impacts and consequences
- Prevention: detect, deter and mitigate threats
- Protection: safeguard people, critical infrastructure, property from criminal acts
- Response: manage and coordinate the response to criminal acts or other emergencies
- Recovery: manage efforts to restore operations after criminal acts or other emergencies.

2. Who are the principal players in SCS?

The table below describes the supply chain participation roles of the principal players in SCS.

Role	Supply chain participants
Role	Third Party Logistics Provider (3PL)
	Buyer (consignee, importer)
Transaction Facilitation	Buying Agent
	Freight Forwarder or NVOCC
	Customs Broker
	Ship's Agent
Transport Task (physical movement of cargo / container)	Empty Container Depot Operator
	Warehouse/Container Freight Station Operator
	Multi - modal Terminal Operator (e. g. road - rail, road - barge, rail - barge)
	Trucker/Intermodal freight transport (short - haul, long - haul)
	Rail Carrier
	Barge Operator
	Ocean Carrier
	Port Terminal Operator
	Other Port Service Operators
Authorizing/ regulatory	Customs & Immigration Authority
	Import/Export Licensing Authority
	Agriculture, Sanitary, and Veterinary Authority
	Port Authority
	Import/Export Statistical Agency
	Others (Chambers of Commerce, Consulates, etc.)
Financing	Banks (Seller's or Advising Bank, Buyer's or Issuing bank)
	Insurance Provider (Carriage Insurance)

3. Why is it important to know about SCS?

Many governments and many players in the private sector may ask the question: "How does SCS affect me?" The answer is different for these groups.

For the governments, the majority has signed the World Customs Organization (WCO) SAFE Framework of Standards (FoS) which requires the implementation of a national supply chain security program, which includes elements such as technology, certification and mutual recognition thereof, risk management and Advance Cargo Information (ACI). This implies that most governments are committed to develop their own national program. Thus, for WCO signatory governments it is key to understand the pillars and requirements of the WCO SAFE FoS and to start making the necessary plans to implement a national SCS program.

The WCO offers many tools to accomplish this and we point to these tools throughout this document as references.

After the implementation of a national SCS program, mutual recognition with other existing programs is the next "hot" issue. This requires a political effort on the part of the national bodies concerned and is often a matter of time and especially trust in the nation – to – nation relationship. Mutual recognition is discussed in this document as one of the as yet unresolved issues since only few states have signed agreements mutually recognizing the national supply chain security certification of one another. Despite such problems, there is however no need to reinvent the wheel, since, for example, the WCO SAFE Framework of Standards' (WCO SAFE FoS) proposed tools offer an internationally, thus multilateral, accepted platform, which will help to facilitate downstream mutual compatibility and recognition – if adequately implemented.

For the private sector the motivations are different. Competitive forces, industry demands, and an increasing number of incidents such as theft, piracy and natural disasters at outsourced locations have all caused a spike in the awareness level of security. This is especially true in the area of risk management. Today the business case for investing in security is focused on two areas: 1) business continuity in the event of a catastrophe or other disruptive event causing a discontinuity in business operations and 2) the reduction of theft/crime. It is also important that the private sector weighs the costs against the benefits of participating or not in the various national and international programs.

For the private sector, more and more it is becoming: "If you are not 'in', you are 'out'", meaning that although SCS programs are voluntary in most cases, if you are not participating, the company runs the risk of being left out of the international trade and transport process or may find itself at a competitive disadvantage compared to competitors who are "in".

4. What is Supply Chain Security Management (SCSM)?

According to Hintsa (2009), SCSM covers all processes, technologies and resources exploited in a systematic way to fight against end – to – end supply chain crime. The primary goal of each single SCSM measure is either to prevent a crime, to detect a crime, or to recover from a crime incident in the fastest possible time. Single SCSM measures fall typically into one of the following five categories: cargo, facility, human resources, information technology, and management systems. The typical supply chain crime includes theft, smuggling, counterfeit, sabotage for financial gain, terrorism for destruction, and any type of fraud and corruption (the detailed crime definitions subject to national and international regulations).

SCSM can be defined as the application of policies, procedures, and technology to protect supply chain assets from theft, damage, or terrorism and to prevent the introduction of unauthorized contraband, people, or weapons of mass destruction into the supply chain (Closs & McGarrel, 2004).

5. What is Risk Management?

Risk management focuses on identifying and implementing measures to limit exposure to risk, or the likelihood of an event occurring with a negative or unwanted outcome. In trade, the focus of risk management is to systematically identify imports and exports that represent the greatest risk of noncompliance with

Customs laws and regulations, and the greatest risk to national security and safety. By using multiple risk management strategies in a layered approach Customs authorities can identify and target those areas that pose the greatest risk, and allocate resources accordingly. Cargo security programs generally implement similar risk management strategies based on the following: collecting data elements and detailed shipment information from a variety of sources; analyzing and assessing risk using rules – based computer programs and Customs targeting teams; prescribing action, such as undertaking non – intrusive or physical inspection or seizure; and tracking and monitoring the risk management process and its outcomes (Laduba, 2005).

6. What is a Layered Approach?

The assumption behind the layered approach to supply chain security is that by having two or more security layers one can achieve " better security outcomes", than by investing the same amount of money into just one layer. Compromised security at any node or transport link in the supply chain can prejudice the entire chain. Hence, attempts to secure the supply chain have relied on the concept of layered security. Such an approach builds redundancy and additional protection measures into the system, so that security breaches at one level can be addressed in a subsequent level. For example, in practical terms, a layered approach could consist of a combination of the following: 1) an Advance Cargo Information (ACI) regulatory requirement, 2) Implementation of risk management approach, 3) Preferable use of NII equipment, 4) Authorized Economic Operator program (a "trusted economic operator" certification program). With multiple layers of supply chain security, each layer addresses the potential weaknesses of the other implemented layers thus ensuring that the combination of elements will ensure security in a much better way than any layer on its own.

7. What is Mutual Recognition?

Mutual recognition is the acceptance of common security parameters and the acceptance of that certification by various countries. Currently the US C – TPAT program shares mutual recognition with the countries of Jordan, New Zealand and Canada. The US Customs and Border Protection and the European Union have already developed a mutual recognition roadmap that envisages achieving mutual recognition of the C – TPAT Program and the EU AEO program before the end of 2009.

8. What is the role of the Port/Cargo community?

The Port/Cargo community is one of the most important key players in supply chain security. This is both in terms of the fact that these represent nodal points in the supply chain and that relevant cargo data is captured and disseminated via systems used specifically by these players that are in this community. Evidence of their importance is demonstrated by the early adoption and implementation of the International Ship and Port Facility (ISPS) Code, even before other global measures were undertaken.

It is relevant that the port/cargo community is often one of the early adopters as they implement new measures in order to gain a competitive edge in a sector where the competition is fierce, especially when there is a difficult economic climate.

Inevitably, although these players are among the most significant, all international trade players are important in SCS as it is clear that the chain is only as strong as its weakest link.

9. What is the current situation of Supply Chain Security?

Supply chain crime and SCS are not new phenomena. There is a long history of crime and security. Pirates, bandits and smugglers have always affected our trade routes while the private and public sectors have always argued over what type of security should be implemented, how much security is needed, and most importantly, who should pay for the security.

The role of government agencies traditionally has focused more on issues with respect to revenue collection and protection, especially Customs for border crossings; major theft investigation, especially police; pirated products, Customs and police, and traditionally nations have set only a few binding regulations, mainly regarding dangerous goods transport and storage, and aviation. Today there are numerous SCS programs or schemes that are being set into motion by multiple sectors, often without collaboration. Differences in schemes and objectives between governments and businesses, different government offices or ministries, different countries, and different continents, will all require the involvement of the international community in order to piece together a collaborative standard. An example of a collaborative standard is outlined in the WCO SAFE Framework of Standards.

10. How did Supply Chain Security Management (SCSM) evolve?

Supply chain crime, as piracy, can be traced back over 3,000 years. The earliest documented act of piracy was pioneered by a group called "The Sea Peoples". These seafaring raiders lived around 1200 B. C. and sailed to the eastern shores of the Mediterranean, causing political unrest, and disruption in all trade. Not much has changed, as we can observe today along the Eastern shores of Africa.

The terrorist attacks of 9/11 have become a defining moment for SCSM. Until then, the focus of governments was on trade facilitation, tax compliance, and the harmonization of trade rules and practices as a result of the climate imposed by the Kyoto Convention. After 9/11, global trade has experienced an extreme change in the current paradigm from facilitation and harmonization to security and anti – terrorist measures. This drastic change has modified the approach to the overall SCS discipline.

Prior to Sept. 11, 2001, most discussions of freight transportation security focused on controlling theft and reducing contrabands such as drugs, illegal immigrants, and the export of stolen cars and construction equipment. After Sept. 11, the highest – order definition of freight security changed from theft – proof to tamperproof (Lee & Wolfe, 2003).

Some elements of this new focus are:

- Not allowing any biological or chemical agent to be introduced to the product
- Not allowing any illegal commodity to be intermingled with the shipment
- Not allowing the replacement of the product with an illegal commodity or person
- Not allowing the shipment to be used as a weapon. (Rice & Caniato, 2003).

This new security oriented approach toward anti – terrorism also implied new requirements in supply chain management. The perception of security as limited to "inside the company" has been expanded to the entire supply chain. A country or regional specific focus approach has been expanded to a global focus due to the interdependencies of world trade.

The 9/11 attacks dramatically illustrated the interdependence that exists in the supply network not just among the trading partners, but also with the government agencies involved in the flow of goods and the transportation infrastructure. Today's operating environment also calls for new organizational capabilities. Specifically companies will need to forge new relationships with those government agencies that are now working to make supply networks more secure. Similarly, deeper relationships need to be developed with suppliers and customers to co - create a more secure network. Internally, the biggest organizational challenge may be to give individuals a solid understanding of the interdependencies and operational imperatives that now exist (Rice & Caniato, 2003).

As a result of these new security requirements and government - business interdependency needs, security initiatives have been launched by governments, international organizations and sometimes associations, including the following:

- 24 hour manifest rule
- C - TPAT
- Container Security Initiative (CSI) in the USA
- Business Alliance for Secure Commerce (BASC) in Latin America
- Authorized Economic Operator (AEO) program
- WCO SAFE Framework of Standards (WCO)
- Transported Asset Protection Association (TAPA)
- International Ship and Port Facility Security (ISPS) Code at a global level.

The common denominator in all these initiatives is the objective of minimizing the risk of any disruption in the supply chain, while facilitating the seamless flow of trade goods globally.

11. What is compulsory today?

There are only 8 live compulsory SCS programs implemented in the world:

- The ACI "24 hour manifest rule" to USA (2003)
- The ACI rules to Japan, Canada and Mexico (2007)
- The ACI 10 + 2 rule (2009 - 10) to USA
- The Pre - arrival and Pre - departure ACI rule (EU) (2009 - 2011)
- The ACI rules to China (2009)
- The ISPS Code (2004)

The 100% scanning rule, by US law, will be implemented as from 2012.

12. What is the role of Advance Cargo Information (ACI)?

Beyond the ISPS Code, the only other compulsory SCS components hinge on Advance Cargo Information (ACI). The information is provided by all the actors in the supply chain, to allow Customs authorities to make informed targeting and intervention decisions with dedication of resources to the high risk issues and cargoes. The ACI requirement is one of the cornerstones in any SCS program with the most relevant examples being the US 24 – hour manifest rule, the US 10 + 2 requirement and the EU, China and Mexico.

13. What is required when a SCS initiative becomes compulsory?

First and foremost, many ports have already implemented the ISPS Code which goes a long way in explaining the basics of SCS. In general, SCS programs are voluntary and not compulsory, but as more and more ports and logistics operators enter the programs and initiatives, there are less and less "outsiders" who will therefore be subject to more intense controls and treatment. Thus, if an organization does not become SCS certified and the rest of the competitors do get certified, this organization will be the one that is systematically controlled. In addition, the trade partners will "deselect" the uncertified partners. This implies that voluntary adherence eventually becomes a standard practice and a necessary requirement if an entity wants to stay in business as part of the international trade supply chain.

A good parallel example to this is the prevalence, nowadays, of the requirement in many contracts for companies to be ISO 9001 certified in order to do business with certain clients. In fact, many retailers in the US and Europe are already requesting SCS certification from their trade and logistics partners and suppliers as a necessity in order to continue to be considered at all to do business with them.

14. What is the status of SCS from a regulatory point of view?

Programs have been implemented in quite a number of countries globally, the most notable two being the US C – TPAT program and the EU AEO. In addition, one of the most high profile and most controversial laws is the US SAFE Ports Act which requires 100 % container scanning at origin for all cargo destined for the US by the year 2012.

A most important "regulatory" model instrument (with the term "regulatory" used loosely) is the WCO SAFE Framework. As this has been signed by an overwhelming majority of the WCO members, in fact, this Framework represents the best consensus basis for a global SCS approach.

强制性供应链安全项目

（原文摘自《供应链安全指南》，世界银行编写）

（缉私局　刘欣平　机场海关　孙茜倩　译）

一、美国提前货物信息（ACI）

提前货物信息是第一个强制性供应链安全要求——2003 年美国海关实施的 24 小时舱单规则的支撑性概念。此外，美国海关与边境保护局运用自动目标甄别系统来支持提前货物信息理念。目标自动甄别系统实际上是基于内网的执法决策辅助工具，它是美国海关与边境保护局所有目标甄别和风险管理的基础。美国海关与边境保护局运用目标自动甄别系统优化大量提前货物信息的收集、使用、分析、筛选和分发工作。这些收集到的提前货物信息主要用于锁定、甄别和防止潜在的恐怖分子和恐怖分子使用的武器进入美国。

提前货物信息也是《世界海关组织全球贸易安全与便利标准框架》（以下简称《标准框架》）中的组成部分，是四大核心要素之一。世界海关组织指出，《标准框架》统一了进出口和转运货物提前递交的电子货物信息。在美国，提前货物信息在《贸易安全与便利港口法案》中作了规定。

供应链中的所有参与者通过船公司提交的提前货物信息使海关得以筛选进口集装箱，作出有情报根据的目标甄别和干预决定，并把资源集中用于高风险问题和货物。这种建立在风险管理基础上的方法被认为是大多数供应链安全项目的“基石”。

以下介绍一些建立在提前货物信息基础之上的最重要的项目，包括美国 24 小时规则、“10 + 2” 申报和中国海关的提前舱单申报管理办法、墨西哥的 24 小时规则和日本的提前货物信息。

二、美国 24 小时规则（2003）

24 小时规则要求海运承运人和无船承运人在最后境外港口输美集装箱装船前的 24 小时前，向美国海关与边境保护局提供集装箱内装货物的详细说明。这项制度适用于一切停靠美国港口的船舶、所有输美货物或经过美国港口的货物。

此项规则不适用于不在美国港口靠岸的支线船舶和转运船舶。然而，若货物转运至停靠美国港口的船舶上，那么此项规则仍适用。

简单地说，24 小时舱单规则可以做如下阐释：

如果船公司没有在装船前 24 小时向美国海关与边境保护局电子申报有关货物内容、集装箱托运人和收货人的详细提单（舱单）信息，该集装箱就不被允许装上驶往美国港口的轮船。如果在申报 24 小时内海关与边境保护局没有发出明确拒绝指令，那就默认其允许装船运往美国。

该规则要求提供的信息包括：

1. 发货人姓名和地址；
2. 收货人或货主姓名和地址；
3. 通知地址；
4. 提单号；
5. 提单上的唛头和号码；
6. 集装箱号和特征；
7. 封志号；
8. 货物描述；
9. 毛重或体积；
10. 件数；
11. 危险品国际代码；
12. 承运人接货的第一外国港口/地方；
13. 货物装船的外国港口；
14. 直接出口的国外卸货港/目的港以及出口的运输方式；

15. 保税数据。

如果违反此规则，最严重的后果就是不准装卸货物，导致货物运输和供应链中断。此外，美国海关与边境保护局也会对承运人和负责向海关与边境保护局提交货物申报信息的相关者予以罚款或其他处罚。这项规则使美国海关与边境保护局工作人员在输美集装箱在国外港口装船前，而不是在其抵达美国港口后分析集装箱信息，甄别潜在的恐怖威胁。对空运货物，舱单信息必须在飞机起飞后直接传输至海关。此项规则最明显的作用就是规定了舱单或舱单前申报数据时限，也就是要更早地把相关装运数据提交给管理部门。其他要求还包括鉴别供应链上各式商业伙伴所需的更具体的货物描述和数据。

三、国际船舶和港口设施保安规则（ISPS 2004）

《国际船舶和港口设施保安规则》是一项国际海事组织（目前有 167 个成员国）各成员国政府间的国际协定。作为一项国际性规则，它对各签约国政府具有强制性。《国际船舶和港口设施保安规则》解决供应链中港口设施和船舶部件的安全问题，旨在建立需要签约国政府、政府部门、当地管理部门和航运、港口产业多方合作的国际框架，从而实现以下目标：

1. 发现、评估安全上的威胁，采取协调一致的预防方式应对影响用于国际贸易的船舶和港口设施安全的事件；

2. 在国际和国内层面，确立所有相关方各自的定位与责任以保障航运安全；

3. 保证相关安全信息的及时、有效的合作和互换；

4. 提供安全评估方法，相应实施计划和程序以应对变化的安全级别；

5. 确保离岸或到岸的商船具备充分、到位的海事安全措施。

《国际船舶和港口设施保安规则》适用于所有 500 总吨及以上货轮、客轮、移动式离岸钻井装置和为国际航运船舶提供服务的港口设施。在安保要求方面，主要是船舶和港口设施需进行安全评估，制订并实施安全计划，任命安保人员。安全评估必须甄别出资产和基础设施在应对安全问题时出现的薄弱环节。安保计划必须明确针对3个安全层级的主要威胁将采取的三级措施，以解决查明的薄弱环节。这项计划至少要包括访问控制、安全监控、限制区域、货物、仓储、分运行李，训练与操作以及安全职责和培训等内容。

《国际船舶和港口设施保安规则》在港口和船舶之间建立起一种长效的精心组织的强制性对话机制，要求他们互相申报或确认各自的安全级别。如果其中一方有违反安全的记录，则另一方要相应提高警告级别和程序，通常为加强其基础安保措施如访问控制、车辆搜查和加强巡查。

反复不遵守规则的船舶会受到越来越多的管制，将逐渐难以找到可停靠和进行操作的港口。船舶运营人会越来越不愿意在违规的港口靠岸。违规船舶和港口因此互相产生负面影响。最后，经常违规者会发现即使之前他们没有被逮捕或抵制，他们也已受到市场的排挤。

四、欧盟到达前和离境前项目（2009—2011）

这个项目是欧盟版的提前货物信息规则，欧洲委员会2005年开始提出建议，于2009年7月实施，2011年全面生效。该项目的制定旨在满足与跨国境货物有关的安保需要，包含了与美国集装箱安全倡议相关的要求，同时，和日后欧盟的电子海关计划保持一致。其目的是向海关提前提供进出欧共体关境的货物信息，以得出更精确的风险分析，并加快通关效率，使得不会因提早申报而给贸易商造成更多成本和不便。

五、日本提前货物信息（2007）

日本政府于2007年实施提前货物信息项目，这项规则适用于进入日本的海运和空运货物。对于海运船舶，规则要求船舶到达日本港前12小时至24小时递交以下货物信息：装船地点、目的地、唛头和号码、货物描述、数量、货物收发货人、提单号和集装箱号。

与此类似，空运货物在到达日本机场的前3至5小时之内必须提交货物信息。若不遵守，如未在指定时限内提交信息或者发送假信息，将受到以下处罚：（1）对往来外国和日本之间运输的船舶和航空器处以50万日元以下的罚款；（2）对其他船舶和航空器处以30万日元以下的罚款。

六、墨西哥24小时规则（2007）

墨西哥的24小时规则与其他国家的一些安保措施类似，要求运往墨西哥的海运货物运输者于货物在境外装货港装船前的24小时向墨西哥海关提交货物电子舱单。只要这些签发提单的海运承运人、货运代理和无船承运人把货物运往墨西哥，就必须向墨西哥海关申报他们的货物，无法替货物代理或无船承运客户申报的海运承运人除外。

七、美国"10+2"申报制度（2009—2010）

2009年1月，美国海关与边境保护局引入了一个新的项目——进口商安全申报，通常被称为"10+2"。它要求有关运往美国的货物安全的信息至少应当在货物装船前的24个小时传输至美国海关与边境保护局。这一新规则与《贸易安全与便利港口法案》第203节相符，要求进口商向海关与边境保护局提供10项数据元，承运人需额外提供2项数据元。

该项目的制定理念是海关无法仅依据海运承运人的提单作出最优和有效的风险评估。熟悉海运运输单据的人都知道如果集装箱满的话，在海运提单上的货物描述和装船信息仅仅是发货人的申报，实际上海运承运人根本无法证实。正因为如此，提单上加入了"集装箱中宣称的货物信息"和"发货人装货、理货和点货"条款。"10+2"就是要进口商直接提供另外一组数据来便于海关使用目标甄别和风险管理工具进行筛选。

如上所述，此项新规则自2009年1月26日起生效。海关与边境保护局已经在其实施和执行方面做了阶段性的努力。在最初的12个月里，进口商的违规行为只会受到警告，而不会被罚款。但是在这12个月的宽限期过后（也就是从2010年1月1日起），如果违规，进口商将会面临高达5000美元的罚款。

以下就是进口商安全项目下必须向海关与边境保护局传输的10项数

据元：

1. 生产商名称和地址；
2. 卖方名称和地址；
3. 拼箱公司名称和地址；
4. 集装箱装货地址（货物装入集装箱的地址）；
5. 买方名称和地址（最后的买家）；
6. 货物送达的公司名称和地址（实际收货方）；
7. 进口商的海关登记号；
8. 收货人号码；
9. 原产地；
10. 协调制度商品编号（六位数）。

海关与边境保护局还要求承运人至少在装船货物离开最后一个外国港口后 48 小时或在到达美国港口前 48 小时提供其他两项数据元：一是船运装载位置计划；二是集装箱的状况信息。

这使得海关与边境保护局能够查出输美集装箱在航运过程中的一些异常行为。

八、中国提前舱单申报管理办法

中国政府于 2009 年 1 月 1 日开始实施此办法，要求海运承运人在货物装船前 24 小时向中国海关提交海运提单或舱单（与以上提到的其他项目类似）。这项规则适用于所有进出中国港口和经中国转运的货物。

九、美国 100%扫描（2012）

美国于 2007 年通过了一条名为《〈9·11 委员会法案〉2007 年执行建议》的法案，规定在 2012 年以后对所有目的地为美国的货物集装箱实施 100%境外透视扫描以及非侵入式查验。由美国海关与边境保护局制定的这个项目被看做是以不损害国家经济活力并确保贸易便利的方式，通过阻止大规模杀伤性武器进入美国以加强国家安全的重要举措。

为达到这些要求，《贸易安全与便利港口法案》要求在3个港口推行项目试点阶段，以评估对输往美国的货物实行100%扫描的可行性。这些港口包括：巴基斯坦的昆新港、洪都拉斯的科尔特斯港和英国的南安普顿港。在以上港口，出口至美国的货物100%需经过辐射扫描，并使用大型非侵入式成像设备拍摄货物图像。对辐射警报和扫描图像的分析可由现场海关与边境保护局工作人员或由海关与边境保护局国家目标甄别中心来完成（可参见“美国安全货运计划”一节）。

关于在2012年以后实行这条法律的能力、实用性和效果已有诸多争议。

许多美国的贸易伙伴，更确切地说是欧盟，认为这项法律义务是单边主义，且意味着治外法权。据许多分析人士认为，实行100%扫描所需要的技术在操作层面上几乎不可行。鉴于该法案要求的100%扫描的规模，有人担忧其对熟练的人力资源的大量需求最终会分散更专业化的非重复劳动中原本就短缺的人力资源。

该项目不仅预计投资和运行的成本极高，更有争议的是这条法律会带来的影响——人为转变运输流量和模式，从而更有利于较大的港口，不利于较小的港口。

为了说明整个商界，尤其是港口和水上运输产业对此感到的深度困惑，以下海关与边境保护局代理局长杰森·P. 阿亨于2009年4月1日在美国众议院拨款委员会国土安全分委会上就货运和集装箱安全问题所作声明的摘录内容说明了一切：

“对每年来自国外港口进入美国的所有1130万集装箱进行扫描在操作、技术以及外交上提出了巨大挑战，包括：

一是在极端气候条件和特定港口环境下扫描设备的可持续性；

二是实时将数据传回美国（国家调查中心）所需的各种高昂费用；

三是在不影响港口工作效率并得到当地政府同意的情况下重新规划港口布局以安放设备；

四是建立当地警报判断应对机制；

五是解决当地政府、货车业以及工会关心的健康和安全问题；

六是明确由谁来承担运行和维护扫描设备的费用；

七是通过货运安全倡议系统在处理集装箱之前获得必要的贸易数据；

八是解决扫描数据中存在的数据隐私问题；

九是与伙伴国家和终端操作方就设备的所有权、运行和维护，信息共享，进口关税因素方面的角色和职责问题达成书面协议；

十是为国外海关服务和终端操作方提供所需要的人员；

十一是确定扫描技术的许可要求；

十二是试点计划结束之后当地政府对前往美国的集装箱进行 100% 扫描的继续支持，以及相应地对美国出口的货物要求扫描的潜在可能。”

2008 年，在世界海关组织的资助下，勒阿弗大学对相关成本进行了评估。经计算，若每年扫描 42 万只至 5000 只集装箱，扫描每个集装箱的成本约在 10 美元至 440 美元之间。

由于美国超过 50% 的进口货物在中国装载，新法律对亚洲港口运行的影响预计将是最大的。亚洲发货人委员会主席约翰·陆认为这项法律将会“减缓货物流动速度，使港口陷于拥堵”。

Compulsory SCS Programs

(Obtained from "*Supply Chain Security Guide*", The World Bank)

(Translated by Liu Xinping, Bureau of Anti – Smuggling, and Sun Xiqian, Pudong International Airport Customs House)

1. US Advance Cargo Information (ACI)

ACI is the concept that underpins the first compulsory SCS requirement, the 24 Hour Manifest Rule implemented by the US Customs in 2003. Additionally, US Customs & Border Protection (CBP) uses an Automated Targeting System (ATS) to support the ACI concept. ATS is in fact an Intranet – based enforcement and decision support tool that is the cornerstone for all CBP targeting and risk management efforts. CBP uses ATS to improve the collection, use, analysis, filtering and dissemination of the massive quantity of ACI information that is gathered for the primary purpose of targeting, identifying, and preventing potential terrorists and terrorist weapons from entering the US.

ACI is also an integral part of the World Customs Organization's SAFE Framework of Standards as one of the "four core elements". The WCO states that the "Framework harmonizes the advance electronic cargo information requirements on inbound, outbound and transit shipments". ACI is recognized in the US through the SAFE Ports Act.

ACI provided by all the actors in the supply chain via the shipping lines allows Customs authorities to screen the imported containers, and make informed targeting and intervention decisions and to concentrate resources on the high risk issues and cargoes. This procedure, based on a Risk Management approach is considered one of the "cornerstones" in most SCS programs.

Some of the most relevant programs based on ACI are described hereunder, including the US 24 Hour Rule, the US "10 + 2" requirement, China 24 Hour Advanced Manifestation Rule, Mexico 24 Hour Rule and Japan ACI.

2. 24 Hour Rule (US) (2003)

The 24 Hour Rule requires sea carriers and Non – Vessel Operating Common Carriers (NVOCCs) to provide US Customs and Border Protection with detailed descriptions of the contents of sea containers bound for the US 24 hours before a container is loaded aboard the vessel at the last foreign port. The Rule applies to all vessels which will call at a US port and all cargo destined for the US or carried via US ports to a non – US destination.

The rule does not apply to feeder or transshipment vessels without a port call in the US. However, the Rule does apply when the cargo is transshipped onto a vessel with a port of call in the US.

In basic terms, the 24 hour manifest rule can be explained as follows:

The shipping lines are not allowed to load a container onboard a vessel bound to a US port if they have not previously electronically communicated the basic bill of lading (manifest) details of the cargo contents, shipper and consignee of the container to US Customs 24 hours before loading. If the loading of a container is not expressly rejected by US Customs within 24 hours of the declaration, by default, it is allowed to be loaded to the US.

The required information includes the following:

1. Shipper's name and address.
2. Consignee's or Owner's name and address.
3. Notify Address.
4. Bill of Lading Number.
5. Marks and Numbers from Bill of Lading.

6. Container Numbers and Characteristics.

7. Seal Numbers.

8. Cargo Description.

9. Gross Weight or Measurement.

10. Piece Count.

11. Hazmat Code.

12. First Foreign port/place carrier takes possession.

13. Foreign Port where cargo is laden abroad.

14. Foreign discharge/destination port for Immediate Exports and Transportation for Exports.

15. In – bond data.

In the case of non – compliance with the Rule, the most important consequence is denial of loading or unloading and a consequent disruption of cargo flows and supply chains. Furthermore, the US CBP may impose fines or other penalties on the carriers and others responsible for the submission of cargo declarations to US CBP. The rule allows US CBP officers to analyze the content information of the container and identify potential terrorist threats before the US – bound container is loaded at the foreign seaport, and not after it has entered a US port. As far as air transport is concerned, the information shall be submitted to CBP directly after the departure of the flight. The most obvious impact of this rule deals with the timing of the manifest/pre – manifest data, i. e. the need to send shipment – related data to the regulatory bodies at an earlier stage. Further requirements include the more detailed description of the goods and data requirements to identify the various business partners within the supply chain.

3. International Ship and Port Facility Security (ISPS) Code (2004)

The ISPS Code is an international agreement between government member states of the International Maritime Organization (IMO), which currently number

167. Being an international code, ISPS imposes itself upon the Government of the signatory States. The ISPS Code addresses the security of the port installations and vessel components of the supply chain. The objective is to establish an international framework involving co-operation between signatory governments, government agencies, local administrations and the shipping and port industries to:

1. Detect/assess security threats and take harmonized preventive measures against security incidents affecting ships or port facilities used in international trade.

2. Establish the respective roles and responsibilities of all the parties concerned, at the national and international level, for ensuring maritime security.

3. Ensure the early and efficient collaboration and exchange of security-related information.

4. Provide a methodology for security assessments so as to implement plans and procedures to react to changing security levels; and

5. Ensure confidence that adequate and proportionate maritime security measures are in place, both ashore and on board merchant vessels.

The ISPS Code applies to all cargo ships of 500 Gross Tons (GT) or above, passenger vessels, mobile offshore drilling units and port facilities serving such ships engaged on international voyages. The security requirements generally call for ships and port facilities to conduct security assessments, develop and implement security plans, and appoint security officers and security personnel. The security assessments must identify the vulnerabilities of assets and infrastructure to a security incident. The security plan must specify the measures that will be implemented at three escalating security levels representing the prevailing threat environment to address the identified vulnerabilities. At a minimum, the plan must address access control, security monitoring, restricted areas, cargo, stores and unaccompanied baggage, drills and exercises, and security duties and training.

ISPS establishes a mandatory permanent and structured dialogue between ports and vessels, which have to mutually declare/confirm their respective level of security. When one registers a security breach, the other has correspondingly raise its own alertness level and procedures, generally by intensifying basic security measures like: access control, searching of vehicles, increased patrolling.

Recurrently non – compliant vessels will be subject to more and more controls, and will gradually experience difficulties to find ports that will welcome and operate them. Vessel operators will become more and more reluctant to call at repeatedly non – compliant ports, as non – complaint ports or vessels mutually taint each other. Eventually, serial offenders will find themselves ostracized by the market itself, if they are not arrested or boycotted before.

4. Pre – arrival and Pre – departure (EU) (2009 – 2011)

This program is the EU version of ACI. The program proposed by the European Commission began in 2005, will be implemented in July 2009 and will come into full effect in 2011. It has been designed to meet the need for safety and security in relation to goods crossing international borders, including requirements linked to the US CSI, while, at the same time, remaining in step with the EU e – Customs plans for the future. Its intention is to provide Customs authorities with advance information on goods brought into, or exported from the Customs territory of the European Community. This is intended to provide for better risk analysis, but at the same time, for quicker process and release upon arrival, resulting in a benefit for traders that should be equal to, if nor exceeding, any cost or disadvantage of providing information earlier than at present.

5. Japan ACI (2007)

Implemented by the Japanese government in 2007, this ACI program is applicable to sea and air cargo arriving in Japan. For ocean – going vessels it requires that the following cargo information: place of shipment, place of destination, marks & numbers, cargo descriptions, quantities, shippers and consignees of goods, bill of lading number and container number is made available at least 12 hours, but no longer than 24 hours, before the arrival of the vessel at the port of destination in Japan.

Similarly, air cargo information is required at least three hours, but no longer than five hours before cargo arrives at the airport in Japan from overseas. Failure to comply, such as not filing information by the specified deadline or providing false information, is subject to the following penalties: 1) for a vessel or aircraft which moves/flies between a foreign country and Japan for foreign trade 500,000 JPY or less; 2) for a vessel/aircraft other than above 300,000 JPY or less.

6. Mexico 24 – hour Rule (2007)

The Mexico 24 – hour Rule, similar to the security regimes developed in other countries, requires all transporters of maritime cargo to Mexico to electronically submit cargo manifests to the Mexican Customs 24 hours prior to loading Mexico – bound shipments at foreign ports of loading. Oceans carriers, freight forwarders and NVOCCs who issue bills of lading to transport cargo to Mexico must file through Mexico Customs for their shipments, with the exception that ocean carriers cannot file on behalf of their freight forwarder/NVOCC customers.

7. "10 +2" (2009 – 2010)

In January 2009, the US CBP introduced a new program, called the Importer Security Filing (ISF) or more commonly called "10 +2", which requires cargo information for security purposes to be transmitted to CBP at least 24 hours before goods are loaded on a vessel for shipment to the US. This new rule is pursuant to section 203 of the SAFE Ports Act, and requires importers to provide 10 data elements to the CBP with the carrier providing 2 additional data elements.

This program originates from the realization that CBP cannot derive the optimal, most efficient cargo risk assessments based only on ocean – carrier bill of lading data. Those familiar with maritime transport documentation will recognize that the cargo description and shipment information mentioned on a maritime bill of lading is, in the case of full containers, solely a shippers declaration, which, by nature, the ocean carrier has no means to verify. Hence the "container said to contain" and "shippers' load, stow and count" clauses on the bill of lading. "10 + 2" is meant to provide another set of data directly from the importer for screening by CBP's targeting and risk management tools.

As mentioned above, the new rule came into effect on January 26, 2009. CBP is taking a phased approach in terms of implementation and enforcement. During the first 12 months, importers will be warned of infractions instead of being fined. After this 12 month grace period, (that is, as from January 1st 2010), importers can face fines up to US $5,000 for each violation.

The following are the ten data elements that must be transmitted to CBP as part of the ISF Importer Security Filing (ISF):

1. Manufacturer's name and address.
2. Seller's name and address.
3. Consolidator's name and address.
4. Container stuffing location (Address at which goods loaded into a container).
5. Buyer's name and address (Last named buyer).
6. Ship to name and address (Party physically receiving the goods).
7. Importer of record's number.
8. Consignee's number.
9. Country of origin.
10. Harmonized tariff schedule number (to the 6th digit).

CBP also requires two additional elements to be provided by the ocean carrier at least 48 hours after departure from the last foreign port, or prior to arrival for voyages less than 48 hours in duration:

1. Vessel stowage plan.

2. Container status message.

This will enable CBP to detect erratic or abnormal behavior by a given container during sea – passage.

8. China 24 – hour Advance Manifest Rule

Starting in 1 January 2009, implemented by the Chinese government, requires ocean carriers to submit the manifest or the bill of lading (similar to those of other programs mentioned above) to the Chinese Customs 24 hours prior to loading of the cargo. This rule is applicable to all export, import, and transshipped cargo via any Chinese ports.

9. 100% scanning (2012)

A bill was passed in the US in 2007 under the title "Implementing Recommendations of the United States 9/11 Commission Act of 2007" mandating overseas radiation scanning and NII inspection of 100% of all cargo containers destined for the U. S. by 2012. Regulated by the US CBP, this program is seen as a major effort to enhance national security by preventing weapons of mass destruction (WMD) from entering the US, but in a way that does not compromise the economic vitality of the country and ensures trade facilitation.

To fulfill these requirements, the SAFE Port Act mandated a pilot project phase in three ports to assess the feasibility of scanning 100% of shipments coming to the United States. These ports included: Qasim, Pakistan; Cortes, Honduras; Southampton, UK. At these ports, 100 % of the cargo exported to the US is scanned for radiation, and an image of the contents is taken, using large scale non – intrusive imaging equipment. The radiation alerts and scan images are analyzed either on the ground by CBP personnel, or back at the CBP National Targeting Center (see also the section on SFI).

There has been much debate surrounding the ability, practicality and effectiveness of implementing this law by 2012.

Many trade partners of the US, more specifically the EU, consider this legal obligation as unilateral and implying extraterritoriality. According to many analysts, the technologies needed to implement 100 % scanning are hardly available at an operational level. On such a scale as imposed by the bill (100% scanning) there are concerns that the massive need for skilled manpower will end up diverting scant human resources from more specialized non – repetitive tasks.

While investment and operational costs are predicted to be on the very high side, it is also argued that one impact of the legislation will be an artificial transformation of the traffic flows and patterns in favor of the bigger ports, to the prejudice of the smaller ones.

To illustrate the deep puzzlement experienced by the Trade Community in general, and the port and maritime transport industry in particular, the below extract from the Testimony of Acting Commissioner Jayson P. Ahern, U. S. Customs and Border Protection, before the House Appropriations Committee, Subcommittee on Homeland Security, on Cargo and Container Security on April 1, 2009 speaks for itself:

"Scanning all 11.3 million containers that enter (yearly) U. S. seaports from a foreign port presents significant operational, technical, and diplomatic challenges. They include:

1. Sustainability of the scanning equipment in extreme weather conditions and certain port environments.

2. Varying and significant costs of transferring the data back to the United States (National Targeting Center) in real – time.

3. Re – configuring port layouts to accommodate the equipment without affecting port efficiency and getting the permission of host governments.

4. Developing local response protocols for adjudicating alarms.

5. Addressing health and safety concerns of host governments and local trucking and labor unions.

6. Identifying who will incur the costs for operating and maintaining the

scanning equipment.

7. Acquiring necessary trade data prior to processing containers through the SFI system.

8. Addressing data privacy concerns in regards to the scanning data.

9. Concluding agreements with partnering nations and terminal operators to document roles and responsibilities regarding issues such as ownership, operation, and maintenance of the equipment; sharing of information; and import duty and tax considerations.

10. Staffing implications for both the foreign customs service and terminal operator.

11. Licensing requirements for the scanning technology.

12. Host government support for continuing to scan 100 % of U. S. bound containers after the pilot ends; and the potential requirements for reciprocal scanning of U. S. exports. "

An attempt to evaluate the related costs was made in June 2008 by the University of Le Havre, sponsored by WCO, gave a range of US $ 10 to US $ 440 per scanned container based on volumes ranging from 420, 000 to 5, 000 containers scanned per year.

Port operations in Asia are predicted to suffer the largest impact of the new law, since over 50% of US imports are loaded in China. John Lu, Chairman of the Asian Shipper's Council commented that the legislation will "slow down cargo and cause a gridlock at ports".

自愿性供应链安全项目

（原文摘自《供应链安全指南》，世界银行编写）

（缉私局　刘欣平　译）

一、运输资产保护协会（TAPA）（1997）

运输资产保护协会是诞生于“9·11”事件之前的项目。它是一个非营利性协会，于1997年在美国成立，并于1999年和2000年分别在欧洲和亚洲开始进行工作。成立运输资产保护协会是基于美国跨境犯罪的增多。据该协会称，这段时期引入欧盟内部市场为犯罪集团跨境行动提供了方便。欧洲、中东、非洲的运输资产保护协会认为这将对针对运输高价值货物的犯罪产生重大影响。

运输资产保护协会的总体目标是找出其成员遭受损失的领域，以及共享有效的日常程序和做法。该项目致力于高科技产品的运输，只有达到平均规模的公司才有可能成为该项目的成员。原先只有生产或出口高科技产品的公司才能够成为成员，后来范围延伸至生产其他高价值商品的公司。

正因如此，运输资产保护协会具有小范围专属性质，主要的知名公司都参与其中。运输资产保护协会的安保措施的重点在于货车运输，不涉及海上集装箱运输。

运输资产保护协会成立时就确立了两大倡议：事故信息服务（IIS）和运输供应商最低安全要求（FSR）。事故信息服务指的是运输资产保护协会向其成员提供交换安保相关信息的服务。运输供应商最低安全要求是对供应链总体安全提出的要求，包括外部安全、场所和安保程序在内的其他内容。

二、海关商界反恐伙伴关系计划（C－TPAT）（2001）

世界海关组织在《21 世纪海关》战略文本中指出，21 世纪的海关应与值得信任的经营者建立战略伙伴关系。海关需要了解商界关注的问题，商界需要知晓海关的规定。最重要的是，有必要将这种关系定义为双方共赢互利的伙伴关系。

海关商界反恐伙伴关系计划（以下简称“C－TPAT”）是美国政府和商界就货物进口至美国的问题共同努力而达成的结果。该项目是美国海关与边境保护局在“9·11”事件之后不断与时俱进的体现，认识到如果海关将商界纳入检查和确保货物安全过程，将大大提高边境安保效率。这项举措始于 2001 年，联合了 7 家美国大型企业，旨在应对可能存在的针对供应链的恐怖行为，尤其是威胁集装箱安全的恐怖主义行为。之后，C－TPAT 的规模不断扩大，现在已经有超过 8000 家公司积极地参与到此项行动中来。美国海关与边境保护局已经参与了 4000 余个认证复审过程，与 50 多个国家的海关商界反恐伙伴关系成员举行了会商。

目前 C－TPAT 所涵盖的运输路线包括所有出口货物至美国的国家，并且适用于所有的运输方式。

只要同意 C－TPAT 关于成员资格的指导条款，绝大多数进口商品到美国的企业，包括货物承运人、经纪人、制造商、进口商等都可以成为 C－TPAT 的成员。除了支持美国的全球反恐战争，C－TPAT 的成员还享有一定的切实利益。其成员较少受到海关的查验，如需查验，其集装箱将被挑拣出来优先于非 C－TPAT 成员的集装箱进行查验。

美国海关与边境保护局大致评估了 AEO 项目成员享有的“绿色通道”待遇：“C－TPAT 成员资格通常意味着较低的安保检查率；C－TPAT 进口商被要求接受安全检查的概率是其他人的 1/6，被要求接受合法性检查的概率是其他人的 1/4。”

C－TPAT 的成员需要核实其合作伙伴、分包商和供应商是否达到了安保要求。此外，除非其合作伙伴也是 C－TPAT 成员，否则无法享受 C－TPAT 成员的权益。C－TPAT 成员也可以利用 C－TPAT 培训平台对员工进行培训，使他们学到更多加强其供应链安全的方法。如果例行检查中发现有不合法的情况，企业将被取消 C－TPAT 成员资格，需要重新认定。

虽然绝大多数的大公司因 C－TPAT 提供显而易见的好处加入伙伴关系，C－TPAT 成员资格申请对任何行业都是自愿性的。另外，美国公司的身份并不是加入 C－TPAT 的必要条件。美国海关与边境保护局的战略是建立在由以下 5 个目标组成的多层次安全手段基础之上的：

一是确保 C－TPAT 参与方按照 C－TPAT 安全标准加强其供应链安全。

二是提供激励措施和优惠加快处理发送至 C－TPAT 伙伴的 C－TPAT 货物。

三是通过与国际社会的协调合作推进 C－TPAT 核心原则的国际化进程。

四是支持海关与边境保护局其他安全和便利化倡议。

五是提高 C－TPAT 项目管理水平。

C－TPAT 成员资格的特殊要求使得它的成员必须同意对其服务供应商和商业伙伴施加影响以提升他们的安保措施。事实上，许多公司都要求它们的商业伙伴加入 C－TPAT 或者遵守其安保指南，并且以此作为建立商业关系的前提条件。如果一个商业伙伴被认证和批准加入 C－TPAT，那就没有必要获取更多有关其是否遵守 C－TPAT 安保标准的信息。

三、集装箱安全倡议（CSI）（2002）

美国海关与边境保护局为了解决潜在的恐怖主义利用海运集装箱威胁边境安全和全球贸易的问题，于 2002 年创设了集装箱安全倡议（以下简称“CSI”）。参与这个倡议的国家与美国海关和边境保护局携手建立起一种安全制度，以确保所有具有高恐怖主义风险的集装箱在装上驶往美国的货轮之前都被识别出来并进行查验。此外，CSI 还旨在对集装箱进行甄别和预扫描，并且开展与输美货物恐怖威胁相关的额外调查。正如美国海关与边境保护局所指出的一样，其目的就是“将安全区域的范围向外进行延伸，从而使美国的国境成为最后一道防线，而不是第一道。”在 CSI 创设之前，没有其他国家对输美集装箱货物进行查验。“9·11”事件之前的海运集装箱安保措施仅仅局限于到达美国国境时的目标甄别和查验，这种方法必然使美国背负更为巨大的风险。美国国土安全部认为，这种针对海运集装箱环境设计的安全制度极大地加强和补充了美国海关与边境保护局在C-TPAT中所运用的多层次安保方法。

在CSI项目中，货物安保措施如X光和辐射扫描将被用来甄别和查验高风险货物。例如，在对集装箱进行查验之后，将附上具有高安全性的机械封志与防揭胶带以保证集装箱在进入美国时的完整性。目前在欧洲、亚洲、非洲、中东地区、南北美洲共有58个CSI运行港口，这也就意味着涵盖了所有输美的海运集装箱货物的86%，此外还有35个海关机构承诺加入CSI。

自愿性CSI项目旨在与参与该倡议的外国政府建立协作性的工作关系，以推进信息情报、当地趋势、最佳实践的共享等事宜。这项行动被期望能够在风险加剧、威胁程度不断提高、发生安全事件重新建立商业流的时期扮演一个重要的角色。美国海关与边境保护局官员已经提出请求，即所有参与CSI的国家的海关能够在风险提高时期加强对运输货物的筛查和查验工作。

希望本国港口成为CSI港口的国家，必须符合大量的特定要求。这些国家的海关必须在技术上有能力对本国的进口、出口、转运、通运货物实施非侵入式查验。接受评估的港口必须拥有直达、定期和大量前往美国的港口的集装箱流量。港口管理机构与海关必须有能力制订出能辨别潜在高风险集装箱的风险管理计划。此外，这个国家的政府当局必须准备好与美国、美国海关和边境保护局一起集中力量应对高风险物品，分享各自的信息，并且同意引入针对此类信息交换的自动化机制。

四、世界海关组织国际贸易安全与便利标准框架（2005）

2005年6月，在布鲁塞尔举行的理事会年会上，世界海关组织（WCO）成员国一致通过了《世界海关组织全球贸易安全与便利标准框架》（以下简称《标准框架》），以为全球贸易提供安全和便利。这项框架的目标为：

一是在全球层面建立支持供应链安全与便利的标准，以增加其确定性和可预见性；

二是整合供应链的综合管理以适应各种运输方式；

三是加强海关的作用、功能和能力以迎接21世纪的挑战和机遇；

四是推动各国海关之间的合作以提高发现高风险货物的能力；

五是增强海关和商界之间的合作；

六是通过安全的国际贸易供应链促进货物无缝流动。

《标准框架》包含4个核心元素：

一是这个框架统一了有关货物入境、出境和转运的提前货物信息要求；

二是每个加入该框架的国家承诺运用一致的风险管理手段应对安全威胁；

三是该框架要求，应货物接收国在可比较的风险目标甄别方法基础上提出合理的要求，货物发出国的海关将对高风险的集装箱和货物实施出口查验，查验倾向于使用诸如大型X光机和辐射探测仪之类的非侵入式检测设备；

四是该框架明确了海关对符合供应链安全标准和最佳实践最低要求的企业将给予的权益。

建立在上述4个核心元素上的《标准框架》，其内容涵盖两大支柱：即海关与海关之间的联网协议以及海关与商界之间的伙伴关系（见图1－1）。这两个支柱包含了一整套的标准以保证该框架易于理解并在国际上快速实行。

世界海关组织已经带头制定了《标准框架》。从实质上说，世界海关组织《标准框架》为施行具有国家性、地区性、国际性特点的供应链安全标准方法提供了蓝图。《标准框架》自通过之后，就在不断改进中，主要是将已经另文制定的有关经认证的经营者的详细条款纳入了该框架的文本之中。

目前为止，世界海关组织174个成员中已经有156个成员签署实施《标准框架》的意向书，这些成员代表了全球国际贸易总量的大约95%。此外，110个成员海关已经通过哥伦布项目要求获得世界海关组织的能力

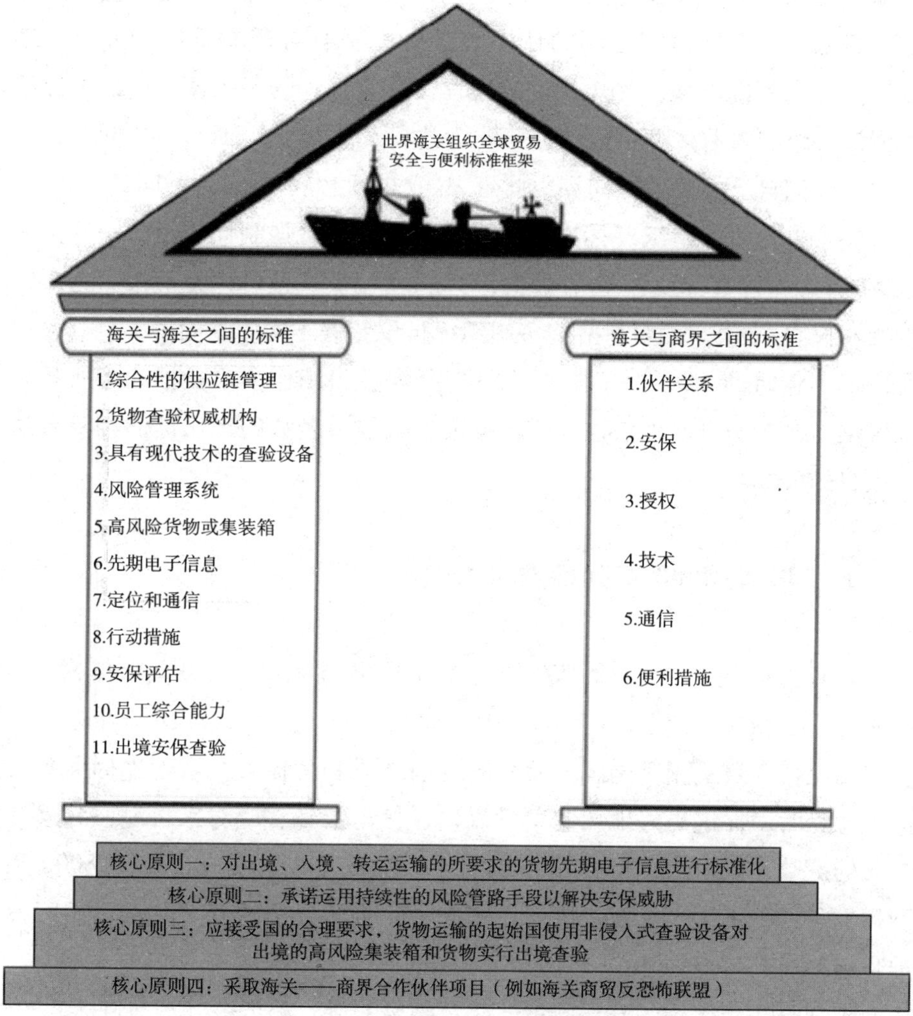

图1－1 《世界海关组织全球贸易安全与便利标准框架》的两大支柱

建设帮助。现在，已经有超过107个成员接待了需求评估团，并收到了评估团的诊断报告。这份报告总结了评估团的调查结果，并提出了一系列建议。超过60个海关已经进入实施阶段。在理事会会议上，各成员国得到了一份阐述执行活动和成果相关信息的“全球趋势和模式报告”，以及阐述评估团调查结果的“地区趋势和模式报告”。

然而据报告所说，《标准框架》的实施正经历着和国际船舶与港口保安设施规则在施行阶段类似的暂时困难——考虑到现有任务的规模，这并非意料之外。不同国家之间的认识和准备水平有着截然不同的差异。因此，实施《标准框架》相关规定的进程仍存有极大的不平衡，而这也促使世界海关组织采取多种手段来进行能力建设和大规模培训。与此同时，商界也对他们自己的发展方向和由此带来的成本产生了极大的疑问。

关于世界海关组织《标准框架》是自愿性还是强制性项目的争论由来已久。一方面，它是以一个平台的形式展现出来并且自称为框架。它最初的版本仅有40页，而且世界海关组织成员仅签署了实施意向书，且其并没有设定实施期限。另一方面，考虑到世界海关组织作为主要推动者所具有的影响力，人们可以确信该框架将决定未来绝大多数的经认证的经营者认证项目的模式。

五、ISO 28000 系列标准（2005）

针对供应链的安全管理系统标准 ISO/PAS 28000：2007（称为 ISO 28000）是解决供应链安全问题的 ISO 系列标准。这项标准由国际标准化组织制定，并且适用于国际上所有的运输路线和运输方式。这项标准背后的理念是为了促进更好地控制运输流动、打击走私、应对来自海盗和恐怖主义的威胁，以及为国际供应链创造出一项安全管理方法。ISO 28000 系列标准是一种基于“规划—执行—核查—行动”方法的安全标准，国际标准化组织对其解释如下：

规划：按照组织的安保政策，确定必要的目标和步骤以实现目标。

执行：引入考虑中的方法。

核查：基于安全政策、目标和目的检查和评估程序。

行动：持续改善安全管理系统。

ISO 28000 系列标准中提出的系统包括许多方面，例如财政、生产、信息管理以及货物的包装、储存和运输。这个系统的执行主体可能是各种规模的组织，涵盖小规模至跨国性主体，它将致力于：

一是建立、实行、维持和改善安全管理系统；

二是确保符合已经制定的安全管理政策；

三是向他方表明上述符合性；

四是获得由可信任的第三方认证机构颁布的对其安全管理系统进行的认证/注册；或者

五是进行符合 ISO 28000 系列标准的自我认定或自我声明。

特别需要指出的是，ISO 28000 系列标准能够为当地供应链安全项目的实行提供切实的最佳实践数据。

一个机构的管理层应起草并通过一项综合性的安全政策，这项政策应符合该机构的其他政策，并甄别针对该机构的威胁。这种政策需要有纸质版本并予以公布，而且该机构的所有成员都应当被告知此政策。该机构可以选择拥有一个机密的具体安全政策供内部使用，以及一个非机密的简要版本供该机构外的各方使用。

可以料想，ISO 28000 系列标准将为跨境贸易和货物运输提供便利，提升供应链内各方在战略和运行层面运用相关机制以解决安全薄弱环节，并制订预防性行动计划。各方可以对其安全措施进行持续评估以保护自身的商业利益，并确保符合国际监管要求。

通过鼓励供应链中的各参与方实施这些标准，各个国家能够在维持最理想的安全水平的同时，最大限度地利用政府资源。

ISO 28000 系列标准的确与世界海关组织《标准框架》、欧盟的 AEO 制度、美国的 C－TPAT 以及国际海事组织的《国际船舶和港口设施保安规则》（ISPS）等政府间、国际性、海关安全倡议互为补充。

六、欧盟经认证的经营者（AEO）制度（2008）

根据世界海关组织的定义，经认证的经营者（以下简称“AEO”）是指，承担某国海关机构认可的功能或者代表某国海关机构，在遵守世界海关组织或者其他同等供应链安全标准的同时，参与到国际货物流动之中的某一方。这个定义来源于世界海关组织《标准框架》中的一项宗旨，即创造出一整套与供应链安全有关的国际标准以促进各个海关组织之间的统一性和可预见性。欧盟经认证的经营者制度是由欧洲委员会设计出的一个旨在为可信赖的贸易商提供贸易便利措施的计划，该项目对欧盟成员国具有强制性，而对公司是自愿性的。

虽然对公司来说这不是强制性的，但企业通过 AEO 认定能够享受多重优惠，例如，货物通关加速、过境运输时间缩短、在贸易波动或威胁水平上升时期获得特别的措施以及货物查验的优先权。所有希望成为经认证的经营者的公司需要采用一套预先制定的安全标准和最佳模式来对他们的全球供应链进行自我评估。在这项评估中，供应商需要表明他们能够遵守相关政策和程序，以此确保货物在到达目的地、脱离海关监管之前其完整性不受到任何损害。

自我评估的程序必须包括下内容：

一是预先制定的安全最佳实践包含在现有商业运行之中；

二是由经认可的海关机构进行验证；

三是利用现代技术维护货物的完整性（包括集装箱）；

四是与海关当局坦诚沟通，获取最低安全标准的更新和供应链安全最佳实践。

Voluntary SCS Programs

(Obtained from "*Supply Chain Security Guide*", The World Bank)

(Translated by Liu Xinping, Bureau of Anti – Smuggling)

1. Transported Asset Protection Association (TAPA) (1997)

TAPA is a pre – 9/11 program. It is a non for profit association which was formed in the US in 1997 and which started working in Europe in 1999 and in Asia in 2000. TAPA's rationale for coming into existence was motivated by an observed rise in cross – border crime in the United States. According to TAPA, the introduction of the EU's inner market during this period, made it easier for criminal gangs to move across borders. TAPA EMEA (TAPA Europe, Middle East and Africa) considers this to have had a major impact on crime directed towards the transport of goods with a high value.

TAPA's overall goal is to identify the fields in which members experience losses, and to share information on effective routines and practices. The program concentrates its efforts on the transport of high tech goods; the possibility to become a member of the program is limited for an average sized company. Initially, only companies that produce or export high tech goods could become members, but this was later extended to include companies producing other high value goods.

Due to this TAPA has an exclusive image, and mainly high – profile companies are involved. TAPA's security measures focus on truck transportation and do not extend to container transport at sea.

Since TAPA began it has established two main initiatives: the Incident Information Service (IIS) and the Freight Suppliers Minimum Security Requirements (FSR). IIS is a service for the exchange of security related information that TAPA provides for its members. FSR are requirements that are placed on general security in the supply chain and which include, among other things, external security, premises and security routines.

2. Customs – Trade Partnership Against Terrorism (C – TPAT) (2001)

In CUSTOMS IN THE 21ST CENTURY, WCO indicates that customs in the 21st century should enter into strategic pacts with trusted economic operators. Customs needs to understand the concerns of business, while business needs to know the requirements of Customs. Most importantly, there is a need to translate this relationship into a partnership that results in mutually beneficial outcomes.

The C – TPAT program is a joint effort between the US government and businesses involved in importing goods into the US. It is part of the ever – evolving nature of the US CBP post 9/11, and recognizes that border security will be much more efficient if Customs involves businesses in the process of securing and inspecting cargo. The approach, which began in 2001 with 7 large US companies, was geared towards acting against possible supply chain terrorism, especially to do with container security. Since then C – TPAT has grown markedly to the extent that over 8, 000 companies are now actively involved with the C – TPAT process. CBP Agents have participated in over 4, 000 validation reviews and have met with C – TPAT Partners in over 50 countries.

Currently, the C – TPAT covered route encompasses any country importing into the US and is applicable to all transport modes.

Membership in C – TPAT is available to most businesses that import goods into the US including freight carriers, brokers, manufacturers, and importers, as long as they agree to the guidelines of C – TPAT membership. In addition to supporting the US global war on terrorism, C – TPAT membership also carries a number of tangible benefits. Members are less subject to Customs inspections, and C – TPAT containers that are singled out for inspection go straight to the front of the line, ahead of non – C – TPAT boxes.

A rough estimation of "green lane" benefits of AEO – programs membership is proposed by CBP: "C – TPAT membership often results in reduced security inspections; C – TPAT importers are 6 times less likely to incur a security examination and 4 times less likely to incur a compliance examination."

The C – TPAT member has to verify that its own partners, subcontractors, suppliers, address the required security elements and it is only the C – TPAT member that derives the benefit and not the partners, unless they are also C – TPAT members. The C – TPAT members can also take advantage of C – TPAT training for their employees, to learn about more ways to strengthen the security of their supply chain. If routine inspection shows non – compliance, C – TPAT membership is withdrawn and the company must re – certify.

C – TPAT membership is voluntary for any business, though most large companies have joined due to the perceived advantages it offers. Additionally, a company does not have to be American to join C – TPAT. CBP's strategy relies on a layered security approach consisting of the following five goals:

1. Ensure that C – TPAT partners improve the security of their supply chains pursuant to C – TPAT security criteria.

2. Provide incentives and benefits to include expedited processing of C – TPAT shipments to C – TPAT partners.

3. Internationalize the core principles of C – TPAT through cooperation and coordination with the international community.

4. Support other CBP security and facilitation initiatives.

5. Improve administration of the C – TPAT program.

Special requirements of C – TPAT membership entail that members must agree to leverage their service providers and business partners to increase their security practices. In fact, many companies are demanding that their business partners enroll in C – TPAT or adhere to its security guidelines, and they are conditioning their business relationships on these requirements. If a business partner has been certified and validated in C – TPAT, there is no need to obtain further information from that partner in terms of their compliance with C – TPAT security criteria or guidelines.

3. Container Security Initiative (CSI) (2002)

CSI was established in 2002 by the US CBP to address the threat to border security and global trade posed by the potential terrorist use of a maritime container. Participating countries establish a security regime in cooperation with the US CBP to ensure all containers that pose a high risk for terrorism are identified and inspected before they are placed on vessels destined for the US. Moreover, CSI aims to target and prescreen containers and to develop additional investigative leads related to the terrorist threat to US – bound cargo. As the CBP puts it, the intent is to " extend [the] zone of security outward so that American borders are the last line of defense, not the first" . Prior to the establishment of CSI, there was no foreign inspection of US – destined containerized shipments. The security of maritime containers pre 9/11 was limited to targeting and inspection upon arrival in the US, an approach deemed to be burdened with significantly greater risk. The US Department of Homeland Security (DHS) considers that this security regime, designed for the maritime container environment, greatly enhances and complements the Layered Security methodology being employed by CBP in C – TPAT.

In the CSI program high risk shipments are identified and examined by using cargo security measures, such as X – ray and radiation scans. For example, high security Mechanical Seals and Tamper Evident Tape are applied after the examination of containers in order to maintain the integrity of the container while intransit to the US. Currently, there are 58 operational CSI ports in Europe, Asia, Africa, the Middle East, and North and South America. This translates to 86% of all maritime containerized cargo destined to the US being covered. A further 35 Customs administrations have committed to join CSI.

The voluntary CSI program aims to foster a collaborative working relationship with the participating foreign governments, promoting, among other things, the sharing of intelligence, local trends, and best practices. The program is envisioned to play a vital role during periods of increased risk, heightened threat levels, and in reestablishing the flow of commerce in the event of a security incident. The CBP Commissioner has requested all of the director generals of CSI partner countries' Customs administrations to heighten screening and examination of cargo shipments during periods of increased risk.

The countries that want their ports to be CSI ports must fulfill a large number of special requirements. Their Customs administration must be technically capable of implementing Non – Intrusive Inspection (NII) of all goods that are imported, exported, in transit, or transshipped through the country. The port in question must have direct, regular and substantial container traffic to ports in the US. The port authorities, together with the Customs, must undertake to produce a risk management program that can identify possible high risk containers. Furthermore, the country's authorities must be prepared to share information with the US and CBP to facilitate a joint focus on high risk objects, and be prepared to introduce an automated mechanism for this exchange of information.

4. World Customs Organization SAFE Framework of Standards (2005)

At the June 2005 annual Council Session in Brussels, the WCO Members unanimously adopted the "SAFE Framework of Standards to secure and facilitate global trade". The Framework aims to:

1. Establish standards that provide supply chain security and facilitation at a global level to promote certainty and predictability.

2. Enable integrated supply chain management for all modes of transport.

3. Enhance the role, functions and capabilities of Customs to meet the challenges and opportunities of the 21st Century.

4. Strengthen cooperation between Customs administrations to improve their capability to detect high risk consignments.

5. Strengthen Customs/business cooperation.

6. Promote the seamless movement of goods through secure international trade supply chains.

The SAFE Framework consists of 4 core elements:

1. The Framework harmonizes the ACI requirements on inbound, outbound and transit shipments.

2. Each country that joins the Framework commits to employing a consistent risk management approach to address security threats.

3. The Framework requires that at the reasonable request of the receiving nation, based upon a comparable risk targeting methodology, the sending nation's Customs administration will perform an outbound inspection of high risk containers and cargo, preferably using non - intrusive detection equipment such as large scale X - ray machines and radiation detectors.

4. The Framework defines benefits that Customs will provide to businesses that meet minimal supply chain security standards and best practices.

The Framework, based on the previously described four core elements, rests on the Twin Pillars of Customs - to - Customs network arrangements and Customs - to - Business partnerships (see figure 1. 1). The pillars involve a set of standards that are consolidated to guarantee ease of understanding and rapid international implementation.

The WCO has taken the lead to develop the SAFE Framework. In essence, the WCO SAFE Framework provides a blueprint for implementing a national, regional and international SCS approach. Since the adoption of the SAFE FoS, work has progressed on improving the program, principally by incorporating into its text detailed provisions concerning AEO which had been initially developed in a separate document.

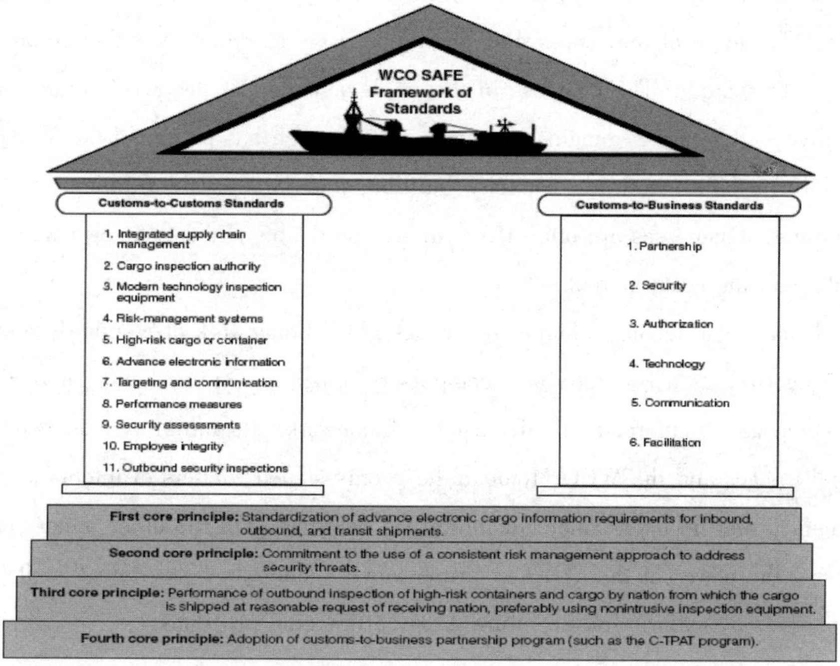

Figure1. 1 The Twin Pillars of the WCO SAFE Framework of Standards

Source: U. S. Government Accountability Office, Report GAO – 08 – 538.

To date, out of 174 WCO Members, 156 have signed the letter of intent to implement the SAFE FoS, representing approximately 95 % of global international trade. In addition, 110 WCO member Customs administrations have requested capacity building assistance from the WCO through the Columbus Program. So far, over 107 WCO Members have received a needs assessment mission and a diagnostic report summarizing the findings of the mission and providing a series of recommendations. Over 60 administrations have entered the implementation phase. At Council sessions WCO Members are provided with a "Global Trends and Patterns Report" that presents information on implementation activities and achievements, and with "Regional Trends and Patterns Reports" which presents findings from the diagnostic missions.

It is however reported that – not unexpectedly, considering the scope of the task at hand – the implementation of the SAFE Framework is suffering from similar teething problems as experienced during the implementation phase of the ISPS Code. The level of awareness and preparedness is extremely variable from one country to another. The progress in the implementation of the SAFE Framework directives, therefore, remains largely uneven, which has prompted the WCO to multiply its efforts towards capacity building and large scale training. In the meantime, businesses are often left with serious doubts about their own way forward, and the costs thereof.

It has been debated whether the WCO SAFE Framework of Standards should be categorized as a voluntary or a compulsory program. On one hand, it is often presented as a platform and calls itself a framework. Its initial version counted only 40 pages and the WCO Members have only signed "letters of intent" to implement it and no enforcement deadline has been set. On the other hand, considering the power of the WCO as prime mover, one can be certain that it will shape the vast majority of the future AEO certification programs.

5. ISO 28000 series (2005)

ISO/PAS 28000: 2007, Specification for Security Management systems for the supply chain (commonly referred to as the ISO 28000) is the ISO series of standards addressing security in the supply chain. The standards are regulated by ISO and can be applied internationally to all routes and transport modes. The idea behind this standard is to facilitate better controls of flows of transport, to combat smuggling, to meet the threats of piracy and terrorism, and to create a secure management approach to the international supply chain. ISO 28000 is a security standard based upon the so – called Plan – Do – Check – Act method which the ISO explains in the following way:

PLAN: to specify necessary goals and procedures to achieve results, in line with the organization's security policy.

DO: to introduce the routines in question.

CHECK: to check and measure procedures on the basis of the security policy, goals and objectives.

ACT: to continuously improve security management systems.

The system proposed in ISO 28000 includes aspects such as financing, production, information management and packing, storing and transport of goods. It shall be possible to implement by organizations of all sizes, from small scale to multinational, that wish to:

Establish, implement, maintain and improve a security management system;

Assure compliance with stated security management policy;

Demonstrate such compliance to others;

Seek certification/registration of its security management system by an accredited third party certification body; or

Make a self - determination and self - declaration on compliance with ISO 28000.

In particular, ISO28000 offers down-to-earth best practice data for local SCS implementation.

The management of an organization shall draft and adopt a comprehensive security policy. This policy shall be adapted to ensure that it corresponds with the organization's other policies. It shall also be adapted to identify threats against the organization. The policy shall be documented and published and all members of the organization shall be informed about it. The organization can choose to have a detailed security policy for internal use which can be confidential and a brief and a non - confidential version, which parties, outside the organization, can be given access.

It is expected that ISO 28000 series will facilitate trade and the transport of goods across borders. It will also increase the ability of organizations in the supply chain to effectively implement mechanisms that address security vulnerabilities at strategic and operational levels, and to establish preventive action plans. Organizations can then continually assess their security measures to protect their business interests, and ensure compliance with international regulatory requirements.

By encouraging the implementation of these standards by the various actors in the supply chains, countries will be able to maximize the use of government resources, while maintaining a level of optimal security.

The ISO 28000 series is indeed a complementary approach to governmental, international and Customs agency security initiatives, including the WCO's SAFE FoS, the EU's AEO, the US's C – TPAT and the IMO's ISPS.

6. EU Authorized Economic Operator (AEO) (2008)

As defined by the WCO, an AEO is "a party involved in the international movement of goods in whatever function that has been approved by or on behalf of a national Customs administration as complying with WCO or equivalent supply chain security standards." This definition comes from the WCO SAFE Framework where there is a tenet to create a set of international standards with respect to SCS to promote uniformity and predictability across Customs organizations. The EU AEO program is a plan devised by the European Commission with the goal to provide reliable traders with trade facilitation measures. The program is mandatory for EU member countries and voluntary for companies.

While not a mandatory program for companies, there are thought to be numerous benefits through becoming AEO certified, such as, expedited cargo releases, reduced transit times, access to special measures during times of trade disruptions or elevated threat levels, and priority during cargo checks. All companies looking to become AEO certified will need to engage in a self – assessment of their global supply chains using a predetermined set of security standards and best practices. In this assessment suppliers will need to demonstrate an adherence to policies and procedures that safeguard against any loss of integrity of their shipments until released from Customs control at destination.

The self – assessment process must include the following:

1. Predetermined security best practices are incorporated into existing busi-

ness practices.

2. Validation process has been completed by a recognized Customs agency.

3. Modern technology is utilized to maintain all shipments (including the container) integrity.

4. Open communication with Customs authorities to receive minimum security standards updates and SCS best practices.

其他重要供应链安全项目

（原文摘自《供应链安全指南》，世界银行编写）

（价格信息处　徐致颖　译）

其他重要供应链安全项目包括：商业运作安全、中国－欧盟安全智能贸易航线试点计划、美国安全货运计划、哥伦布计划、中国海关企业分类管理办法、全球贸易交换、自动化商业环境、船舶远程识别与跟踪、自动识别系统和海域感知。具体如下：

一、商业运作安全（2002）

商业运作安全（以下简称“OSC”）是美国政府、私营企业和海运业为形成和分享关于安全、快速运输集装箱货物的最佳实践而共同努力的成果。该项目对部分经选择的全球供应链实施新技术和新计划，旨在提高集装箱在装箱和分拆过程中的安全性、物理上确保运输中的集装箱安全和监控，以及及时可靠的交流沟通。

OSC 的第二阶段包括 18 项提高集装箱供应链安全的试点项目。具体而言，该项目总结并实施了商业上可行的业务程序、技术和计划，来保护商业运输免受恐怖袭击、大规模杀伤性武器、非法走私的威胁，同时将对运输系统的经济影响降到最低。该项目对原有做法进行了分析，并测试了联合运输操作环境中的安全技术。

检查、数据收集与传输按以下方式进行：

一是在起运地使用新的安全技术查验货物；

二是在供应链中对完整性做独立验证，对集装箱和数据进行电子追踪；

三是三项工作贯穿整个供应链；

四是传输安全电子数据至数据处理中心。

二、中国－欧盟：安全智能贸易航线试点计划（2006）

2006 年 9 月 19 日，中国与欧盟于第二次中欧海关联合委员会会议上达成协议，开展此项试点计划。该计划的初衷与长期目标是双方（中国与欧盟）相互承认对方的安全标准与 AEO 企业，通过使用旨在确保平稳高效的海关通关手续的最新科技手段，互相合作，共同促进信息互换并提高风险分析能力。双方希望安全智能贸易航线试点计划能允许对从集装箱装箱后至其到达目的地的整个过程进行“首尾相接的供应链”测试。目前，该项目是欧盟委员会、中国海关、英国海关和荷兰的合作项目。然而，如果试点项目成功，将进一步扩展并覆盖整个欧盟及更多的中国港口。针对此试点计划的评估将于 2009 年完成。

三、美国安全货运计划（2006）

2006 年 11 月，美国国土安全部与能源部启动了安全货运计划（以下简称“SFI”），旨在加强美国政府机构在边境探测核材料和其他放射性物质的能力。美国将此计划作为最终实现 100% 扫描之前的实验性测试阶段。自 2007 年，以下 7 个外国试点港口已应用了最新探测设备：巴基斯坦的昆新、洪都拉斯的科尔特斯、英国的南安普顿、也门的撒拉拉、新加坡、韩国的釜山和中国香港。据美国海关与边境保护局称：“国际集装箱安全计划通过对海运集装箱进行实时射线和光谱扫描，加强了海运货物安全和全球核武器不扩散行动。其通过将数据整合入美国海关与边境保护局程序，为重大科技进步开拓了新层面。”

美国的长远目标是在全世界海港运行辐射探测和集装箱成像设备，形成全球一体化的网络。该网络应允许美国接收和审核扫描影像和辐射探测数据。美国将把这一数据与全球各国政府共享。其另一个特点是基于部分尚未采集的现有数据，开发新的风险评估功能。

四、哥伦布计划

在《标准框架》被采纳以后，世界海关组织于2006年开始实施哥伦布计划。该计划是帮助各成员海关，尤其是来自发展中国家的成员海关实施《标准框架》以及相关的国际义务，如WTO关于贸易便利化的谈判。该计划是迄今为止最广泛、最全面的海关能力建设项目。哥伦布计划由以下三个阶段组成：

第一阶段，需求评估。即利用世界海关组织诊断框架工具就海关现状进行全面的诊断需求评估。该工具已得到了联合国、经济合作与发展合作组织、世界银行、世界货币基金组织及其他组织的认可。需求评估诊断由两位能力建设专家完成。诊断期间，专家将访问包括商界在内的所有相关方。诊断任务通过一系列建议形成一项诊断报告，包括现状、全面实施差距分析以及对未来的建议。

第二阶段，实施阶段。该阶段将为行动计划、援助方配对、试点行动计划和实施提供支持。

第三阶段，监测阶段。该阶段包括监测实施进展。能力建设司开发了一套进展监测系统，已在上海召开的世界海关组织高层战略小组会进行介绍并获通过。将在国家和地区层面进行进展报告，援助方也将参与。

至此文成稿时，已实施或计划了100多个诊断需求评估。在69个国家和14个地区的第二阶段工作已完成。

五、中国海关企业分类管理办法（2008）

此办法由中国海关总署于2008年4月1日颁布实施，该办法覆盖所有涉及中国的以任何运输方式进出口的物品。目标是使中国海关根据进出口企业的安全守法情况和历史记录进行分类。分类等级为AA类、A类、B类、C类和D类。AA类和A类企业享受更为便利的海关政策，例如较低的查验率、快速查验规程和快速放行。AA类企业可通过电子数据进行报关操作，比如，不必提交纸质单证报关。

六、全球贸易交换

全球贸易交换项目是美国国土安全部于2007年启动的一个项目。该项目作为由政府监管、私人运作、用户收费的数据仓库，使美国及其他国家政府得以利用大量的贸易数据促进供应链安全。在贸易团体因数据传播问题对其不断施加压力下，2008年4月，美国海关与边境保护局宣布暂停该项目。

七、自动化商业环境

自动化商业环境（以下简称“ACE”）是美国的商业贸易处理系统，旨在通过使边境操作自动化加强边境安全，以及通过合法的国际贸易推动本国经济安全。ACE最终将替代美国海关与边境保护局现有的进口处理系统——自动商业系统。ACE是美国海关与边境保护局多年来推进现代化举措的一部分，将分阶段进行。ACE为美国海关与边境保护局所有边境安全项目提供了坚实的技术基础，并将：

一是允许贸易方通过提交报告获得并管理其贸易信息；

二是为海关与边境保护局提供高效进出口处理程序，使货物快速通过关境的工具，加快合法贸易通关；

三是促进海关与边境保护局和商界的沟通、合作及守法努力；

四是使进出口商业信息的采集、处理及分析更便捷高效；

五是为各政府机构提供贸易信息共享平台。

八、船舶远程识别与跟踪

船舶远程识别与跟踪（以下简称“LRIT”）系统在全球范围内对船只进行识别与跟踪。1974年《国际海上人命安全公约》V/19－1的规定确立了船只提供LRIT信息的义务，以及缔约国政府和搜救机构获取LRIT信息的权利和义务。

LRIT 系统由船载 LRIT 信息传输装置、通信服务提供者、应用服务提供者、LRIT 数据中心组成，包括所有相关的船舶监控系统、LRIT 数据分配计划和国际 LRIT 数据交换。LRIT 协调人代表所有缔约国政府对 LRIT 系统的部分操作进行审核。

应请求，LRIT 信息将通过使用国际 LRIT 数据交换的国家级和地区级的国际合作数据中心，向 1974 年《国际海上人命安全公约》缔约国政府和经授权的搜救机构提供信息。

LRIT 用于以下船舶（国际航运）：

一是货轮（300 总吨以上，包括快速船）；

二是客轮（包括快速船）；

三是海上钻井平台（仅限移动式）。

以上船舶需每天至少 4 次向船旗国机构报告所在位置。

LRIT 与短程自动识别系统（以下简称“AIS”）相结合后，可被视为供应链安全追踪处理不可或缺的一层。

然而，在防止恶意方利用重要 LRIT 信息追踪定位船舶问题上，LRIT 在船旗国、港口国和沿海国对 LRIT 信息的恰当管理和传递方面似乎存在一定困难（详见下文 AIS）。

九、自动识别系统

船舶追踪服务（VTS）与船舶使用自动识别系统在相对有限的范围内对船舶进行定位和识别。当 AIS 与 LRIT 系统相结合，将为供应链安全提供清晰的追踪层。事实上，AIS 使得船舶可以传送、接收、共享包含船舶标识、位置、航线、速度的实时数据信息。此外，传播最总服务和海事部门可以利用该信息监管船舶航行。根据国际海事组织《国际海上人命安全公约》，所有客轮和 300 总吨以上的货轮必须安装 AIS。

“尽管 AIS 在监管船舶交通方面迈出了重大一步，但它的存在使任何拥有 AIS 接收器的人都可以获知船舶信息。如亚丁湾海盗，据悉已利用 AIS 信息提升了他们拦截和劫持船只的能力。如何确保 AIS 系统信息免落他人之手，并被利用以威胁船舶安全的问题亟待解决。”

十、海域感知

海域感知（以下简称“MDA”）是指对可能影响美国的安全、经济和环境的任何海域有关事宜的实际获悉。

MDA 的目标是在今后十年支持国家核心国防和安全方面的当务之急。MDA 通过达成以下战略目标简化当今复杂不清的安全环境：

一是加强海洋领土的透明度，尽可能提前侦测到、制止和打击针对美国利益的威胁；

二是对所有海事威胁能做出精准、高效、确信的决定和对策；

三是维护其在法律上的适用，从而保障航行自由和高效的商业流动。

MDA 的任务是，实现 MDA 依靠以识别动向和辨别异常的方式对各种行为进行监控的能力。仅有数据是不够的。数据必须进行收集、融合、分析，最好配合计算机数据整合和分析演算来处理大量独立的数据流，使得行动决策者能预计威胁，先发制人。MDA 关键任务清单将是美国政府未来能力发展的指引，其执行将使全球海上利益共同体有效了解海域并进行持续监控，以下是清单中的任务：

一是对全球海洋领土进行持续监控：包括各类船舶、货物、船员和乘客以及所有利益相关区域；

二是获取并保存有关船舶、设施和基础设备的数据；

三是收集、融合、分析并向决策者发送信息，便于其有效了解相关情况；

四是获取、开发并保存 MDA 相关行动运行情况的数据。

Other Significant SCS Programs

(Obtained from "*Supply Chain Security Guide*", The World Bank)

(Translated by Xu Zhiying, Division of Valuation and Information)

Other significant supply chain security programs include Operation Safe Commerce (OSC), EU – China Smart and Secure Trade Lane Pilot Project (SSTL), US Secure Freight Initiative (SFI), Columbus Program, China Customs company classification program, Global Trade Exchange (GTX), Automated Commercial Environment (ACE), Long – Range Identification and Tracking of ships (LRIT), Automatic Identification System (AIS), and Maritime Domain Awareness (MDA).

1. Operation Safe Commerce (OSC) (2002)

Operation Safe Commerce (OSC) is a collaborative effort between the US government, private business and the maritime industry, to develop and share best practices for the safe and expeditious movement of containerized cargo. New technologies and initiatives are being implemented in selected global supply chains. These are aimed at improving security during the process of stuffing and deconsolidating containers, physically securing and monitoring containers for transportation, and exchanging timely and reliable communication.

Phase II of OSC consisted of 18 pilot projects designed to improve container SCS. More specifically, the project identified and implemented commercially viable business processes, technologies and initiatives to protect commercial shipments from threats of terrorist attack, weapons of mass destruction, smuggling and contraband, while minimizing the economic impact on the transportation system. This project analyzed existing practices and tested security techniques in an operational intermodal transport environment.

Inspections, data collection and transmission activities were performed as follows:

1. New security techniques for inspecting goods at point of origin.
2. Independent verification of the integrity and electronic tracking of the container and data.
3. Throughout the supply chain.
4. Transmission of secure electronic data to a data clearing.

2. EU – China: Smart and Secure Trade Lane Pilot Project (2006)

During the second session of the Joint EU – China Customs Cooperation Committee (JCCC) meeting on 19 September 2006, the EU and China reached an agreement to initiate this pilot Project. The initial motivation and longer – term goal is that the two sides (EU and China) will give mutual recognition of each other's security standards and AEOs, and collaborate to improve information exchanges and risk assessment by means of the latest technologies aiming at ensuring smooth and prompt Customs clearance. It is hoped that the Smart and Secure Trade Lane Pilot project will permit tests of "end to end supply chains" from the point in time when a container is loaded through its entire journey up to its final destination. Currently the project is a cooperation project between the EU Commission, the Customs authority in China and the Customs authorities in UK and the Netherlands. However, if the pilot project is successful, it will be progressively extended to cover the whole EU and more ports in China. An evaluation for this pilot project is scheduled for completion in 2009.

3. US Secure Freight Initiative (SFI) (2006)

In December 2006, the US government's DHS and Department of Energy launched the SFI initiative that aimed at strengthening the ability of the American authorities to trace nuclear and other radioactive substances at borders. This program is considered by the US as a laboratory and testing phase for the ultimate goal of 100 % scanning. Since 2007 the latest technological equipment has been placed in seven foreign test ports: Port Qasim in Pakistan, Puerto Cortés in Honduras, Southampton in the UK, Salalah in Oman, Singapore, Busan in South Korea and Hong Kong in China. According to the US CBP, the International Container Security project strengthens maritime cargo security and global nuclear non-proliferation efforts by providing real time radiographic and spectrographic scanning of maritime shipping containers. It adds a new dimension to be significant technological advancements by integrating those data elements into the US Customs and Border Protection (CBP) process.

The further ambition is to develop a globally integrated network of radiation detection and container imaging equipment to be operated in seaports worldwide. This network should allow streaming scanning images and radiation detection data for verification in the US. The arrangement is that this data will be shared by governments across the world and the government of the US. An additional feature is the development of a new risk scoring feature, partly based on existing, but uncollected data.

4. Columbus Program

Following the acceptance of the SAFE Framework, the WCO started in 2006 what is termed the Columbus Program, which is specially designed to help Members, especially those from developing countries, implement the SAFE Framework and related international obligations, such as the WTO negotiations on trade facilitation. The program is the largest and most comprehensive Customs capacity building to date. The Columbus Program consists of three phases:

The 1st phase, needs assessment, is a comprehensive diagnostic needs assessment of the current situation in the Customs administration uses the WCO's Diagnostic Framework tool that has been acknowledged by organizations like the UN, OECD, the World Bank, the International Monetary Fund (IMF) and others. The needs assessment diagnosis is carried out by two capacity building experts. During the diagnostic mission, the experts interview all concerned parties including the members of the trade community. The mission results in a diagnostic report including the current situation, gap analysis to full implementation and the suggested way forward through a number of recommendations.

The 2nd phase, Implementation, is support for action planning, donor matchmaking, planning of pilot activities and implementation.

The 3rd phase, Monitoring, involves monitoring of progress. The Capacity Building Directorate has developed a progress monitoring system that was presented to and endorsed by the WCO High - Level Strategic Group in Shanghai. Progress reporting will be made on a country level, on a regional level and will involve donors.

At the time of this writing, over 100 diagnostic needs assessments have been undertaken or are scheduled. 69 Phase 2 national missions and 14 Phase 2 regional missions have been completed.

5. China Customs - company classification program (2008)

Launched on 1 April, 2008, by the Chinese General Administration of Customs, this program covers imports and exports involving China, in all forms of transport. The goal is for the Chinese Customs to classify importing and exporting companies on the basis of their security compliance and historical record with Customs. Classes are AA, A, B, C, and D. AA and A class companies enjoy advanced Customs privileges, such as limited inspection risk, quick inspection protocols and quick release. Class AA companies enjoy electronic communication and declaration procedures, without, for example, the need to submit paper documents.

6. GTX or Global Trade Exchange

GTX was an initiative launched by the US Department of Homeland Security (DHS) in 2007, as a government – controlled, privately operated, user – fee based data warehouse that would have taken the huge quantities of trade data and made this available to the US government and other governments in order to improve supply chain security. Under mounting pressure from the trade community due to data dissemination issues, in April 2008, the US Customs and Border Protection announced that the GTX initiative would be suspended.

7. ACE or Automated Commercial Environment

"The Automated Commercial Environment (ACE) is the United States' commercial trade processing system designed to automate border processing to enhance border security and foster our Nation's economic security through lawful international trade and travel. ACE will eventually replace the current import processing system for U. S. Customs and Border Protection (CBP), the Automated Commercial System (ACS). ACE is part of a multi – year CBP modernization effort and will be deployed in phases. ACE provides a solid technology foundation for all border security initiatives within CBP and will:

1. Allow trade participants access to and management of their trade information via reports.

2. Expedite legitimate trade by providing CBP with tools to efficiently process imports/exports and move goods quickly across the border.

3. Improve communication, collaboration, and compliance efforts between CBP and the trade community.

4. Facilitate efficient collection, processing, and analysis of commercial import and export data; and

5. Provide an information - sharing platform for trade data throughout government agencies."

8. LRIT or Long - Range Identification and Tracking of ships

"The Long - Range Identification and Tracking (LRIT) system provides for the global identification and tracking of ships. The obligations of ships to transmit LRIT information and the rights and obligations of Contracting Governments and of Search and rescue services to receive LRIT information are established in regulation V/19 - 1 of the 1974 SOLAS Convention.

The LRIT system consists of the ship borne LRIT information transmitting equipment, the Communication Service Provider (s), the Application Service Provider (s), the LRIT Data Centre (s), including any related Vessel Monitoring System (s), the LRIT Data Distribution Plan and the International LRIT Data Exchange. Certain aspects of the performance of the LRIT system are reviewed or audited by the LRIT Coordinator acting on behalf of all Contracting Governments.

LRIT information is provided to Contracting Governments to the 1974 SOLAS Convention and Search and rescue services entitled to receive the information, upon request, through a system of National, Regional, Cooperative and International LRIT Data Centers using the International LRIT Data Exchange."

LRIT applies to the following vessels (international movements):

1. Cargo vessels (300 gross tons and above, with high speed included);
2. Passenger vessels (high speed included);
3. Offshore drilling platforms (mobile only).

At least four times per day the vessels must report their position to the administration which is associated with the flag of that vessel.

When used in conjunction with the short range Automatic Identification System (AIS), LRIT can be considered to be an integral layer in the supply chain security tracking and tracing process.

However, LRIT seems to experience some difficulties concerning the proper control and dissemination of LRIT information by flag states, port states and coastal states when it comes to prevent that critical LRIT information reaches the hands of malevolent parties who might use it to attempt to spot and trace vessels (see AIS below).

9. AIS or Automatic Identification System

Vessel Tracking Services (VTS) and ships use the Automatic Identification System (AIS) for locating and identifying ships within a relatively limited range. When AIS is combined with the Long Range Identification and Tracking (LRIT) system, this provides a clear tracking and tracing layer in supply chain security. Practically, the AIS enables vessels to transmit receive and share real – time data covering ship identification, positioning, course, and speed. Additionally, vessels tracking services and maritime authorities can use this information to monitor and control vessel movements accordingly. According to the IMO SOLAS convention AIS must be installed on all passenger ships and cargo ships over 300 gross tons.

"Although AIS is an important step forward in monitoring vessel traffic, its existence places vessel information in the hands of anyone who has an AIS receiver. Pirates in the Gulf of Aden, for example, have been known to have used AIS information to improve their ability to intercept and hijack vessels. The problem of securing the AIS systems against outsiders' acquisition of information that can be used to compromise the safety or security of the vessels remains to be urgently solved".

10. MDA or Maritime Domain Awareness

Maritime Domain Awareness is the effective understanding of anything associated with the maritime domain that could impact the security, safety, economy, or environment of the United States.

MDA Goals:

MDA supports core national defense and security priorities over the next decade. MDA serves to simplify today's complex and ambiguous security environment by meeting the following strategic goals:

1. Enhance transparency in the maritime domain to detect, deter and defeat threats as early and distant from U. S. interests as possible.

2. Enable accurate, dynamic, and confident decisions and responses to the full spectrum of maritime threats; and

3. Sustain the full application of the law to ensure freedom of navigation and the efficient flow of commerce.

MDA Objectives:

Achieving MDA depends on the ability to monitor activities in such a way that trends can be identified and anomalies differentiated. Data alone are insufficient. Data must be collected, fused, and analyzed, preferably with the assistance of computer data integration and analysis algorithms to assist in handling vast, disparate data streams, so that operational decision makers can anticipate threats and take the initiative to defeat them. The following objectives constitute the MDA Essential Task List, which will guide the development of capabilities that the United States Government will pursue and when executed will provide the GMCOI an effective understanding of the maritime domain and allow for continuous monitoring:

1. Persistently monitor in the global maritime domain:

- Vessels and craft
- Cargo

- Vessel crews and passengers
- All identified areas of interest.

2. Access and maintain data on vessels, facilities and infrastructure.

3. Collect, fuse, analyze and disseminate information to decision makers to facilitate effective understanding.

4. Access, develop and maintain data on MDA – related mission performance.

供应链安全技术

（原文摘自《供应链安全指南》，世界银行编写）

（缉私局　宋洁艳　译）

本质上，全球供应链是一家分拨企业。它需要运输模式（陆路、空路和海路）、转运点（如海港、空港）和内陆运输设施。除了供应链项目、政策和程序，供应链也依赖技术的运用。由于供应链中的经营者从事的是移动货物的业务，所以防止货物丢失、被盗和损坏自然是这些经营者必须解决的问题。

由于“安全”的基本概念随着时间推移发生了一些改变，现在的趋势是满足两个目标：安全和效率。安全专家和效率专家合作的概念50多年前就开始形成。1956年，一个卡车公司老板，也是一个司机——马尔科姆·麦克莱恩改变了航运业。在开发出集装箱之前的20年中，马尔科姆·麦克莱恩一直遵循着一种缓慢、低效且不安全的运输方式。他发明的集装箱能确保货物安全并使货物高效率地运输。集装箱使安全性得以标准化、交易费用得以降低、运输损失得以减少以及互通性得以加强。今天，供应链安全的重点依然是集装箱。

虽然这一章的重点在于介绍应用于供应链安全中的新技术，但人力的参与也不容忽视。如果新的供应链安全计划和立法对技术使用作出规定，成本分摊对发展中的世界而言将继续成为一个难题。

本章将对新兴的和现有的技术、集装箱完整性（CI）、跟单追踪、先进查验技术（AIT）进行研究。由于篇幅有限，我们无法具体分析信息和通信技术（ICTs）、实施数据模型所运用的技术以及其他两个协作工具——电子单一窗口（ESW）和供应链中使用的港口共享系统（PCS）。电子单一窗口和港口共享系统只在此提到。它们不是供应链安全的核心，但是在本质上，它们有助于加强供应链安全。若读者对电子单一窗口和港口共享系统感兴趣，推荐阅读联合国贸易便利和电子商务中心（UN/CEFACT）第33号建议书。

一、技术新趋势

在研究第一章中所提到的供应链安全计划时，大部分人把集装箱作为安全的重中之重。当分析“特洛伊木马”后果或者走私的威胁和犯罪时，解决与集装箱技术有关的安全问题似乎很有道理。这样一来，集装箱或者集装箱式的多模式运输就不是唯一目标了。全球供应链依赖不同的运载工具。运输管道、散装车、轮渡这些方式都会在许多情况下易受或受到过阻截。事实上，我们目前能得到的多数数据显示，供应链中几乎85%的损失来自于内陆运输。随着世界贸易量继续迅速增长以及边境日益开放，犯罪和恐怖网络也变得越来越有组织性并且复杂化。“智能集装箱”——对犯罪科技含量不断增加的一种应对方式，应运而生。如今的“智能集装箱”包括导航和路由引导系统、卫星定位、内部传感器和无线射频识别，以确保货物安全地从原产地到达目的地。可以预计，这本指南第一次出版时，已经有几千个“智能集装箱”投入使用了。目前，全世界的集装箱使用量已达1600万个（2400万标箱）。

“智能集装箱”探测仪可以探测出异常现象，例如：一是门开启过或移动过；二是顶部、边侧及底部有切开的洞孔；三是装有人或动物，如使用被动式红外传感器；四是危险的化学、生物及放射性物质，如使用核生化与爆裂物探测仪；五是位置，如使用全球卫星定位系统或者“伽利略系统卫星无线”追踪设备。

这些探测仪会被连接上某种形式的中央数据记录器。记录器中的探测数据可以被港口或者边境站的可兼容封志读取器识别出来。或者，这些数据通过一个远程通信系统到达监控点，例如通过卫星或者全球移动通信系统。到目前为止，企业认为“智能集装箱”的使用及相关的技术、系统带来了多方面好处。

以下为格尔曼斯基（2008）撰写的大纲，强调了“智能集装箱”的前景：

“智能集装箱”已经投入运行。德国和美国2006年的情况表明：“智能集装箱”的成本非常小，几乎不比电子锁和封志高，“智能集装箱”可以通过电子化方式携带及传输物流和感官数据。虽然“智能集装箱”没有统一的定义，但我们可以把它大体定义成：符合世界海关组织标准、遵守美国法律（比如：安全港口法案）和计划（例如：海关－商界反恐联盟），从原产地至目的地再到海关时，根据海关需要和要求，把从原产地至目的地的数据和安全情报以电子化方式携带和传输给海关的运输工具。如今的“智能集装箱”至少执行7项有明确定义的任务：

一是作为协调供应链各方面所必需的系统方法的一个部分，使得自原产地起我们就能确保可见性和安全性；二是通过电子化方式捕捉和传输与其他供应链资料相关的贸易数据，例如集装箱号、订舱号；三是遵守世界海关组织、美国海关商界反恐伙伴计划和欧盟经认证的经营者的要求，通过探测集装箱的某个开口来了解全貌，以保证集装箱的完整；四是实时报告或者阻止任何违规行为；五是提供详细的地理位置，若偏离预设路线，则自动报告所处位置；六是识别和记录被授权在目的地打开集装箱人员的身份；七是“智能集装箱”必须能适应不同的探测仪，能与供应链中发货人和承运人所使用的不同软件包兼容。

然而，此行业的一些人却认为所谓的“智能集装箱”能开发出来几乎是不可能的。有人认为，不管集装箱中运用了多少科技的力量，集装箱永远不可能“智能”。还有人认为，至今进行的“现场测试”都是层层保护的，一旦到了现实中很难应验。

集装箱运输已经高度标准化（参见ISO标准）和商品化。把集装箱分为“智能”和“非智能”，确实是一个挑战。

最初，“智能集装箱”虽为承运人使用，但是为发货人所有。这样就产生了“智能集装箱”被使用完后必须空箱归还至发货地的问题。因此，一些集装箱租赁公司就提供“智能集装箱”的出租业务。另一个更可行的方法是使用可移动的“智能装置”。这种装置可以固定在任何标准化的集装箱上，和集装箱液袋或微型冷藏探测设备相似。

“智能装置”也被称为资产监视设备（AMU）、集装箱监视设备（CMU）或者资产防护设备（APU）。供应商的科技、方法和高科技“供应链可视性”的理念促成了“智能装置”的产生。高科技“供应链可视性”理念提出了“严格的库存管理”这个话题。一些货物比另一些货物更加需要关注。属于前一类货物的有：高价值的货物、药物、敏感化学品、军用物资。另外，促销活动中所使用的时尚商品也需要这种高能见度的设备。这些设备大多数由物流运营商提供。另一方面，虽然普通的进口商很乐意享受时刻监视货物的服务，但是他们没有一丁点儿付费购买该设备的意愿。

生物识别也开始被运用到供应链之中。在取货点、即时发货站甚至目的地，对司机的识别和确认都是非常重要的。生物识别可以提高司机身份确认和识别的效率，特别是频繁卸货和提货的司机，减少偷窃和恐怖袭击的风险，同时，可以加快卡口和接待程序。生物识别工具（例如指纹和虹膜识别）可以植入智能身份卡，也可以与舱单、载货工具及司机资料库联系起来。将来，运输安全管理局将为全美的运输工人开发运输工人身份卡。

二、现有技术

本部分，我们将简要概述供应链安全中使用的技术以及这些技术如何应用。鉴于对商业市场上现有技术作全面的整体介绍将对本指南的读者有帮助，世界海关组织网站上已经有了一个现成的介绍。该组织为其 174 个成员维护着先进技术数据库，其成员可以从该组织网站获取这些数据。这个资料库搜集在市场上出现的科技设备的信息，并提供以下方面详细、最新的技术资料：一是试验和检测设备；二是 X 光设备；三是机械和电子集装箱封志。

三、确保集装箱完整性的供应链安全技术：集装箱安全设备和封志

集装箱安全设备对于在供应链中确保集装箱的完整性和便利贸易与海关手续非常关键。我们可以通过使用机械和电子封志来提高货物的安全

性。机械和电子封志就像壁垒一样，防止集装箱和拖车中的货物在运输途中被盗窃、走私和损坏。若封志破损或者识别码与货物的文档记录不同，这就显示集装箱或者拖车可能在运输中被未经授权的人打开过。机械和电子封志拥有唯一的识别码，这个号码可供我们追踪货物信息。封志的识别码将在货物交管时被记录下来，这样我们可以得知集装箱或者拖车在何时何地被移交，以及在那个时候封志的状态如何。

理想的情况是，由直接负责装箱或者核查货物的部门来安装集装箱封志。基于这点，负责装箱或者核查货物的部门是集装箱安全链中第一环并且是最重要的一环。我们必须牢记，使用高安全性的机械封志和移交过程中封志的贴附、监视及记录程序是同等重要的。

（一）机械封志

以下术语和定义都来自 ISO 17712。我们会在下面的内容中概述分类情况。

机械封志是一种标记唯一识别符的装置，通常被标记上封志拥有人或者发行人的印章和/或颜色。机械封志安装在集装箱门外部，以识别是否有篡改或从门口闯入的情况，由此来确保集装箱门始终处于关闭状态。另外，鉴于机械封志的结构，不同封志对于防止有意或者无意破门而入的牢度有所不同。即使在破损的封志处重新安装相同的装置，封志的识别号也不会与原始封志记录的号码相同。密封程序的重要性不亚于封志本身。

正确的密封程序包括以下几项：一是采购封志和装船过程；二是培训员工使用和核对封志；三是跟踪封志的库存情况、安全地储存/分发封志；四是正确装置封志；五是记录封志编码；六是管理和传输封志编码；七是记录封志操作情况和核实有关人员、时间和日期；八是记录封志的异常状况；九是封志的终止使用和报废。

如果缺少正确的密封和核查程序，封志的使用反而会事与愿违。错误的操作将使我们得到错误的集装箱把手/门情况。理论上来说，安全封志应该有效地探测出任何意欲破坏集装箱的行为。

但是事实上，简单的安全封志却不能胜任上述任务。有很多原因造成了这个情况。有可能是因为封志很容易被割坏，可能是缺少正确的封志资料，可能是在集装箱运输中管理不当，也可能是伪造封志和封志号码很容易。对于简单的提示性封志来说，核实封志是人工操作和耗费时间的过程。因此，在运输过程中，如果都要核实，也只是大概地检查一下。最后，这个问题不只出现在安全封志中，惯偷设计出了别的方法，他们可以绕开把手或集装箱门而进入集装箱内部。

我们必须牢记，高安全性封志很重要，但是封志安装、监视以及集装箱交接过程中的记录同等重要。

另外，一旦非法货物在上封前进入集装箱内，这些非法货物像全程拥有了合法的通行证一样。因此，上游供应链安全程序必须将生产、包装货物和把货物装入集装箱的公司、人员和设施纳入进来。

1. 机械封志的种类

高安全性封志。这种封志由金属丝/条、金属钢索等材质制成，旨在降低侵入的概率。一般的，高安全性封志必须用螺旋刀和电缆刀才能移除。它可以显示是否有破坏和闯入的情况。根据10月15日生效的2007年9/11委员会法案，2008年所有运往美国的集装箱必须密封上符合ISO/PAS 17712标准的封志。所有通过货轮进入美国港口的货物都被要求密封上符合ISO/PAS 17712标准的高安全性封志，公司意识到这点非常重要。世界海关组织也已经认可了ISO 17712封志标准。

有许多封志和封志的制造商符合或超过ISO 17712标准。公司应当从合法制造商处采购封志。采购封志的公司应当依据制造商的测试报告来决定是否采购，这些报告由独立的、符合ISO 17025标准的经认证的测试实验室提供。公司必须保留这些文件以备将来查询。虽然本指南不宣传任何一家封志制造商或者任何一款封志产品，一些机构［例如国际封志制造商协会（ISMA）］能够提供生产ISO PAS 17712标准的高安全性封志的厂商的资料。

高安全性封志的种类包括：

挂锁封志：锁体附有半拎环，有金属线钩环挂锁（金属或者塑料锁体）、塑料挂锁、无钥匙挂锁封志。

钢丝封志：包括钢丝及紧固装置。在单件式的封志中，紧固装置永远地固定在钢丝的一端。双件式封志的紧固装置是分开的，它分开装在钢丝上或者预制的钢丝端上。

子弹封志：金属杆（无论是否有螺纹，柔软的或坚硬的）上有成型封头，装有分开的紧固装置。

屏风封志：设计成在集装箱入口处的屏障状。例如，屏风封志将内部锁杆围起来。屏风封志是可重复使用的。

2. **安全封志**

安全封志的材质对侵入的抵抗力是有限的，安全封志需要轻质的工具去移除。我们需要去查看安全封志的情况，以判断集装箱是否遭受过改动或者被侵入过。

金属丝封志：一定长度的钢丝圈装在紧固装置上。例如：卷曲丝、折叠丝及杯型丝封志。

条形封志：金属条或者塑料条装在一个环上，这个环从金属条或者塑料条的一端穿进/穿过另一端的紧固装置。

3. **提示性封志**

封志采用的是非常容易被破坏的材质，我们用手或者简单的切碎工具或者剪刀就可以轻易将它移除。我们需要去查看提示性封志的情况，以判断集装箱是否遭受过改动或者被侵入过。

拉带封志：提示性封志由一条薄带的一段连接在一个坚固装置上，薄带有锯齿也可能不带锯齿。另一端穿过紧固装置上的洞口，根据使用者的需要调整到合适的紧度。拉带封志可以有很多锁定位置。这些封志一般由合成材料制成，例如：尼龙、塑料。它们不可与简单的电扎带相提并论。

转动封志：钢棒或者重轨被穿进紧固锁。使用特定的工具后，使钢棒或者重轨缠绕本身。钢棒或者重轨直径各异。

标签或胶带封志：这种封志是自粘和自行解除的。它们被作为集装箱门的辅助安全方案使用。我们可以用手撕去纸质底层，然后贴在门把手上，或者贴在门把手下面。我们用肉眼去看封志的情况，去判断集装箱是否遭受过改动或者被打开过。标签封志就像一个沉默的哨兵，监视着集装箱的情况，而子弹封志、塑料封志或者其他传统封志都没有这个功能。子弹封志或者其他装在右手封洞位置的封志都很容易被避开。

黏胶门封志：由条形码制成，外面包裹着防伪物质。它可以显示出集装箱门是否被移动过。我们在视觉上很容易发现它的变动，因此它对于想要秘密偷窃的人来说是个障碍。若封志受到损坏，甚至没有受过训练的人都能立刻发现。

（二）电子封志

为了进一步确保高价值货物的安全，我们推动了所谓的“智能”封志的发展。这种封志将实体安全和信息化管理能力结合了起来，而正是后者将它和机械封志区别开了。它可以传输关于集装箱状态和货物内容的数据，所以它和机械封志是不同的。最基本的电子封志系统结合了装有记录和恢复关于集装箱内装物基本信息，如电子货物舱单的数据芯片的机械密封设备和能够读取芯片中所记录数据的机械装置。更高端的电子封志加入了可以电子化通信的系统。当封志被损坏或者被改动时，这些信息会传输过来。这种封志通过无线电频率、红外线和光纤来传输数据。在最先进的技术中，这种封志装上了各种传感物质（例如，辐射线、放射线、化学物质、生物物质、光、二氧化碳），这些传感物质可以记录和传输数据。与全球定位系统（GPS）结合后，警报和状态信息可以实时传输至中央处理系统，这样，我们可以确定集装箱的位置。以下电子封志的内容在经济合作与发展组织和欧洲运输部长会议的集装箱运输安全模式（2005）中作了概述。

1. 电子封志监控什么？

电子封志只监控封志以及和封志连接的传感器的状态——它不监管集装箱内部的状态。这点非常重要。正如前文所说，集装箱完整性不包含封志在内。即使传感器装载在集装箱上，传感到的状况也并不能反映集装箱内部的状况。对传感器的误读是一种特殊的情况，但是我们不能忽视传感器不能胜任监控集装箱内部的问题。

2. 电子封志提供什么？

电子封志不能提供集装箱内部的具体情况。电子封志提供的信息与负责密封的一方所描述的集装箱情况有关。如果原始的发货人负责密封，我们可以认为他所提供的情况基本上是正确的。然而，如果密封方不再是原始发货人，如货物到达中转站时，承运者给集装箱上了未确认的机械封志，那么载入封志内存的运输资料只反映第一个加封人对集装箱内容的最佳可得信息。最糟糕的情况是，装载非法货物的集装箱上了经过确认的封志，那么这个封志可以便利而不是阻止货物的运输。不申报和漏申报是国际运输中经常出现的情况。某些事故，例如贴错标签的装有次氯酸钙或者爆竹的集装箱引发的灾难性结果，强调了这种情况的现实性和风险性。若上述例子为大规模杀伤性武器，后果将不堪设想。

3. 电子封志相关基础设备

若电子封志要成为全球集装箱安全策略的一个有效部分，它必须有配套的读取设备/扫描设备、电脑硬件和正确处理封志数据的信息管理软件。如今，这些设备远远达不到标准，并且不可能在近几年内得到完善。码头经营人很可能是最早在他们经营的集装箱码头中的战略性地点安装电子封志读取装置的人，并利用该系统监控和跟踪封志的状况。一些大型海运承运人也可能安装电子封志读取器。但是，在中期，小型港口不可能安装和有效管理这样的系统。并且，尽管大型铁路和驳船运输公司安装上述基础设备和辅助电子封志的必要硬件具有可行性，小型的公路、铁路和船舶运输公司就算有可能安装也基本不可能在短时间内办到。可能出现的情况是，在整个集装箱运输链中对于电子封志的不平衡使用，即有能力处理电子封志数据的某些高安全节点间穿插着低水平或没有电子封志功能的区域。正确识别出这些区域的界限并制定出妥当的关于集装箱在这些区域间转运的协议是一项综合的集装箱安全计划不可或缺的一部分。

4. 电子封志的种类

根据封志和读取器间不同的通信系统，我们将电子封志分四类：

一是射频识别（RFID）；二是红外线（IR）；三是接触式；四是全球移动通信系统或卫星。下面的数据由美国交通部货物管理和运作办公室提供：

（1）射频识别（RFID）封志

射频识别技术是电子封志中最常见的。从根本上来说，这类封志结合了射频识别发射器和机械密封部件。射频识别标签和封志主要有两类：被动式和主动式。

被动式封志不主动传输数据。只有当读取器控制的装置被激活时才读取。被动式封志的识别码与标准条形码相同时，它获得验证。标签和封志作用相同。免电池的被动式封志简单、便宜且用完即弃。被动式封志是短程的、定向的，因此可以最大化地接收信号。在没有电池的支持的情况下，读取器最大的通信距离是 2 ~ 3 米，也有人认为 2 米之外效果就变差了。

主动式封志主动传输数据。这类标签和封志都需要插上电源，一般来说就是需要一块电池。主动式标签和封志的最大优势在于其远程和多方位通信的潜力，通信最远距离可达 100 米。远程通信和信号的穿透性对于快递公司非常重要。快递公司的需求促使电子封志和射频识别标准化组织制定了主动式封志的标准协议。

理论上来说，被动式和主动式的标签和封志的唯一区别即是否主动传输数据——这也说明了被动式射频识别标签不会主动发出求救信号。但设计者可给被动式标签加上电池，做些改动以匹配其他功能，解决监管、安全和成本问题，并且增加读取范围以及通过增加电池和感应器的方式增加多方位通信的灵活性。以上这些设想交给实验室进行研发讨论似乎是最合适的。

（2）红外线封志

红外线封志（IR）不如射频识别使用广泛。目前红外线封志还没有被标准化，但是对其技术优点却多有质疑。据报道，业内对红外线的不满包括其短程、数据速率慢、受雨雾天气影响以及对信号误诊的可能性。另外，红外线系统的信号传送是定向的，不能绕过拐角的阻碍。

（3）接触式封志

这类封志能在恶劣的气候下使用。接触式和近距离接触式技术包括接触式内存按钮、掌上型电脑和电子钥匙插件、低频率射频识别以及短程红外线。接触式和近距离接触式方案的支持者认为，人工监视封志是很重要的，且有很多好处。支持远距离方案的人则批评其未能节省人力和时间。

（4）远程报告封志

此类封志采用卫星或者移动电话通信方式。最大的好处是在运输中保持可视性，并且可以及时获得情况报告。这是一项高端性能，成本也高。若成本下降，远程报告封志对于安全和管理应用有巨大吸引力，尤其对于高价值和高危险性货物。

表1－2 电子封志技术比较

种 类	优 点	不 足
射频识别封志	功能广泛 被动式成本低廉 主动式功能强且成本适中	没有统一标准但此问题正在解决中；没有全球统一频率，这对主动式射频尤为关键
红外线封志	短程效果明显	没有明确优势或缺陷——矛盾的信息
接触式封志	可在恶劣环境中放心使用	接触式“键”容易丢失或被按错
远程报告封志	迅速识别问题的潜力 全球覆盖的潜力	成本高 需要大量外接电源
以上所有	提高效率和安全性	增加复杂性，开放了新的攻击途径，有令人产生虚假信心的风险 对供应商的索赔需进行独立评估 需对运行影响和技术表现进行评估 对增加的数据流进行管理和筛选、识别错误的正面信息，根据正确的正面信息采取行动

5. 电子封志如何工作?

在电子封志安装于集装箱之前，我们必须确认集装箱的号码、种类和内容，然后用手持设备将电子封志调试好。在每个检测点，射频识别子弹封志和集装箱标签一起，被相同的仪器读取。

一旦射频识别被安装在集装箱上并且被载入数据，它就可以检查集装箱的门是否被移动过。

6. 电子封志标准

若要使电子封志有效地确保国际贸易安全，它必须适用于全球集装箱运输系统。也就是说，安装在集装箱上的电子封志能被任何运输节点中的读取器所读取。反过来说，运输节点的读取器/扫描器能读取所有经过的电子封志。但现实并不是这样，很多竞争激烈的供应商推出了无数系统，有些与电子封志和读取器不相匹配。然而，很多管理部门和贸易界一致认为，若要使电子封志在供应链中被有效地使用，必须出台能被广泛接受的标准。至少，这些标准可以把专有硬件解决方案同信息传输协议和代码区分开来。

（三）对封志的总结

集装箱完整性对于集装箱安全非常重要。然而，从以往的经验看来，防盗设备、集装箱门/把手封志不足以全面保护集装箱免受蓄意侵入。明显地，为了防止集装箱成为恐怖分子的目标，我们必须开发出更好的封志。但是，如果我们认为采用科技方法（先进的机械或电子封志）就可以保证集装箱在航行中不受到破坏，那就错了。集装箱封志本身只是和货物装填以及密封过程同等重要。密封过程必须包括监管下的发货人装箱程序、整个封志使用期间里（不只是集装箱运输过程中）的封志确认和管理。

我们必须将以下两者区别开来：通过电子封志系统记录和管理的与集装箱安全有关的数据（如封志状态和集装箱编号）和可能通过电子封志系统记录和管理的、从供应链管理角度看更有实用性的数据。

射频识别在供应链和安全应用中的运用被减弱是由于统一标准的缺少和被某些人称为的“频率战争”的缘故。这两者是相关的。射频识别没有全球性的协议和标准。例如，在美国传输数据的射频识别不能在其他地方使用。总而言之，只有在那些使用同一频率的地方，射频识别才可以使用。因此，只有射频识别和卫星通信的结合才能为全球供应链提供安全和物流价值，并促使“智能集装箱”的产生。能使集装箱智能化的技术是：射频识别、卫星和移动电话。然而，在人们考虑将智能集装箱在供应链中全面使用之前，我们还需要做很多努力。首先需要我们解决的是规范和互通性问题。

关于规范必须解决以下问题，例如：对装置的具体要求和它的安全价值、可接受的误读频率是多少、使用哪种无线电频率、必要的读取器设备的安装和操作、与海关必要的通信连接和协议、装置的安全隐患、不同供货商的装置和系统的互通性、装置捕捉和传输的数据、数据权限的确认、装置的耐久性和易损性、电源或电池使用时间、装置被检测，或在没有检测就被移除的可能性、数据传输格式、事件日志和数据加密。

四、确保集装箱完整性的供应链安全技术：跟踪/追踪或定位技术

显然，如果管理者担心集装箱会被犯罪分子和恐怖分子滥用，他们就必须具备在整个供应链中对集装箱进行追踪的能力。这非常重要。因为这样不仅可以找到有风险的集装箱并对其进行查验，也能识别并可能追踪到比如因被劫持而失踪的集装箱。

追踪集装箱有两种方法：一是记录集装箱通过运输链“阻塞点”的信息，并通过数据库系统管理集装箱所在位置数据。二是通过运用卫星系统传送集装箱、货物、运输工具所在位置实时数据。发生在中东的一个案例分析中强调了这种方法（表1－3）。

表1－3　中东地区集装箱完整性案例分析

该中东国家对所有通过该国的卡车安装了运输监控工具。该工具使用实时追踪软件系统和报警装置，它能使海关关员看到卡车上装载的过境货物。该系统运用了全球定位系统（GPS）、全球移动通信系统（GSM）和无线电技术，能够：

- 记录并报道任何装有该系统的车辆的位置；
- 追踪车辆动向；
- 发现运输过程中的异常情况（比如发动机状态，打开的车门）
- 收集特殊情况中的准确信息
- 通过分析安装在车辆上的定位和通信元件承载的信息，判断伪报和走私风险
- 为海关决策提供充分资料

该运输监控工具如何工作？利用射频识别（RFID）标签和全球定位系统的数据读取器。

全球定位系统触头安装在卡车上，射频识别电子封志加装在集装箱上，全球定位系统每10分钟连接射频识别电子封志，并且通过全球定位系统每20分钟传送一次数据。

在整个供应链中，大部分的集装箱由“阻塞点”检查系统追踪。东非地区的案例分析中概述了阻塞点系统的一个衍生形式。检查可以由人工完成（比如由司机口头确认集装箱确实装载上车）；半自动化完成（比如使用条形码扫描）；自动化完成，如使用电子封志等方式。追踪这些检查得出的数据的难易程度和速度快慢取决于该地所安装的信息处理系统。虽然对集装箱进行追踪采用多个系统，但能够实现高效追踪。举个例子，海运承运人和货站经理通常使用高效的门、集装箱码头堆场和装船三个“阻塞点”追踪系统，使他们能准确掌握自己职责下的集装箱位置信息。即使是“低技术”含量的解决方案也能十分有效。很多小路运营者只依靠以纸和手机为基础的系统就能快速、高效地追踪货物。

第二项战略涵盖了一些持久和“实时”追踪形式。决定采用何种技术的关键因素与期望追踪的地理范围相关。东非地区的案例分析强调了低技术含量的关键点追踪系统（表1－4）。

表1－4　东非地区集装箱完整性案例分析

与前一案例中技术的作用相反，在这个系统中使用的是手机和互联网：

首先，在装载时，每个集装箱安装一个一次性编码封志。封志号码通过短信息发送到安全工作人员的手机上。从此刻起，对运输过程的护卫开始了，且运用了军方模式的护航技术。按照事先规划好的路线，在各个阻塞点安装有“视觉检查点”，以确保没有偏差，依次编号的封志符合初始信息。最后，在目的地的收货代理也收到所有短信。

这项供应链安全机制基本上包括本指南里提到的各种安全措施。装载时进行检查，先前的数据和已有的舱单信息通过实时短信或电话进行反馈，整个过程都有关于集装箱内装物的物理安全检查。

在相对较小的区域（比如集装箱码头），实时跟踪能够通过射频识别（RFID）标签和读取器共同完成。但是对整条供应链的实时追踪还需要卫星定位系统和相关的数据传输，虽然已有一些商业解决方案，但是相比于已有的追踪系统，这些商业方案还是相当昂贵的。

现在，卫星追踪依靠的是民用美国军方的全球定位系统（以下简称“GPS”）。GPS卫星发送一个较弱的信号，地面接收器将这个信号同步放大以定位接收器。这些接收器体积较小且已经为民用。每套设备根据其不同功能可达数百美元。GPS 技术已广泛运用，但在运用于比如集装箱追踪等关键技术前还有问题亟待解决。

一是现在民用 GPS 信号是军用信号的降低版本，通常需结合地面工作软件弥补此版本的不足。但现在这已不是 GPS 的操作问题。二是现在的 GPS 工作信号极弱。冷战期间苏联研发出的 GPS 堵塞和模仿技术如今被广泛应用于价格便宜的手提设备。根据功率不同，这些设备可以在相当大范围内造成信号堵塞或者发送错误的 GPS 数据。这项技术可能会被犯罪组织利用，通过仿造 GPS 数据掩盖其行动，将 GPS 定位的集装箱在不引起任何警报的情况下运输到另一地点。三是 GPS 在复杂地区和管（隧）道的运用会产生信号传输不畅或没有信号等情况。

（一）全球定位系统（GPS）

GPS 是由美国国防部开发的全球卫星导航系统，它是全球唯一在运作的全球导航卫星系统（GNSS）。该系统利用卫星星座传送精确的微波信号，使卫星接收器确定它们的当前位置、时间、运行速度和方向。

（二）伽利略（GALILEO）

伽利略是由欧盟和欧洲航天局（ESA）建立的全球导航卫星系统，这项斥资 34 亿欧元的项目是欧洲对美国全球卫星导航和俄国格洛纳斯的技术补充和备用。2007 年 11 月 30 日，欧盟 27 国交通部长达成协议，该系统将运行到 2013 年。

（三）格洛纳斯（GLONASS）

格洛纳斯是无线卫星导航系统，由苏联研发，现由俄罗斯空军掌握，为俄政府服务。该系统是俄罗斯对美国 GPS 和欧盟伽利略定位系统的补充和备用。该系统 1976 年开始研发，计划在 1991 年形成覆盖全球的网络。

从 1982 年 10 月 12 日起，大量的火箭把新卫星送进了该系统。到 1995 年，卫星星座布置完成。此后不久，由于俄罗斯经历经济崩溃，该系统无人维护。2001 年，俄政府修复该系统，近年来，和印度政府合作，修改并加快了该项目，计划于2009年恢复全球网络覆盖。

（四）指南针/北斗二号

指南针又名北斗二号，是中国独立开发的卫星导航系统。指南针不是对之前开发的北斗一号的升级，而是理论上与GPS和伽利略类似的一个新的全球导航卫星系统（GNSS），该系统是由35颗卫星组成的卫星星座，其中包括5颗地球同步轨道（GEO）卫星和30颗中地轨道（MEO）卫星，范围覆盖全球。

（五）印度区域性导航卫星系统（IRNSS）

印度区域性导航卫星系统是由印度空间研究所开发的自主区域性卫星导航系统，它将由印度政府全权控制。建立该导航系统要求的提出基于战争时无法保证全球导航卫星系统正常使用的事实。

印度政府在2006年5月批准该项目，计划在2012年建成并实施。印度政府与俄罗斯政府的协议中，就是否会优先于印度区域性导航卫星系统项目来修复俄罗斯格洛纳斯系统，或是否提供额外技术支持来完成印度区域性导航卫星系统的建设，态度尚不明确。

（六）对集装箱追踪的总结

尽管开发全球多式联运“阻塞点”集装箱追踪系统最终将是可行的，然而目前帮助承运人充分利用他们自有的追踪系统，同时保证相关政府部门获得其所需数据可能更有实效。

集装箱追踪的关键问题是时间。现行集装箱系统是否提供充分及时且有用的数据以应付对集装箱潜在的威胁？集装箱追踪关注的不应是“实时”数据而是“适时”数据。在某些情况下，实时数据可能更为合适，但是在更多其他情况下，现有的“阻塞点”追踪系统更适合追踪集装箱。例如，获知一个集装箱晚到了某个检查点，那么了解谁是最后承运人及其联系方式就可能足够。毕竟追踪只能告诉我们特定运输工具的位置而不是运输工具本身的信息 。

最后，各国需要全面评估基于GPS技术的实时追踪系统进行安全敏感度较高的集装箱追踪系统在现阶段是否足够强大。至少，不能完全脱离传统的“阻塞点”控制追踪系统。考虑到 GPS 转运设备的成本，尚无法明确是否会强制所有集装箱运输货物使用该技术。恰当的风险管理实践可能会根据特定用途更好地研究这些系统。

五、先进查验技术

在进一步讨论查验技术之前，必须确定讨论集装箱及其装载物时常用到的三种查验方式的基本定义：

筛查：一项目标甄别和风险管理程序。海关要对所有进口集装箱信息进行筛查。每个被确定为高风险的集装箱都要进行扫描，在必要情况下进行人工查验。

货车扫描或非侵入式查验：无须卸载货物，不会造成时间紧张，在运输工具系统中即可完成查验和确认货物。这种方法经常用于扫描内陆航运集装箱。对集装箱的非侵入式查验和人工查验是为了提供给海关关员足够的信息来辨别由集装箱的承运人所提供的集装箱资料是否准确，同时保证了集装箱完整性和查验效率。货车扫描很重要，可能在始发时或者负责填装和密封集装箱的合法的中小型企业已被犯罪组织利用，在这样的情况下，其他层面上提供的安全消息可能是虚假的，因为在实际情况非法时货物也可能表现出“合法”状态。

人工查验：基于筛查和扫描结果，打开集装箱，掏出货物，亲眼核查所装货物。这会造成额外支出和时间延误。

筛查、货车扫描或非侵入式查验和人工查验三种方式互为补充，但各不相同。若一个政府选择集装箱 100% 筛查，那是可能实现的。而另一方面，100% 扫描和查验是不可行的，因为口岸海关有繁重的工作量，而且从经济上来说，在任何国家都不具有可行性。额外增加传感或信息装置投入能够优化筛查。额外的数据，不管是否来自集装箱，比如篡改迹象；还是来自基础设施，比如辐射探测门户；又或是来自信息系统，比如额外货物详情，都能够优化筛查或者目标甄别程序。

（一）先进查验技术方法与实践

以下对东非和西非的案例分析的简介为我们提供了对筛查、扫描和人工查验如何互为补充的深入了解（表1－5）。

表1－5 西非和东非港口转运流程先进查验技术案例分析

两国都通过风险管理系统使用先进查验技术对每项进口交易给予适当程度的干预，确保更有效的海关资源分配，包括“快速通道放行”（只进行单证检查），X光扫描和人工查验。以下程序在这些港口中应用，并进行随机扫描： • 收集情报，如利用舱单数据来分析异常情况和集装箱与其单证的其他差异。 • 对集装箱进行风险排序、扫描，以及如有必要检查箱内货物。 • 仅在一个设计良好的系统框架内运用技术（如扫描设备），以使对物流的影响降至最低。 这种以风险为基础的扫描筛查和目标甄别方法增加了处理量和税收，也增强了安全性。

一般而言，可以区分出两种扫描的衍生形式：

主动扫描：依靠X射线和γ射线生成集装箱图像的系统。

核探测：基于放射等级不同来探测核物质和其他放射性物质的被动系统。

（二）核探测

2006年9月，一项针对《美国贸易安全与便利港口法案》的修正案被提出，该修正案建议将核探测作为运往美国集装箱货物的强制查验手段。欧洲、亚洲和美国的很多大型港口正在安装放射物探测门。这些项目几乎全由各国海关负责。

但让决策者感到尴尬的是，最近对由美国政府资助的新一代放射探测门——高级能谱门式探测器的测试引起了人们对其放射性物质探测效能是否显著优于目前的放射探测门产生了质疑。另一方面，一台新一代高级能谱门式探测器（ASP）在使用寿命期间的总费用预计超过80万美元，是现行放射物探测仪的3倍①。

---

① 据美国GAO报告09－655“Combating Neuclear Smuggling”，2009年6月。

对不影响物流又能检查出危险物的非侵入式查验的研究和发展一直没有间断，然而一项技术不能探查一切，所以多项技术的综合运用以及人力的操作就十分重要。好的扫描系统的确有诸多好处和优势，所以安装扫描系统是有必要的。提高扫描能力不但能探测核武器或大规模杀伤性武器，还能打击走私，促进税收，建立投资者信心以吸引更多投资。

（三）X射线和γ射线放射技术

先进查验技术最先在核对舱单上崭露锋芒，它让国家能更好地征收进口关税。权威人士认为X射线生成的图像质量有利于禁止如药品、金钱、武器等违禁物品的走私。X射线查验系统能够穿透30～40厘米厚的钢板、时速为13公里的货车。高穿透力也意味着更高的价格和维修费。过去几年，X射线扫描的用途已经由最初防止走私大规模杀伤性武器转变为安全保护。货物集装箱X射线查验系统已经在许多港口得到运用，这种激增的使用量反映了对港口安全的需求，该系统的特性使整箱扫描和成像的时间缩短至几秒。即使用于大范围扫描，生成的图像结果与传统的机场扫描相比，其能识别的货物可小到棒球的尺寸。

这种层次的扫描便于海关执法者对同一集装箱的进出港进行查验，并且可以对集装箱进行不同形式和层次的查验。以下着重介绍扫描的内置图层。

主动查验利用γ射线，γ射线是X射线的补充，但它是以电波作为放射元素。

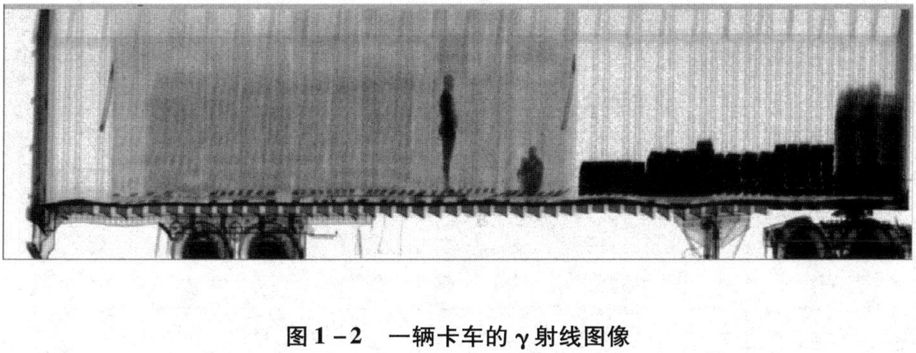

图1－2　一辆卡车的γ射线图像

图1－2为一辆卡车的γ射线图像：装载发泡胶托盘的集装箱里藏匿了2名偷渡者。该集装箱从加拿大入境美国水牛城纽约，图像拍摄使用了1.25兆电子伏光子。

X射线扫描在港口和边境越来越常用，它对集装箱运输的影响也常常被论及。这本质上是一个系统吞吐量问题。选择不同的X射线系统和在不同的港口设施中操作会产生不同的系统吞吐量。由于X射线系统已经解决了很多重要的问题，其在世界各个港口得到广泛使用。争论在于扫描是为了税收还是为了安全？所有利益相关人都应该记住，集装箱查验对安全和税收都是很重要的，效率（吞吐量）和操作经不起耽搁。但是在表1－6中可见，扫描结果和申报的不一致量一直在增加，税收可能会在进口商的错误或有意避税申报下流失。从安全的角度看也可以想象这些不一致将带来什么后果。

查验的人力因素也应该考虑在内，扫描图像需要有经过良好培训的人员来分析图像和其他指标。专家认为对海关关员进行扫描图像分析、数字化改革和由此带来的效率提高、创新扩展以及扫描制造部门的发展的培训将增加安全性并提高效率。分析表1－6中的数据，2001年到2008年之间的趋势表明对操作者的培训间接有利于供应链的安全。

表1－6　在西非港扫描的集装箱

年份	扫描集装箱数	申报与扫描结果不符的集装箱数	不符比例
2000	7480	103	1.38%
2001	13878	542	3.91%
2002	19767	770	3.90%
2003	13563	489	3.61%
2004	9595	344	3.59%
2005	13163	803	6.10%
2006	12079	1055	8.73%
2007	13811	1176	8.51%
2008	13842	1140	8.24%

与有关效率的讨论相对的，是对发展中国家负面影响的讨论。发展中国家认为安装进出口扫描系统是额外的负担，较小的港口可能因此被边缘化，而在枢纽港的货物转运方面，发展中国家关注的是专业性流失比如风险评估技巧和机会丧失。

（四）扫描的双重角色

扫描服务于两种不同目的：

一是协助侦查打击有组织或者有恐怖主义性质犯罪的非法物资流动；

二是协助海关保护并增加税收以减少贸易商或其代表错报或误报。

在同等技术、设备或者人力资源的前提下，这两种功能又相互重叠。在一个港口安装一台仪器查验进口货物以保持和增加税收，不应该被视为是解决供应链安全问题的全部。事实上，对潜在的武器、爆炸物和类似物品走私的监控是供应链安全中一个重要部分，是与税收利益相关的。有很多发展中国家尤其是非洲国家的进口货物扫描与税收相关。其中一个植入模式是：供应商授予建造、营运和移交（BOT）特许权，以安装和操作进口扫描设备。特许权通常包括有形设施，供应和运行的一个或多个扫描仪和一个风险管理系统、能力建设、转让技术诀窍和培训当地海关人员。虽然促进税收目标不断实现，在某些情况下甚至超过了期望值，但是扫描过程中的物理介入并不是很顺利，这就需要港口运营者、贸易组织和政府机构之间更多的关注。在港口经常可以听到关于物流操作、货物税款和由于港口和物流操作造成延迟产生的抱怨。在一些案例中，能力建设和专利的有效性遭到质疑。

本指南的目的不在于深入分析税收扫描机制，而是从这些经验中尽可能获取实际教训。

（五）快速扫描

扫描的一个明确的未来方向是“快速扫描”。它意味着海运集装箱可以在减速运动状态下在港口完成扫描。其在原理上和高速公路自动付费系统相似。为了回应美国提出的100%扫描计划，一些主要港口已经在对这种扫描方式进行调研。当然，快速扫描也有缺点。第一，由于货车在运动中，驾驶员要参与其中。这种低穿透力的扫描提供的图像不能以细节显示出集装箱内的全部内容。第二，由于图像细节少，补充查验即经常成为弥补不足的必要手段。

快速查验目前处于开发的初级阶段，早期系统包括公路和铁路的门式扫描装置，它们或被那些被喻为技术的“先遣采用者”的港口列入测试计划，或正在被测试。这些港口想要在当前和未来的供应链安全环境中确保竞争力。

总的来说，快速扫描包含3个完整的技术要素：

1. 识别货物/集装箱技术［射频识别（RFID），光学字符识别的集装箱号码或其他类似的技术］。

2. 集装箱X射线扫描。

3. 放射性威胁探查。

查验结束后，集装箱要装上高安全封志，这样任何篡改都将被记录。如果在港口处理中发现有封志不完整，则需要重新查验。值得注意的是，快速查验不仅仅依靠图像，也需要类似风险管理系统的风险分析。

快速查验不能独立存在，当发现异常时就需要高穿透力的扫描或者人工查验来辅助。快速扫描通常只对离港的集装箱实施，对于通过公路和铁路进入港口的集装箱需要重新考虑。所有进口集装箱将来都需要进入快速查验系统，这也就需要相应严格的准入控制。很多大型港口已经在准备和测试快速扫描，以作为应对100%扫描一旦实施的前期措施。

六、供应链安全技术讨论/总结

除对技术初步的明显共识之外（没有人愿意被视为“反技术”），对这一章的多种解读反映了对技术这一问题的不同观点、角度和解决路径。争论激烈并且仍将继续，本指南的目的就是如实反映当前的情况。有热情的技术开发者，也有来自港口和海运业的怀疑者，而这些怀疑者最终将采用这些技术或者为这些技术提供资金。立法者则凭借他们的智慧、精明、实用主义和现实主义，以及客观的态度处于两者之间。

研究和发展应朝着用低支出发展出大量远程感应和查验新技术的方向

努力。现有的探测武器和非法货物的技术很昂贵，并且会在物流环节造成拖延。安全的关注点应该在集装箱识别技术和操作流程上，风险管理的目的是减少集装箱扫描带来的负担。所有手段都有共同的弱点：它们都可以被规避。防篡改的封志会被恶意仿造或用电子手段篡改。当犯罪分子获知了哪些特征会启动特征描述算法时，这一算法对他们来说就沦为了一种游戏。新的检测技术对爆炸物和辐射物进行远程扫描，这能更好地确保集装箱运输系统。

技术的发展应该和市场需求相一致，能提供工业真正需要的设备。

在供应链关键点上对货物进行扫描需要通过数据取得、传输和分析，而技术在此具有重要作用（如货物舱单的安全传输）。问题的关键是，最需要技术的国家缺少技术能力。

最大的挑战不是技术问题而是发展中国家能否把获得的技术应用于相应的系统。这需要国内机构之间的合作、场景构建、制订计划书和来自财务部门领导的高层支持，以及领导们认识到成功与否依赖于资源和政府的意愿。

同时，动员企业参与提供信息通信技术服务非常重要，在必要的情况下，可以研究如何通过技术能力建设项目为企业参与提供资金支持。

企业已经在管理其国内和国际供应链时积极采用信息通信技术。在适当的政策和国际合作的配合下，这些发展可能获得有力支撑，以新的途径达成电子化政府，从而获得更佳和更多信息，提高边境保护能力。

发展中国家的相关支出和获益。

着手提出一项安全倡议要考虑的主要问题是每一个安全措施在效率基础上的利益和效果。经合组织的一项研究表明，低效率贸易流程的成本支出占货物本身价值的1%到15%。在发展中国家，各种复杂要求增加了进出口货物的时间和金钱成本，使得其成本更高。一般而言，发展中国家不采用复杂的安全程序和技术来提高效率。虽然几乎所有国家都认可先进技术带来的利益和联合措施能提高贸易便利和安全，但是对于如何达到这样的结果，由谁来主导现在以及未来全球都可接受的行为准则的问题，欧洲、美国以及发展中国家和各国的企业之间意见并不一致。

发展中国家基本上认可贸易便利和协调手段所产生的利益。另一方面，有很多人认为重视安全所带来的支出过高且无用。他们指出现行贸易内容复杂，包括基础设施不足、复杂地形和贸易伙伴相距甚远等。更多的是严格的预算限制和过分依赖外国贸易与投资，已经证明这是一个困难的结合体。所以这些国家提出："为什么让我们全面参与其中而这样会给我们带来更多困难?"

近期的调查着重指出了这些担心，比如胡默尔指出发展中国家运输费用平均高达发达国家2~4倍，货物量却远远少于发达国家。这意味着船舶需要停靠更多港口以提高运能利用率。下面是一组发展中国家经常碰到的问题：

货物重复装卸；

超载和阻碍影响港期；

复杂的海关手续；

复杂和不透明的文件、资料要求；

有限的计算机化，导致高成本的信息管理；

对合法贸易文件（如海运提单、信用证）是否有效的不确定性。

发展中国家有理由认为，国际组织和发达国家在实施如经授权的经营者（AEO）、100%扫描等国际标准时应当考虑他们的实际情况。他们提出，安全认证带来的支出已经过高，成为负担，并且导致恶性循环："随着越来越多的国家在供应链安全中引进认证项目，会产生一种风险，即那些缺少资源及信息交流和安全控制系统的国家不能分享项目带来的利益，甚至会对他们继续参与国际贸易的前景带来不利影响。"

注：本编五篇文章的原文选自世界银行出版物《供应链安全指南》，由世界银行提供（www. worldbank. org）。

有关中译本的免责声明如下：

该中译本不是由世界银行翻译，也不应被认为是世界银行的官方中译本。对于中译本的内容及可能存在的错误，世界银行概不对此负责。

Supply Chain Security Technologies

(Obtained from "*Supply Chain Security Guide*", The World Bank)

(Translated by Song Jieyan, Bureau of Anti – Smuggling)

The global supply chain is a distribution enterprise by nature. As such, it needs transport modes (land, air and sea) and transfer points, like maritime ports, air ports and inland transport facilities. In addition to the programs, policies and procedures outlined in the previous chapter, the supply chain also requires the use of technologies. Since operators in the supply chain are in the business of moving goods, protecting those goods from loss, theft and tampering is also inherently part of what these operators must address.

While the basic concept of security has changed little over time, there is now a trend to serve two purposes: security and efficiency. This collaboration between security and efficiency specialists actually began as a concept over 50 years ago. In 1956, it was a truck company owner driver who changed the shipping industry. Malcolm McLean observed a slow, inefficient and non – secure process for 20 years before he developed a container to secure his freight and move it in an efficient manner. This container standardized security, lowered costs of trade, lowered intransit losses, and allowed for interoperability. Today the container is still the center of the focus of SCS.

While this chapter will focus on the new technologies applied in SCS it will also display that the human component cannot be ignored. The issues of cost absorption will continue to be a problem for the developing world if new SCS schemes and legislature dictate technology use.

This chapter will review emerging and existing technologies; container integrity (CI), track/trace efforts, Advanced Inspection (AIT). Due to space constraints, information and communications technology (ICTs) , and technologies used to actualize data models, and two other collaborative tools, Electronic Single Windows (ESW) and Port Community systems (PCS) used in the supply chains will not be analyzed in detail. They are only mentioned in this introduction. They are not core to SCS, but, by nature, can contribute to its enhancement. For the reader interested in ESW and PCS, it is recommended to read: United Nations Centre for Trade Facilitation and Electronic Business (UN/CEFACT) Recommendation nr 3334.

1. Emerging trends in technology

In reviewing the numerous SCS schemes outlined in Chapter 1, most consider the container to be the main focus of security. It seems to make perfect sense to address the security issues linked to container technology once the consequences of a Trojan horse scenario or smuggling threats and crimes are analyzed. With that said, containers or containerized intermodal transport is not the only target. The global supply chain relies on various loading units or conveyances. Pipelines, bulk, roll on/roll off are all susceptible to, and have suffered interdiction on many occasions. In fact, according to most statistics available today, approximately 85% of loss within the supply chain occurs during hinterland transport. As world trade volumes continue to multiply and borders become more open, criminal and terrorist networks have become more organized and sophisticated. One avenue explored to combat the increased technology use in the modus operandi of criminal elements; so - called "smart containers" have been developed. Today's "smart containers" include a navigation and routing guidance system, satellite location, interior sensors, and radio frequency identification to secure the box from origin to destination. It can be estimated that a few thousand "smart containers" are in use at the time of the first publication of this guide.

The world - wide fleet of containers currently in use consists of 16 million units (24 million TEUs).

"Smart containers" sensors can detect anomalies such as:

- Door opening or removal.
- Cutting of holes in the roof, sides or floor.
- People or animals inside, e. g. by using passive infrared sensors.
- Dangerous chemical, biological or radiological material, e. g. by using CBRNE sensors.
- Location, e. g. using GPS or Galileo for track and/or trace applications.

The sensors would be connected to some form of central data logger. Sensor data from the logger could either be read at a port or border crossing point equipped with a compatible seal reader, or is sent by a long range communication system, e. g. satellite or GSM, to a monitoring point. So far, there are varying claims of benefits to the private sector for using "smart containers" and their associated technologies and systems.

The following synopsis by Giermanski (2008) highlights the potential of the "smart containers": "smart containers" have already been demonstrated to work. In 2006 between Germany and the US it was shown that the cost to the shipper is minimal, hardly more than electronic locks and seals… "smart containers" can carry and transmit electronically both logistics and sensory data. While there is no single definition of a smart container, it should be defined generally as a conveyance that meets World Customs Organization standards and complies with U. S. law, like the SAFE Port Act, and U. S. programs like C - TPAT by carrying and transmitting electronically, data and security intelligence from origin through destination to Customs when needed and on demand. "smart containers", as they exist today, perform at least seven clearly defined operations:

- Functioning as a part of a system approach necessary to coordinate all facets of the supply chain process to ensure visibility and security, beginning at origin.
- Capturing and transmitting electronically certain trade data that will link

to other supply chain documentation. Examples would be the container number, or booking number.

• Complying with the WCO, C – TPAT and the European Union's Authorized Economic Operator requirements to maintain the integrity of the entire container, by detecting a breach anywhere into its body.

• Reporting any breach in real time or close to real time.

• Providing worldwide geographic positioning throughout the supply chain when queried, and when programmed, automatically report its position if it is off its designated course of travel.

• Recognizing and recording the identity of the authorized person opening the container at destination.

• The container should be adaptable to different sensors and be able to communicate with or be adapted to divergent software packages used by shippers and carriers within the supply chain.

Some in the industry, however, regard so – called "smart containers" more as a miracle cure promoted by some technology providers. It has been commented that a container will never be smart, regardless the amount of technology propped into it. It is also argued that some of the "live tests" conducted so far have been nursed and cocooned from end to end, and would probably find it hard to routinely survive real life stress.

Container transportation, by nature, is heavily standardized (see ISO norms for maritime containers) and commoditized. Introducing a segregation between "smart" and "non – smart" containers, in itself, could be a challenge.

Initially, "smart containers" would be owned by the shippers who have a specific use for them, and treated as "shippers owned" by the sea carriers. This entails the problem of returning them to origin when emptied. Some container leasing companies have started to offer such equipment to lessees. Another avenue being explored, probably more viable, is to have removable "smart kits" that can be affixed onto any standard container, in a way somewhat similar to flexi – tanks or remote reefer cargo probe sets.

These "smart kits", sometimes called Asset Monitoring Unit (AMU), Container Monitoring Unit (CMU) or Asset Protecting Unit (APU), depending on the vendor, derive much of their technology, methodology and general philosophy from the high-tech "supply chain visibility" line of thought, which addresses tight inventory management issues. Some types of cargoes indeed do justify, and can afford a much closer attention than ordinary cargo, such as high value cargo, pharmaceuticals, sensitive chemicals, military supplies, and fashion goods linked to promotional campaigns do indeed resort to this kind of high visibility devices, generally provided by the logistics operators. On the other hand, while ordinary Importers would also enjoy the extra level of 24/7 visibility service, there is no sign in the market that they even remotely appear interested in paying for it.

Biometrics is also being introduced to the supply chain. Driver identification and verification is an essential function at cargo pickup points, intermediate delivery terminals, and even at destinations. Biometrics can improve the effectiveness of the function, reducing the risks of theft and terrorism while facilitating gate and reception processes, especially for drivers who make frequent pick-ups and drop-offs at the terminal. Biometric identification tools, such as fingerprint and iris recognition, may be incorporated in smart identification (ID) cards and integrated with on-line access to manifest, vehicle, and driver databases. Looking ahead, the Transportation Security Administration (TSA) Transportation Worker Identity Card (TWIC) aims to deploy a common biometric smart ID card for all US transportation workers.

2. Existing technologies

The following sections will provide a brief overview on the different types of technology used in SCS and how they are applied. While a complete overview of all existing technologies available on the commercial market would be beneficial to the readers of this guide, a current catalogue is available online with the WCO. The WCO maintains, for the benefit of its 174 Members, a Databank on Advanced

Technology accessible via the Organization's website. The Databank assembles information on technical equipment available in the market place and provides detailed and updated information of currently available technologies listed such as:

- Test & detection equipment.
- X – Ray equipment.
- Mechanical and electrical container seals.

3. SCS Technologies for Container Integrity: Container security devices and seals

Container Security Devices (CSD) play a crucial role in ensuring the integrity of the container along the supply chain and facilitating trade and Customs processes. Cargo security can be enhanced through the use of both mechanical and electronic seals. Both mechanical cargo seals and E – Seals act as barriers against pilferage, smuggling, and sabotage of cargo within containers and trailers en route to their destination. If either type of seal is found to be broken or if its identification (ID) number is different from the one on the cargo document, this is an indication that the container or trailer door might have been opened by an unauthorized person at some point in the transportation route. The unique ID numbers on both mechanical and e – seals provide tracking information. It is expected that the ID number on either type of seal will be recorded at each handoff in the chain of custody to provide information about when and where the container or trailer was handed over and the seal status at that time.

Ideally, seals should only be placed on containers by the party directly responsible for stuffing and/or visually verifying the contents of the container. In this respect, it should be stressed that the party responsible for stuffing and sealing the container is the first, and most important, link in a "secure" container transport chain. One must however remember that even high security mechanical seals are only as good as the procedures in place to affix, monitor and document them at each transfer of responsibility.

(1) Mechanical Seals

For the purposes of this document, the following terms and definitions from ISO 17712 apply. The classifications and types are outlined below.

A mechanical seal is a device marked with a unique identifier and is often marked by the seal owner's or issuer's stamp and/or color. It is externally affixed to the container doors and designed to evidence tampering or intrusion through the doors of a container and to secure closed doors of a container. In addition, depending on its construction, the seal provides varying degrees of resistance to an intentional or unintentional attempt to open it or to enter the freight container through the container doors. Even if a tampered seal were to be replaced with a similar unit after entry, the seal's unique identification number might not match with the one that was recorded when the original seal was affixed. The sealing process for security seals is as important if not more important than the seal itself.

Proper sealing protocols are comprised of a number of elements including the following:

- Purchasing/sourcing and shipping procedures for seals
- Training in seal use and verification
- Tracking of seal inventories and safe storage/release procedures
- Correct application of seals
- Recording seal numbers
- Managing and transmitting seal numbers
- Recording seal operations and identification of people involved and time and date
- Recording seal anomalies
- End - of - use and end - of - life disposal of seals.

Without proper sealing and checking protocols, the use of seals can be counter - productive as they can instill a false sense of security as to the status of the container handle/door. In theory, security seals should prove effective in detecting any attempt to tamper with the container.

In reality, however, simple security seals are relatively easy to defeat. The reasons are numerous but include the ease with which they can be cut, the possible lack of proper seal documentation, the possibility of poor security management in the container transport chain and the relative ease of replicating certain seals and their numbers. As with simple indicative seals, verifying the seal is both a manual and time – consuming process and thus many seals are only summarily checked, if checked at all, while in transit. Finally, and this is not a problem unique to security seals, experienced thieves have devised ways to bypass the handle or the container doors entirely when gaining entry to the container.

One must however always remember that even high security mechanical seals are only as good as the procedures in place to affix, monitor and document them every time the container changes hands (at each transfer of responsibility). In addition, once illegitimate cargo stealthily finds its way into a container prior to affixing the seal, the sealed container will be as good as a legitimate passport all the way to destination. This is why upstream supply chain security procedures must include the company, personnel and facilities that produce, pack and stuff the cargo into the container.

i. Types of mechanical seals

High security seals. This is a seal that is constructed and manufactured of material, such as metal or metal cable, with the intent to delay intrusion. High security seals generally must be removed with quality bolt cutters or cable cutters. They require inspection to indicate whether tampering has occurred or entry has been attempted. According to the 9/11 Commission Act of 2007, effective October 15, 2008 all containers in transit to the United States shall be required to be sealed with a seal meeting the International Organization for Standardization Publicly Available Specification 17712 (ISO/PAS17712) standard for sealing containers. It is crucial that companies are aware that all cargo arriving by vessel at any port of entry in the United States are required to be sealed with a seal meeting the ISO/PAS 17712 standard for High Security seals. The WCO has also endorsed the ISO 17712 standard for seals.

There are many types of seals on the market that meet or exceed the ISO 17712 standard and many seal manufacturers. Businesses are responsible for acquiring seals from legitimate manufacturers. Companies purchasing seals should be backed by the seal manufacturer's test report issued by an independent ISO 17025 certified testing laboratory. Businesses should maintain this documentation for future reference. While this guide does not endorse any particular seal manufacturer or product, there are organizations, such as the International Seal Manufacturers Association (ISMA) that can provide information on seal manufacturers offering ISO PAS 17712 high security seals.

A variety of High security Seals is shown below:

PADLOCK SEAL: Locking body with a bail attached: either wire shackle padlock (metal or plastic body), or plastic padlock and keyless padlock seals.

CABLE SEAL: Cable and a locking mechanism. On a one – piece seal, the locking or seizing mechanism is permanently attached to one end of the cable. A two – piece cable seal has a separate locking mechanism which slips onto the cable or prefabricated cable end.

BOLT SEAL: Metal rod, threaded or unthreaded, flexible or rigid, with a formed head, secured with a separate locking mechanism.

BARRIER SEALS: Designed to provide a significant barrier to container entry. A barrier seal may, for example, enclose a portion of the inner locking rods on a container. Barrier seals may be designed to be reusable.

ii. SECURITY SEALS

Seal that is constructed and manufactured of material that provides limited resistance to intrusion and requires lightweight tools for removal. Security seals require inspection to indicate whether tampering has occurred or entry has been attempted.

Wire seal: length of wire secured in a loop by some type of seizing device. Some examples are crimp wire, fold wire and cup wire seals.

Strap seal: metal or plastic strap secured in a loop by inserting one end into or through a protected (covered) locking mechanism on the other end.

iii. INDICATIVE SEALS

Seal that is constructed and manufactured of material that can easily be broken by hand or by using a simple snipping tool or shear. Indicative seals require inspection to indicate whether tampering has occurred or entry has been attempted.

Cinch or pull – up seal: indicative seal consisting of a thin strip of material, serrated or non – serrated, with a locking mechanism attached to one end. The free end is pulled through a hole in the locking mechanism and drawn up to the necessary tightness. Cinch or pull – up type seals may have multiple lock positions. These seals are generally made of synthetic materials such as nylon or plastic. They should not be compared to simple electrical ties

Twist seal: steel rod or heavy – gauge wire of various diameters, which is inserted through the locking fixture and twisted around itself by use of a special tool.

Label or Tape seal: These seals are self – adhesive and self – voiding seals. They are used as an adjunct security protocol on doors for any container. They are hand applied by removing the protective paper backer and sticking them to the container over or under the keeper bars. They are used to visually indicate tampering or opening of the doors while unattended. These seals work as a silent sentry to monitor doors where bolt seals, plastic seals or other conventions seals cannot. Bolts or any seals placed in a normal right hand seal hole are easy to circumvent.

Tape door seals are manufactured with barcode, coated with anti counterfeiting components. This application procedure will indicate if the doors had been removed. These seals are easy to visually interrogate and they provide a formidable barrier to thieves against surreptitious entry. As a chain of custody tool, anyone seeing them violated will immediately know with little or no training.

(2) Electronic Seals

The need to further secure containers containing high value goods has led to the development of several types of so – called "smart" seals. These types of seals have integrated physical security and information management capabilities. It is the latter functionality that sets these aside from their mechanical counterparts since they can transmit data regarding their status as well as the information regarding the contents of the container. At a minimum, an electronic seal system combines a physical sealing device with a data chip capable of recording and restituting basic information regarding the container contents, such as an electronic cargo manifest, and a mechanism for reading the information recorded on the chip. A higher level of functionality is added by systems capable of electronically communicating whether the seal has been broken or otherwise tampered with. These seals use radio frequency (RF), infra – red (IR) or fiber optics to transmit data. In their most advanced iterations, electronic seals can be coupled with a variety of sensors (e. g. radioactive, radiological, chemical, biological, light, CO2, etc.) that can record and communicate data regarding the in – container environment. In combination with a global positioning system (GPS) transceiver, alerts or status messages regarding the container can be transmitted in real time to a central processing system that can pinpoint the container's location. The following section on e – seals is outlined in the Organization for Economic Co – operation and Development and European Conference of Ministers of Transport Container transport security across modes (2005).

i. What do e – seals monitor?

E – seals only monitor the seal's status and that of any sensors connected to the seal – they do not monitor the condition inside the container. This nuance is important. As pointed out earlier, a container's integrity can be compromised without compromising the integrity of the seal. Even when sensors are attached, the seal records sensor events which may or may not reflect what is actually happening within the container environment. "False – positive" readings from sensors are a particular concern but one should not overlook the possibility that sensors can be defeated by more or less sophisticated means.

ii. What do shipping – related information e – seals provide?

E – seals cannot provide detailed information on the contents of a container. What they do provide is information regarding what the party responsible for sealing the container said was in the container. If that party was an originating shipper, one might assume that the information is more or less correct. However, if that party is once or twice removed from the originating shipper like in the case of a carrier placing an E – seal on a container that arrived at the terminal with a non – conforming mechanical seal, then the shipping documents loaded into the seal's memory only reflect the E – seal – affixing party's best available information as to the contents of the container. In a worst case scenario, a conforming E – seal on a container containing illegitimate cargo might actually facilitate the transport of that cargo, rather than prevent it. Non – declaration or mis – declaration of goods is not an unknown phenomenon in international transport, and the catastrophic outcomes of certain incidents such as mislabeled calcium hypochlorite or fireworks – containing containers, highlights both the reality and the risk of such situations. Any sense of security instilled by the presence of an E – seal on an intentionally mis – manifested container containing a WMD would have dramatic consequences.

iii. E – seal infrastructure

For E – seals to be an effective part of a global container security strategy, they must be accompanied by a host of reading devices/scanners, computer hardware and a suite of underlying information management software systems capable of properly processing the seal data. Today, these requirements are far from being met, and their fulfillment throughout the container transport chain is not at all assured in the near future. It is likely that major terminal operators will be the first to place E – seal readers at strategic locations within their container terminals and to use such systems to monitor and track the status of such seals. Some of the major maritime carriers might start to deploy E – seal readers as well. However, it is not at all sure that smaller ports will be able to deploy and effectively manage such systems in the medium term. Furthermore, while it is feasible that major railroads and barge operators might also be able to deploy the underlying infrastructure and hardware necessary to support E – seals, it is highly unlikely that small road carriers and smaller barge/rail operators will be in a position to do so any time soon – if ever. What is likely to emerge is uneven support for E – seals across the container transport chain with certain high security nodes capable of processing E – seal data punctuated by areas of low or no E – seal functionality. Properly identifying the boundaries of these zones and developing appropriate container transfer protocols among these zones are necessary components of a comprehensive container security plan.

iv. Types of E – seals

There are four types of E – seals, classified by the four different communication systems used between the seal and its "reader:"

- Radio frequency identification (RFID)
- Infrared (IR)
- Direct contact, and
- Mobile GSM or satellite.

The following data is provided by the US Department of Transportation office of Freight Management and Operations:

- RFID Seals

RFID technologies are most common among electronic seals. Fundamentally, they marry RFID transponders or their components with manual seal components. There are two main types of RFID tags and seals, passive and active.

Passive seals do not initiate transmissions—they respond only when prompted by the device used by a reader. A passive seal can identify itself by reporting its ID similar to a standard bar code. The tag can also perform processes, such as testing the integrity of a seal. A battery – free passive seal is simple, inexpensive, and disposable. Passive seals tend to be short range and directional to maximize antenna exposure to reader signal strength. Maximum read range for electronic seals without battery – assisted communications tends to be two – three meters, with some debate in the industry about efficacy beyond two meters.

ACTIVE SEALS can initiate transmissions as well as respond to interrogation. All active tags and seals require on – board power, which generally means a battery. A major attraction of active tags and seals is the potential for longer – range and Omni directional communications——up to 100 meters. Expressed user needs for greater range and the ability of signals to wrap around obstructions in terminal operating environments prompted the international standards group working on electronic seal and read/write container RFID standards to add active RFID protocol (s).

Theoretically, the only difference between passive and active tags and seals is the ability to initiate communications from the tag——a distinction that means passive RFID tags could not initiate mayday calls. However, a designer could add on - board power to a passive tag, match other functionality and, setting aside regulatory, safety, and cost issues, increase read range and directional flexibility by increasing power and adding antennas. This perspective seems most appropriate to laboratory R&D discussions.

- Infrared Seals

IR is a less common choice than RFID. It does not appear to be any standards issues about IR, but there are unresolved disagreements about its technical merits. Reported industry concerns include short range, slow data rates, effects of fog and rain, and susceptibility of some designs to generate false positive tampering signals. In addition, infrared systems are directional, offering line - of - sight performance without an ability to wrap around corners.

- Contact Seals

These seals work in most harsh weather environments. Contact and near - contact technologies include contact memory buttons, PDA and electronic key plugins, low frequency RFID, and short range IR. Proponents of contact and near - contact solutions argue that it is important to have a human being visually observe the seal, and their solutions provide that added benefit. Proponents of longer - range solutions criticize the missed opportunity for labor and process timesaving.

- Remote Reporting Seals

Remote reporting uses satellite or cellular communications. The great advantage is the ability to maintain visibility en route and to obtain near real - time event reports. It is a high - end capability, usually at high cost. As costs drop, it will become increasingly attractive for security and management applications, especially for high - value and hazardous cargo.

Box Comparison of E - seal technologies

Type	Pros	Cons
RFID	Broad array of capabilities Passive can be very low cost Active can be high capability and moderate cost	Lack of standards, but this is being addressed Lack of global frequencies, especially in regard to active RFID
IR	Clearly effective at short ranges	Lack of clarity on strengths and shortcomings—contradictory information
Contact	Some are highly reliable in harsh environments	Contact " keys" subject to loss and misuse
Remote	Potential for immediate identification of problems potential global coverage	High cost Usually requires significant outbound power
All	Potential to improve efficiency along with security Source: US Department of Transportation	Risks of increasing complexity, opening new avenues of attack, and generating false confidence Need for independent assessment of vendor claims. Need to assess performance Requirement to manage and sift increased data flow, identify false positives, and act on true positives operational impacts as well as technical

v. How do they work?

Before its installation on the container the E - seal must be programmed with a handheld device by validating the container number, container type and eventually the content. The RFID bolt seal is then read at each check point using the same readers as the Container tag. Once the RFID is installed on the container and the data is loaded it will signify if the door has been tampered with.

vi. E - seal standards

For E - seals to be effective in helping to secure international trade, they must be useable throughout the global container transport system. This means that any E - seal affixed to a container must be readable in any transport node equipped with E - seal readers, and, conversely, reading/scanning equipment in any transport node worldwide should be capable of reading any E - seal passing through. This is not the case today as many competing vendors have proposed numerous and sometimes incompatible systems. However, many administrations and the trading community in general now agree that broadly accepted standards are necessary if E - seals are going to be effectively deployed throughout the supply chain. At a minimum, these standards should separate proprietary hardware solutions from information transmission protocols and codes.

(3) Conclusion: seals

Ensuring container integrity is fundamental to ensuring container security. However, past experience with anti - theft devices and container door/handle seals have revealed the inadequacy of these devices to fully protect containers from and/or reveal unauthorized access by determined criminals. Clearly, better seals must be deployed if the container is to be targeted by terrorists. However, it would be incorrect to believe that a technological fix in the form of an advanced mechanical or electronic seal alone would be sufficient to ensure that containers are not tampered with during their voyages. Any container seal is only as good as the container stuffing and sealing process in which it is involved. This process must include controlled stuffing procedures by the shipper, seal identification and management throughout the seal's lifespan (and not just during the container voyage).

Distinction should be made between the data recorded and managed by an E - seal system that has particular security relevance such as seal status and container number, and the data that could potentially be recorded and managed by E - seal systems that have more utility from a supply chain management perspective.

Adoption of RFID in supply chain and security applications is hampered by a lack of standards and by what some call "the frequency wars." The two issues are interrelated. RFID has no global protocols or standards. For instance, RFID on which the data ride in the US will not work anywhere else. In short, RFID for container security is applicable only to those areas of the world that have agreed on the same frequency. Therefore, only a combination of RFID and satellite communication integrally linked to a human agent provides both security and logistics value in a global supply chain, and by its nature becomes the "smart container." The technologies that would make the container smart are RFID, satellite, and cellular. However, there is still a long way to go before the "smart container" can be considered a candidate for generalized use in the supply chain. To start with, the question of specifications and interoperability needs to be solved:

Specifications must address issues such as:

- what specifically the device would be required to do and its security value.
- what acceptable false positive and false negative reading rates would be.
- what radio frequency would be used.
- the requirements for the installation and operation of the necessary device reader infrastructure.
- the requirements applicable to the necessary communications interface and protocols with Customs.
- the security vulnerabilities of such devices.
- the necessity of interoperability of various vendors' devices and systems.
- the data to be captured and transmitted by the device.
- identification of who will have access to the data in the device.
- survivability and vulnerability of the device.
- power or battery life requirements.
- the probability that the device can be detected, or removed without detection.
- required data messaging formats, event logs, and data encryption.

4. SCS Technologies for Container Integrity: Track/Trace or Positioning technologies

It seems evident that if authorities are concerned about the potential misuse of containers by criminals or terrorists, they should have the ability to track containers throughout the transport chain. This is not only important so that containers identified as risky can be found and inspected, but also so that containers that have gone missing like in the case of a hijacked container, can be identified and possibly found.

There are two ways containers can be tracked. The first involves recording the passage of containers through "choke points" in the container transport chain and managing the location data via database systems. The second involves utilizing a transponder or satellite – based system to deliver real – time data on the location of the container, cargo, or transport. This method is also highlighted in a case study conducted in the Middle East.

Box Case Study on Container Integrity in the Middle East

This Middle Eastern Country incorporated a transit monitoring tool for all trucks transiting through the country using a live – feed tracking software system and alarm that provides Customs officers full visibility of transiting goods aboard truck transport. This system utilizes GPS, GSM positioning and Radio technology in order to:

- Record and remotely report the location on land of every vehicle equipped with the system
- Trace all movements by the vehicle
- Detect abnormal patterns throughout the transit trip (e. g. engine status and open doors)
- Collect accurate information on specific events
- Assess risk of fraud and smuggling by analyzing information conveyed by the positioning and communication unit installed on the vehicle
- Provide adequate information to support decision making by Customs.

How Does it Work? RFID Tag and Reader with GPS

A GPS antenna is installed on the truck and an RFID e – seal is affixed onto the container. The GPS is pinging the RFID seal every 10 minutes and the data is transmitted every 20 minutes by GPS.

Most containers are tracked in the supply chain using some iteration of a "choke point" checking system. A variant of a choke point system is outlined in the case study conducted in East Africa. The checks can be accomplished manually (e. g. by a driver orally or otherwise confirming the loading of a particular container onto a truck) semi – automatically (e. g. through some form of barcode scanning) or automatically, as envisaged in several active e – seal solutions. The data generated by these checks is tracked and can be restituted with more or less ease, and more or less quickly, depending on the particular information management system in place. Container tracking within each individual system, however, can be highly effective. For instance, maritime carriers and terminal managers typically operate highly effective gate, container yard and vessel loading "choke point" tracking systems that allow them to have a precise knowledge of where containers under their responsibility can be found. However, even "low – tech" solutions can be effective. Many small road operators simply using paper and cell phone based systems can track their consignments both quickly and effectively.

The second strategy involves some form of continuous and "real – time" tracking. The main determining factor in deciding which technology option to use relates to the desired geographic scope for the tracking. The case study in East Africa highlights a low – tech choke – point tracking system.

Box　Case Study on Container Integrity in East Africa

In contrast to the technology deployed in the previous case study, the technologies used in this system are cell phones and the internet: first, at loading, a disposable numbered seal is attributed per container. This seal number is broadcast via SMS on mobile phones to the security staff. From this point, an escort follows the transport and military style convoy techniques are applied. Along the pre – planned route, there are "visual check points" that are strategically placed at choke points to ensure there is no deviation and that the serial numbered seal matches the initial communication. Lastly, at destination the receiving agent has also received all SMS.

Basically, this SCS scheme consists of all the security layers outlined in this guide. Inspection is conducted at loading, advanced data and manifests exist via e – mail or real – time SMS feeds or voice calls, and there is physical security around the contents at all times.

In the case of relatively small areas (such as in a container terminal), real – time tracking can be accomplished via a combination of RFID tags and readers. However, real – time tracking throughout the supply chain necessarily requires some form of satellite positioning system and a related transponder. Already, several commercial solutions are available based on this principle but these are considerably more expensive than existing tracking systems.

Currently, satellite tracking is accomplished through the civilian use of the US military GPS. GPS satellites emit a weak signal that ground receivers triangulate and synchronize according to a satellite – timing signal in order to pinpoint the receiving station's location. These receivers are small and are becoming common for civilian use. Each unit, however, can cost upwards to several hundred dollars depending on its functions. While GPS is currently a widespread technology, several issues remain that should be addressed before its deployment for critical use applications – such as container tracking.

The first issue is that the civilian – use GPS signal is a degraded version of the military GPS signal. GPS systems typically integrate a software work – around to compensate for this. However, this is not so much an issue for operational GPS use anymore. The second issue is that GPS systems operate on extremely weak signals. During the cold war, the Soviet Union developed GPS – jamming and GPS emulation techniques that are now widely available in relatively inexpensive handheld devices. Depending on their power levels, they can jam or generate false GPS readings over considerable ranges. As this technology and its use are widespread, it is conceivable that a criminal organization could use an emulated GPS signal to hide its actions and deliver a GPS – tracked container to a location without raising any external alarms. Finally, GPS use in complex urban environments and in tunnels is compromised by reflected, scattered and/or unavailable satellite signals. The GPS systems are outlined below.

(1) GPS

GPS is a Global Navigation Satellite System (GNSS) developed by the

United States Department of Defense. It is the only fully functional GNSS in the world. GPS uses a constellation of satellites that transmit precise microwave signals that enable GPS receivers to determine their current location, the time, and their velocity (including direction).

(2) GALILEO

Galileo is a global navigation satellite system currently being built by the EU and European Space Agency (ESA). The 3.4 billion project is an alternative and complementary to the US Global Positioning System (GPS) and the Russian GLONASS. On November 30, 2007, the 27 EU transportation ministers involved reached an agreement that it should be operational by 2013.

(3) GLONASS

GLONASS is a radio – based satellite navigation system, developed by the former Soviet Union and now operated for the Russian government by the Russian Space Forces. It is an alternative and complementary to the United States' GPS and the planned Galileo positioning system of the EU. Development on the GLONASS began in 1976, with a goal of global coverage by 1991. Beginning on October 12, 1982, numerous rocket launches added satellites to the system until the constellation was completed in 1995. Following completion, the system rapidly fell into disrepair with the collapse of the Russian economy. In 2001, Russia committed to restoring the system, and in recent years, with the Indian government as a partner, has diversified, and accelerated the program with a goal of restoring global coverage by 2009.

(4) COMPASS / Beidou – 2

The Compass system (also known as Beidou – 2) is a Chinese project to develop an independent global satellite navigation system. Compass is not an extension to the previously deployed Beidou – 1, but a new GNSS system similar in principles to GPS and Galileo. The new system will be a constellation of 35 satellites, which includes five geostationary orbit (GEO) satellites and 30 Medium Earth Orbit (MEO) satellites that will offer complete coverage of the globe.

(5) Indian Regional Navigational Satellite System (IRNSS)

The Indian Regional Navigational Satellite System (IRNSS) is an autonomous regional satellite navigation system being developed by Indian Space Research Organization, which would be under total control of Indian government. The requirement of such a navigation system is driven by the fact that access to Global Navigation Satellite Systems is not guaranteed in hostile situations.

The government approved the project in May 2006, with the objective to have the system completed and implemented by 2012. It is unclear if recent agreements with the Russian government to restore their GLONASS system will supersede the IRNSS project or feed additional technical support to enable its completion.

(6) Conclusion: Container Tracking

While in the end, developing some form of global multimodal "choke point" container tracking system may be desirable, presently it is probably more effective to help carriers to optimize their own tracking systems and to ensure that appropriate government agencies have access to this data as needed.

One of the key questions related to container tracking is the issue of timing. Does the container tracking system in use provide sufficiently current and useful data so that threats can be acted upon? The focus of container tracking should not necessarily be real - time data but "right - time" data. In some instances, real - time data may be appropriate and useful (as in the case of hazardous substances and/or in regions known to harbor terrorist operatives), but in many others, existing choke point tracking systems might be perfectly adapted to tracking containers. It may be sufficient to know, for instance, that a container was arriving late at a checkpoint and know who the last carrier was and how contact can be made.

After all, tracking just tells us with some certainty where the transponder is, not necessarily the vehicle itself.

Finally, countries should fully assess whether real - time tracking systems based on GPS technology are sufficiently robust at this stage for security - sensitive operations such as container tracking. At a minimum, these should not be deployed without the back up of a more traditional chokepoint control tracking system. Furthermore, given the cost of GPS - enabled transponder devices, it is not at all clear that their use should be mandated for all containerized consignments. Again, appropriate risk management exercises might better target these systems for specific uses.

5. Advanced Inspection Technologies (AIT)

Before inspection technologies can be further discussed, a baseline definition must be established for the three types of inspections that are commonly used when discussing the container and its contents:

i. Screening: described as the targeting and risk management process. Customs should screen information on 100 % of import containers (see ACI). Each and every container identified as high risk is subsequently scanned and, if needed, physically inspected.

ii. Cargo scanning or non - intrusive inspection (NII) is a method of inspecting and identifying goods in transportation systems without a time intensive unloading process. It is often used for scanning of intermodal freight containers. NII and the physical inspection of a container's contents are conducted in order to provide Customs officials with the ability to verify the accuracy of information provided by shippers on a container's contents and the effectiveness of container integrity measures. Scanning is important because it can help identify dangerous cargo when the originating shipper, or the party responsible for stuffing and sealing the container, appears to be legitimate (AEO) but has actually been infiltrated by a criminal group. In these cases, other layers of security may provide a false sense of security because the shipments appear to be outwardly "legitimate" when in fact it is illegal.

iii. Physical Inspection: Based on the results from screening and/or scanning the container is opened and unstuffed for a visual verification of contents. This generates extra - costs and delays.

Screening, scanning, and physical inspection of containers, while complementary, are not the same. 100% container screening is possible, should an administration choose to do so - 100% scanning and inspections, on the other hand, are not viable due to the backlog at Customs in ports, nor is it economically feasible for all countries. Screening can be improved with additional sensor - based or information - based inputs. Additional data, whether from the container, i. e. tamper indication, from the facility infrastructure, i. e. radiation detection portals, or from information systems, additional shipment detail, could be used to improve the screening/targeting processes.

(1) AIT Methodology and practice

The following snapshot from case studies in East and West Africa provides insight in how screening, scanning, and inspection complement each other.

Box AIT Case Study of AIT process of Ports in West and East Africa

Both of these countries use AIT through a Risk Management system to ensure a more efficient allocation of: Customs resources by designating the appropriate level of intervention required for each import transaction. This ranges from "Fast Track Release" (documentary check only), X - Ray scanning and then inspection through a physical examination. The following process is employed in these ports, random scans are conducted:

- Collect intelligence, e. g. manifest data to analyze anomalies and other discrepancies of container and their documentation.
- Rank containers by risk, then scanning and (if needed) inspect the contents of containers as appropriate
- Employ technology (e. g. scanning devices) only in a well - crafted systems framework to minimize the impact on the flow of trade.

This risk based approach of screening and targeting for scanning has increased throughput, increased revenue, and increased security.

Generally, two types of scanning variants can be distinguished:

- Active scanning: A system making container images based on X – rays or Gamma ray beams.
- Nuclear detection: A passive system detecting nuclear and other radioactive materials based on their radiation levels.

(2) Nuclear detection

In September 2006, an amendment was proposed for the US SAFE port act in which Nuclear Detection will become mandatory for US – bound containerized cargo. Many of the largest ports in Europe, Asia and the US are in the process of installing radiation detection portals. Almost all these programs take place under responsibility of Customs.

However, adding to the predicament of the decision – makers, recent tests of the new generation of radiation detection portals, the Advanced Spectroscopic Portal (ASP), developed under the aegis of the US Government, have cast doubts on its ability to detect radioactive material significantly better than the existing generation. On the other hand, the estimated lifecycle cost for one of the new generation ASP exceeds US $ 800, 000 or almost the triple of the cost of existing radiation scanners. ①

While the continuous research and development of NII technologies are needed to detect hazardous cargo without interrupting the flow of goods, one technology cannot detect everything. Thus, the combination of technologies and attentive human operators is necessary. In order to justify the eventual installation of scanning devices, it can be noted that multiple benefits and objectives might result from a good scanning system. Improving scanning ability could serve not only to detect Nuclear or other WMD weapons but also to reduce smuggling, to improve tax collection and to earn the trade community's trust to attract

---

① US GAO report 09 – 655 "Combating Nuclear Smuggling", June 2009 more trade.

(3) X - ray and Gamma - ray radiography

Advanced Inspection Technologies (AIT) first gained prominence for manifest verification, allowing countries to better enforce import tariffs. Authorities also found that the image quality achieved with X - ray scanning allowed them to interdict contraband, including drugs, cash, weapons, and other illicit materials. X - ray radiography systems can penetrate up to 30 - 40 cm of steel in vehicles moving with velocities up to 13 km/h. They provide higher penetration but also cost more to buy and operate. During the last few years, attention has shifted to security concerns, where X - ray screening is expected to become a major tool in prohibiting the smuggling of weapons of mass destruction. X - ray inspection systems for cargo containers have now become a more familiar feature in numerous ports. This rapid adoption has been accelerated by the needs of port security, but made practical by the systems' unique ability to penetrate entire containers and generate images of the contents in just a few seconds. Even at this large scale, the resulting images are comparable to those obtained through traditional baggage scanning at airports and capable of identifying objects smaller than a baseball.

The inspection layer also allows for Customs administrations of both the originating and importing ports to conduct inspections on the same container and can require the container to pass through different types and increasing levels of inspections. The following highlights the built - in layers of a scanning operation.

Active scanning using Gamma - ray radiography

Gamma - ray radiography is an alternative to X - ray but uses a radio - active source for the radiation.

Gamma - ray image of a truck with two stowaways in a container of Styrofoam trays entering US from Canada at Buffalo, N. Y. Image taken using 1. 25 MeV photons.

As X - ray cargo scanning becomes more common at ports and border

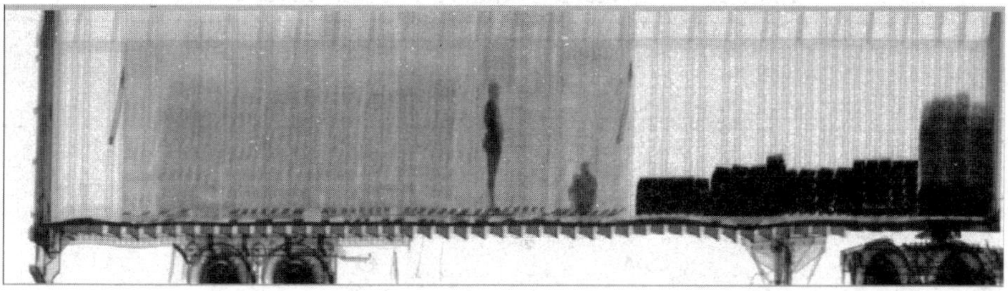

crossings, its impact on container traffic is frequently discussed. This is essentially a question of system throughput, which varies by the type of X – ray system chosen and how it is operated within a port facility. X – ray cargo screening has been adopted at ports and border crossings throughout the world because this technology has solved a number of important problems. This is where the scanning debate lies: is it for revenue or security? All stakeholders should keep in mind the fact that, while container inspections are critical from both security and revenue perspectives, efficiency (throughput) and port operations cannot afford to slow down. However, as shown in Table 3 – 1 Customs continues to increase the rate of discrepancies that capture revenue that would have otherwise been lost to importer error or deception. From a security stand point one can imagine what some of these discrepancies revealed.

The human side of the scanning process should also be examined so that the inspectors are well trained to interpret the x – ray images and other indicators. Experts argue that better training of Customs staff on analyzing scanned images, the digital revolution and related efficiency gains, diffusion of innovation, as well as growth and specialization in the scanning manufacturing sector will enhance security and efficiency. When analyzing the data in Table 2 – 1, the trends between 2001 and 2008 show an increased age in the number of proven discrepancies. With this data it becomes evident that with more training the proficiency of the operator increases, thus indirectly resulting in a more secure supply chain.

Table 2 – 1 Containers scanned in West Africa Port

Year	Containers Scanned	Discrepancies Proven	Percentage
2000	7480	103	1. 38%
2001	13878	542	3. 91%
2002	19767	770	3. 90%
2003	13563	489	3. 61%
2004	9595	344	3. 59%
2005	13163	803	6. 10%
2006	12079	1055	8. 73%
2007	13811	1176	8. 51%
2008	13842	1140	8. 24%

In contrast to the efficiency argument is the adverse effect these technologies could possibly have on developing countries. The added burden for these countries to implement systematic scanning on exports, the possibility of smaller ports being marginalized, cargo diversion in favor of hub ports, loss of expertise, such as Risk Assessment techniques and some opportunity costs are all concerns.

(4) The Dual Role of Scanning

Scanning can serve two clearly distinct purposes:

- Assist in detecting and counter illegal material movements by organized crime, be it contrabandist or terrorist in nature.
- Assist Customs to protect and enhance tax collection against fraud and mis – declaration by the trade or their representatives.

The two functions sometimes overlap, often through the use of the same technology, facilities and/or operating personnel.

Having one scanner in one port to inspect imports to protect or enhance tax revenue should not normally be considered as fully addressing supply chain security per se. In fact, improved monitoring of possible smuggling of weapons, explosives and similar, an important objective of SCS, is actually a collateral benefit of tax – related scanning.

There are examples of tax collection – related import cargo scanning operations in developing countries, particularly Africa. One of the implantation models is the following: a provider is granted a Build, Operate, and Transfer (BOT) concession to install and run import scanning operations. The concession often encompasses physical installations, supply and operation of one or more scanners and a risk management system, capacity building, transfer of know – how and training of the local Customs officers.

While the tax – collection improvement objectives are reportedly achieved and even exceeded in some cases, the physical insertion of the scanning procedures and sites have not always been well thought of, and the necessary consultation with the port and trade communities, as well as between concerned government agencies have sometimes been lacking. Complaints have been heard in some ports about the high costs being recouped from the logistics operators and cargo interests, as well as about the delays and interferences sometimes caused on the cargo flows and port operations. The effectiveness of the capacity building and know – how transfer components has also been questioned in some cases.

It is not the purpose of this guide to analyze in depth these tax – collection scanning schemes, but practical lessons might be drawn from these experiences.

(5) Fast Scanning

One of the clear future directions of scanning is "fast scanning". Fast Scanning implies that the shipment container could be scanned while in motion at a reduced speed in the port. It is in a way similar to the automated prepaid highway toll principle. This type of scanning is already undergoing investigation by a number of major ports due to their concern in addressing the US 100% scanning requirement as discussed in this document.

There are some limitations however to fast scanning. First, as the cargo is in movement and as conveyance vehicle operators are often involved, the scanning beams have to be of relatively low power and penetration. With this type of lower penetration scan, the images do not provide the same capability to discern the container contents to the full level of detail. Second, due to this less detailed image, secondary inspections will be required on a more frequent basis in order to address this weakness.

Fast scanning is in the early stages of development – early systems include road and rail portals that are either planned for testing or currently undergoing testing by ports that are "early adopters" of technology who want to ensure their competitiveness in the current and future supply chain security environment.

In general fast scanning consists of three integrated technology elements, more specifically:

- Identification of the goods/container (RFID, optical character recognition of the container number or other similar technologies)
- X – ray scanning of the container
- Radioactive threat detection

Once the scanning is complete the container needs to have a high security seal affixed (if not already the case), so that any tampering with the contents can be noted. And if the seal is found to be not intact at any point in the port process, a new scan will need to be done. It is also important to note that with fast scanning it is envisaged that not all images will be viewed and analyzed as there will be risk based decisions made using additional tools such as a risk management system and profiling.

Fast scanning cannot be implemented as a stand alone system as there will be requirements for secondary high penetration scans and even physical goods inspections if and when anomalies are found. Implementation of fast scanning is normally oriented solely toward outgoing shipping containers and will require re – thinking of port logistics for containers coming into the port by road and by rail. All incoming containers will need to be routed through the fast scanning systems, so this implies strictly controlled access, although in practice this has already been implemented in most ports. Many of the larger ports are already preparing for and testing fast scanning as an early implementation measure if and when the 100% scanning requirement is implemented.

6. Supply Chain Security Technology Discussion/Conclusion

Beyond the initial apparent consensus about technology – nobody wants to be seen as "anti – technology" – the heterogeneous look of this chapter, is reflecting diverging opinions, angles and approaches on the issue. The debate is live, lively and ongoing, and it is the role of this guide to mirror this current situation. There are enthusiasts on the side of the technology developers, and doubters in the port and maritime industries who would end up having to deploy – and probably finance the technologies. The lawmakers are in – between with their wisdom, sagacity, pragmatism, realism and objectives.

Research & Development should target new technologies for low – cost, high – volume remote sensing and scanning. Current sensor technologies for detecting weapons or illegal shipments are expensive and typically impose delays on the logistics system. As a result, security efforts have focused on technologies or processes for identifying containers that have been tampered with, for making it harder to tamper with containers, and for risk management purposes to reduce the burden of volume on screening containers. All these approaches have a common weakness: They are easy to circumvent. Tamper – resistant seals can be fooled, spoofed or "e – tampered". Profiling processes can be gamed as criminals learn what characteristics trigger profiling algorithms. New detection technologies for remote scanning of explosives and radiation would provide valuable capabilities for better securing the container shipping system.

Technology development must also be coordinated with market requirements to produce devices with low development and deployment costs that contribute to attend real needs from the industry.

Technology plays a particularly important role in providing for screening of cargo at the critical nodes of the supply chain through data acquisition, delivery, and analysis (e. g. the secure transmission of cargo manifests). The main issue in this context is a lack of capacity in the countries which most need it.

The bigger challenge is not technical but whether developing countries can apply the available technology into viable and responsive systems. This will require cooperation among domestic agencies, scenario building and high level support from finance ministries and leaders to understand that success depends on resources and political will.

Also, the mobilizing of private sector participation in providing the ICT capacity and services required is important, and if necessary, how to finance that participation through capacity building programs.

The private sector is already actively adopting ICT in managing their domestic and international supply chains. These developments might, with appropriate policies and international coordination, both be bolstered, through new approaches to e – government, and enhance border protection capabilities through better and more accessible information.

Relevance of Costs and Benefits for Developing Countries.

A major issue when thinking about the formulation of a security initiative is the benefits and effects any security measure has on efficiency. An OECD study estimates that the transaction cost of inefficient trade procedures amounts to between 1 and 15 % of a products value (Walkenhorst and Yasui, 2003). This "higher figure is more often the case in developing countries where it is complicated and costly in terms of both time and money to fulfill the requirements laid down for the import and export of goods" Kommerskollegium (2008). To compound matters, developing countries do not possess sophisticated security procedures and technology to improve efficiency. While the potential benefits of improved technologies and a coordinated approach for improved trade facilitation and security are agreed upon amongst nearly all countries, the means of getting there and who gets to determine what exactly are the current and future globally – accepted norms has created much disagreement between the EU, the United States, developing countries and their respective private sector operators.

Developing countries are generally in agreement with the benefits of trade facilitation and a coordinated approach. On the other hand, many feel that the costs associated with addressing threats to security are very high and in many cases unnecessary. They point out that an already difficult trading context exists, including inadequate infrastructure, difficult terrain and great distances between trade partners. Moreover, when added to severe budget limitations and their immense reliance on foreign trade and investments this proves to be a difficult combination. These countries therefore argue: "Why make it even more difficult for us to participate fully?"

Recent research highlights these concerns. Hummel, for example, shows that the transport costs of developing countries are on average two to four times higher than in developed countries (Hummel, 2001). In addition, the volume of goods is generally far less, meaning that ships need to call at more ports for the purpose of better capacity utilization. There are a number of difficulties that are a common feature for many developing countries:

- Frequent reloading of goods.
- Overloading and bottlenecks which affect port time for feeder ships.
- Complicated Customs procedures.
- Complex and non-transparent requirements which often apply to documentation.
- Limited use of computerization which leads to high costs for information management.
- Uncertainty regarding the extent to which legal trade documents such as sea freight notes and letters of credit are valid.

Developing countries might legitimately consider that their circumstances should be taken into consideration by international governing bodies and the developed world before global standards such as AEO and 100% scanning are implemented. They suggest that the high financial costs imposed by security certifications are overburdening. However, they are caught in a vicious circle: "As more and more countries introduce certification programs for security in the supply chain there is a risk that countries that lack resources and have inefficient systems for the exchange of information and security controls will not share in the benefits proposed by these programs and even experience a deterioration in their prospects of participating in international trade".

Articles in this part obtained from the World Bank publication Supply Chain Security Guide, courtesy of the World Bank - www. worldbank. org.

The disclaimer to the translation as follow:

This translation was not created by The World Bank and should not be considered an official World Bank translation. The World Bank shall not be liable for any content or error in this translation.

第二编

海关三大技术支柱

WTO 估价知识简介

（普华永道合伙人 Damon Paling）

（缉私局　宋洁艳　刘欣平　根据录音整理翻译）

我认为估价是个很有挑战性的课题，很复杂，需要很多年的学习、研究以及实践。

按照计划，先简要介绍估价的历史和估价的原则。然后，了解 6 种估价方法。重点讲解第一种，即成交价格估价方法。最后，讨论成交价格的调整，这是在估价时最常遇到的情形。

第一部分，我们主要来看背景。首先，我们看历史。很多年前，存在一个名为 BDV 的规则，它的全称是布鲁塞尔价格定义。这是在全球范围内使用过的一个老系统。这个系统存在很多的价格磋商和不确定因素，使用起来非常复杂。进口商常常发现在与海关关员进行价格磋商前，海关已有定论，为此感到不满。进口商不能理解进口商品的到岸成本。所以说，BDV 是个陈旧而且不好用的系统。早在 1947 年，“二战”之后，相关国家就关税及贸易总协定（GATT）达成一致。1979 年 GATT 估价协议起草成文。我记得到了 1994 年，世界贸易组织（WTO）成立，然后我们就不再沿用 GATT 规则，改用 WTO 规则。于是有了 WTO 估价协议。欧洲和美国率先采用了 WTO 估价协议。亚洲国家中，印度尼西亚在 1998 年应用该估价协议，泰国、菲律宾、马来西亚紧随其后。中国于 2001 年 12 月 11 日加入 WTO。2002 年 1 月，中国采用了 WTO 估价协议。

这个估价协议的目标是什么？对于政府和企业来说，他们都想避免采用“武断的”价格。我举手提包的例子来解释“武断”的意思。一些人认为这个包值 100 美元，一些人认为它值 50 美元，究竟是 100 美元还是 50 美元？很有可能产生毫无根据的争论。所以我们想要避免这种情况，我们想要有个公平、统一、客观的估价方式。这就意味着，商业协议应作为估价的基础。比如说，我是这个手提包的境外供货商，我把这个包以 100 美元的价格卖给你们，这个价格就是我俩所认可的，如果我们没有欺骗海关，没有进行一些特殊的交易，这个价格就应是完税价格的基础。

估价方法不是去设定一个价格。估价协议的规则不是明确这个包的价值是 50、100 还是 150。这些规则用以判定申报价格是否可以接受。如果申报价格可以接受，那么没有问题。如果申报价格不能接受，那么这些规则就告诉我们如何使用估价方法来得出海关的完税价格。没有人可以去宣布这个包值 50、100 还是 150。你也不需要去了解生产成本等信息。估价协议在任何情况下都能让你得到一个完税价格。只要你正确使用估价方法，你就肯定能得出一个结论。这是不是就意味着估价很简单呢？不。正确使用规则非常难，但答案是一定存在的。有时你很快能得出一个结论，有时你需要花很长时间。有时你只需要一点点信息来得到答案，有时你需要从纳税人处得到大量的信息来完成估价。完税价格不一定等于实际支付的货款。也许纳税人会对海关关员说，我付了 100 美元，但是 100 美元并不一定就是完税价格。大多数时候 100 美元就是完税价格，但有时不是。只有满足了特定条件后 100 美元才能作为完税价格。

有人熟悉这 6 种估价方法吗？它们是成交价格估价方法、相同货物成交价格估价方法、类似货物成交价格估价方法、倒扣价格估价方法、计算价格估价方法和合理方法。你必须按照次序来使用这些方法。这意味着你不可以直接选择第三种方法——类似货物成交价格估价方法。你必须从第一种方法开始使用，如果你不能使用第一种方法，那就使用第二种方法，如果第二种也不行，那就依次采取第三种、第四种、第五种、第六种。这与 BDV 的旧规则不同，与转移定价不同。

有一个重要的问题是，这些方法使用频率如何？为什么要提这个问题？因为这告诉我们哪个方法是我们最多用到的。我们用亚洲、全球总体情况、全球平均使用率来说明问题。我们可以看到第一种成交价格估价方法使用率几乎是 100%，全球平均值是 94%。这个就意味着，对于 100 个入境商品交易，94 个交易的估价是使用成交价格估值方法的，只有 6 个交易使用其他方法。人们常常希望迅速使用其他估价方法，那是不对的。正确的方法是，你先使用成交价格估价方法，除非有条件不符合，你再使用其他的方法。这个使用率的统计显示，94%的情况下你要使用成交价格估价方法。我们再来看相同货物成交价格估价方法和类似货物成交价格估价方法。为何他们的使用率如此低？原因是相同货物和类似货物有非常严密的定义。举个例子，这里有两瓶水，一瓶 A，一瓶 B，我们可以说它们是相同的，在同一个国家生产，来自同一个供货商，同等数量等。再举个例子，这个手提包和那个手提包，我们能说它们是同一商品吗？不能。我们可以说它们是类似的吗？也许对于去购物的人来说，它们是类似的。但在估价规则下，它们不属类似，不可互换。它们由不同国家制造，也许出自不同的生产商，所以我们不能用一个手提包的价格来对另一个手提包进行估价。倒扣价格估价方法被使用得稍多一点。

什么是实付、应付价格？实付、应付价格就是成交价格，它是货物出口到进口国的价格。如果我从新加坡将这个手提包卖给你，价格是 100 美元，这就是实付、应付价格。你可以看到这个价格体现在发票上。当进口商提供诸如发票、箱单、提单等单证时，发票金额就是 100 美元，这就是实付、应付金额。进口货物的成交价格应当符合下列四项条件：第一，对买方处置或者使用进口货物不予限制。“不予限制”是买方再卖给谁不受限制。如果我卖给你，你只能卖给这位男士，那么这就是限制。这将会导致我们无法使用成交价格估价方法。如果你可以将手提包卖给这个房间的任何人，那么这就是无限制。第二，不存在无法确定的条件或者因素。我们再拿这个手提包做例子，我以每个 100 美元的价格卖给你，但前提是你会再买 1000 个手提包。这就是影响 100 美元价格的因素，它使我们无法使用成交价格估价方法。第三，除非作出价格调整，卖方不得再从买方处获得收益。举个例子，我以 100 美元卖这个手提包给你，你卖给他 200 美元。但是，我们商定，你每卖出一个包，我可以再得到 10 美元的收益。这个 10 美元就是卖方再从买方处获得的收益，这部分是需要纳税的。第四，买卖双方的关系不影响价格。我们可能是有关联的，我是母公司，你是子公司，这没有问题。只要双方的关系不影响成交价格，买卖双方就可以被当作无关联的公司对待。

关于相同货物成交价格估价方法的定义。货物必须完全是相同的。它们可以在量上或者商业水平上有所差异，其他都必须完全相同。举宝马 3 系列机动车的例子，我们有一辆黑色的和一辆红色的宝马 3 系列机动车，它们都是德国造，进口到中国。我们就说它们是相同的货物。虽然它们一辆是黑色，一辆是红色，但是它们就是相同的。我们再来举洗发水的例子，我们有一瓶强生的洗发水和一瓶宝洁的洗发水。它们两者是相同的吗？不。如果你去超市购物，作为消费者，也许你觉得它们是相同的，但从海关估价的角度看，两者是不同的。它们的制造商、生产国、成本、成分、品牌都有可能不同。什么时候使用相同货物成交价格估价方法？在实际操作中，大宗商品，比如大米、糖、面粉、大豆、矿石、铝。如果我们遇到最基本的、没有经过加工的、来自同一片海洋、同一个矿场，我们可以认为它们是相同的或者相似的商品。日用品不能认为是相同的或者相似的商品。

第三种方法是相似货物成交价格估价方法。第三种方法和第二种方法相似，但它具有弹性。你一定认为宝马和奔驰的轿车是不同的，但你认为强生和宝洁的洗发水是相同的么？不，虽然两者可以替代，但是它们来自不同的生产商、不同的国家、不同的品牌价值。基于此，二者价格不可比较。除非你面对的是最基本的初级制品，否则我认为第二种和第三种方法很难被使用。

第四种方法是倒扣价格估价方法。我们再来拿手提包作例子。消费者以 200 美元的价格购得这个手提包。然后我们减去国内的成本、进口商的利润、国内税款、佣金、运费等等，做完一连串减法后，然后得到倒扣价格。海关可以要求纳税人、进口商提供用于计算倒扣价格的数据与信息计算倒扣价格。

第五种方法是计算价格估价方法，这和第四种方法正好相反。我们不去看境内价格、境内销售和物流成本。我们去看境外发生的相关事件。我们再拿这个手提包做例子。这个包生产的成本是多少？品牌的成本是多少？生产商的利润是多少？把所有这些加起来就是计算价格。对于海关来说，这种方法的弊端是你们在中国，而我可能在新加坡，你们如何相信我？你们怎么知道我提供的数据是否是真实、完整和准确的？我有可能编造数据。所以计算价格估价方法曾经是个好方法，但它需要海关去验证境外的数据是否真实准确。从境内获得数据比从境外获得数据简单得多。所以对于海关来说，最重要的是是否可以依赖境外获得的数据，以及如何验证这些数据的准确性。

第六种方法是合理方法。在过去的 10 多年中，我没有使用过这种方法。这种方法比较罕见。我认为如果你使用前五种方法，你就能得到答案，并就完税价格与纳税人协商一致。当前五种方法不奏效时，你就使用第六种方法。第六种方法不代表你可以编造价格，你不可以认为说这个手提包很好看，车线很精密，那么它就价值 200 美元。第六种方法要求你更灵活地运用前五种方法。你仍然需要遵循基本的计算原则，以基本的逻辑依据去计算进口价格。当然你也需要与进口商磋商价格。第六种方法需要同纳税人解释、交换信息，使得双方协商一致。

总结一下，成交价格估价方法是最重要的方法，但并非放之四海而皆准。相同货物成交价格估价方法和类似货物成交价格估价方法，就是将货物作比较，但是使用起来非常严格。一般使用这种估价方法的货物是铁、矿石、铝、大米、鱼类等。倒扣价格和计算价格有时会被用到。合理价格估价方法只是使你估价时更为灵活地使用另外五种估价方法。不同的估价方法当然就会延缓通关时间，造成纳税人的困扰。如果你不能使用成交价格估价方法，那你必须要有依据。因为纳税人会问为什么，你自己需要明白原因并解释给纳税人听。同时，你还需要将这些原因写在报告中，然后你再逐个使用其他方法：相同货物法、类似货物法、倒扣价格法、合理价格法。你可以参考该商品竞争者的价格。这种方法有难度。除非你面对的是相同货物和类似货物，否则无法参考竞争者的价格。我们以高尔夫球棒为例子，Callaway 和 Mizuno 牌的高尔夫球棒是一样的吗？答案是否。虽然在市场上它们是实力相当的竞争者，但在估价中，它们不是相同货物或者类似货物。所以当你去购物中心或者上网查找信息时，并不意味着你所找到的信息就是可以适用于第二种和第三种方法或者第四种、第五种方法。以上就是第一部分。我介绍了成交价格估价方法的历史，什么是 WTO 估价协议，什么是成交价格，以及其他的估价方法。超过 90% 的场合，我们使用成交价格估价方法。如果你不用第一种方法，你必须有依据。方法二和方法三在实际生活中很难被运用。你可能会用到第四种倒扣价格估价法。这个方法对海关来说很不错，因为数据来自中国境内，你可以验证数据的真实性。方法五对海关来说使用有些困难，因为数据来自境外，这些数据的真实性很难被验证。

然后让我们进入第二部分——成交价格估价方法的使用。在这部分，我们会有一些案例分析。海关总署令第148号中对成交价格的定义：进口货物的成交价格，是指卖方向中华人民共和国境内销售该货物时买方为进口该货物向卖方实付、应付的价款。当我从事估价方面事务时，会先画一个流程图去了解进口过程中发生了哪些事情。谁卖给谁，谁支付给谁，支付多少。当你收到一叠单证时，很难去找出哪些重要哪些不重要。估价时，要确定谁是境外供货商，谁是境内买家。你常期待在发票上看到成交价格。卖家以100美元卖给买家，买家支付100美元，发票金额就是100美元，这就是实付、应付价格，该原则是估价工作的起点。我们不详细讨论其他的估价方法，而是重点关注成交价格估价方法是否可在这些场合应用。下面讨论案例。

问题一：如果买卖双方有关联，我们是否可以用成交价格估价方法？我们举通用公司的例子，一边是美国通用，一边是中国通用，两家关联公司。我们是否可以采用成交价格估价方法？

答案是可以的。但原因并不是那么简单。原则上来说，是可以的。什么是“原则上来说”？我们假设两者的关系不影响成交价格。如果你去审查一家公司，发现买卖双方的关系影响了价格，那么你就不能用成交价格，你必须使用其他估价方法。在大约50%的国际贸易中，你会发现交易双方是有关联的。高达50%！所以说，只要交易双方的特殊关系不影响交易价格，那么就可以使用成交价格估价方法。

问题二：成交价格受到其他因素影响。境外卖东西到中国，价格为100美元，但是价格受到了其他因素影响。我们可以用成交价格估价方法吗？举个例子，我以100美元的价格卖货物A，但条件是我可以以200美元的价格卖给你货物B。

答案是：不可以。原因是当存在无法确定的条件或者因素时，我们不可以采用成交价格估价方法，连带销售就是一个例子。若我们购买附件，我们买的机器可以有折扣。还有个例子是打印机，办公室里都有打印机，打印机里有墨盒。很多时候，我们要是答应配套的墨盒一直是在卖家那里购买的话，我们买打印机时可有折扣。

问题三：免费更换零部件。举个例子，卖家以 100 美元的价格将货物 A 卖出，但是买家说 A 坏了，不能用了。于是卖家就将 A 免费调换货物。我们是否可以使用成交价格估价方法？

答案是“否”。替换 A 的货物并非买卖双方交易的目的。一般我们用被替换的货物来对替换货物进行估价。如果被替换货物入境时价格为 100 美元，我们就以 100 美元的价格作为免费替换货物的价格。

问题四：寄售货物。有人知道什么是寄售货物吗？我来解释一下。境外的供货商将 100 美元的货物运到境内买家处，发票是 100 美元，但是买家并没有支付这 100 美元。物权并没有转移，卖家还拥有货物的物权。买家也许持有货物，但他没有物权。

我们不能使用成交价格估价方法。库存商品并不等同于实际销售。在现在的行情下，也许你可以使用倒扣价格估价方法。

问题五：发票显示购买大量商品会有折扣。比如说，卖方以 100 美元的价格卖给买方，但打折后，货物价格为 90 美元，实际支付 90 美元。我们是否可以使用成交价格估价方法？

答案是只要折扣是无偿提供且应用于该批货物，我们就接受成交价格。折扣并不意味着不能使用成交价格估价方法。

问题六：货物在 6 个月前购买。举个例子，购买日期为 2009 年 1 月 1 日，但是进口日期为 7 月 1 日。6 个月是两者的时间差。在经济下行的时候这种情况很多。很早之前就购买了货物，但并不马上就进口到中国。

答案是有可能。既有可能是，也有可能否。就第一种方法——成交价格估价方法来说，不存在时间的概念。如果你使用“相同货物”和“类似货物”，时间限制是 45 天。你参照的是近 45 天内进口的货物。但是在成交价格估价方法中，不存在这个概念。你必须去查实时间因素是否影响了货物的价格。你必须去查实原来这笔交易是否就是运往中国的，如果是的话，你就可以用成交价格估价方法，如果不是的话，你要用其他的估价方法。

问题七：分红协议。分红是卖家以 100 美元的价格将货物卖给买家，而买家在中国以200美元的价格把它卖给顾客。然后买家将其中的10美元再交给卖家。这多出来的10美元就是来自于货物在中国出售后所获得的利润，所以买家总共支付给卖家的价格是110美元。那成交价格是否适用呢?

答案是原则上适用。分红协定是被我们所接受的，但在确定成交价格时，你需要在成交价格中将100美元加上10美元，因此成交价格就成了110美元，你所运用的估价方法仍旧是第一种方法。如果你阅读第一种方法，你会发现它有四个条件存在，其中一个条件就是没有诸如分红之类的后续环节。但是如果你能够量化所共享的利润，你仍然可以使用第一种方法，即用成交价格估价方法确定价格是110美元。如果货物没有被出售，那分红也就不存在了，这种情况下成交价格就是100美元。

问题八：货物购买价格很低。现在遇上了经济危机，而这就意味着公司会试图出售库存产品。以前顾客拥有很多钱，他愿意支付200美元。现在他没钱了，就只愿意付150美元。卖家会削减货物的价格，所以会出现相同货物从前售价100美元，现在仅售75美元。在货物购买价格很低的情况下，成交价格能适用吗?

“也许能”。只要这个成交价格是真实的，只要你仍旧能够满足第一种货物估价方法的四个条件，就能用成交价格方法。

问题九：买家提供免费设计。我们还是回到这个手提包来说。买家设计包，然后把设计给了卖家。也就是说买家设计了手提包，包括针脚、颜色、材料以及外观。所以买家提供了设计，并且可能是通过电子邮件发给了卖家，而卖家就用这个设计来生产手提包并再把它们卖回中国。因为买家拥有这个设计的所有权，所以他不需要为这个设计支付费用。我们能够运用成交价格吗?

在这个例子中，我们假设这个设计是从中国被提供到海外的。那什么情况下我们能用成交价格方法呢？我们所必须要做的就是针对这些设计援助做出估价调整。只要买卖双方可以将设计成本量化，我们仍然能够使用成交价格方法。

问题十：成交价格的调整。在这个部分中我们应该抛开成交价格，因为它只是你在发票上看到的内容。我们会讨论任何与买家付往海外的钱有关的内容，以及关注有哪些其他情况存在。是否存在其他情况？这些情况是不是需要被归入完税价格？因此调整成交价格就是为了确保我们有一个公平贸易的环境。价格调整既可以提高也可以降低成交价格。如果发票上的价格是 100 美元，我们可以把它调整为 110 美元，也可以调整为 90 美元，这取决于价格调整的目的。你所做出的任何增加或减少价格的行为都需要有法律基础。如果这些调整项目不在法律条文之中，或者不在海关总署第 148 号令的规定之中，你就不能做出增加或减少成交价格的行为。

接下来我们来看调整成交价格的因素。

佣金和经纪费。通常佣金是付给代理商的。举例说，这代理商收取了 10 美元佣金。这笔佣金是否应该征税呢？买方佣金不需要征税，而卖方佣金则需要征税。买方佣金也就是采购佣金。为什么买方佣金不需征税呢？因为代理商是代表买方去购买的商品。为区分买方代理商还是卖方代理商，第一步是看合同。合同中应该有一个协议，看协议签署双方是代理商与买方还是代理商与卖方。接下来看代理商代表谁，他的服务对象是谁。这最好通过佣金的支付者判断。如果我付了佣金，那我就是你的服务对象。谁付了佣金，那他就很有可能是代理商的服务对象。佣金的情况很复杂，因为人们无法判断买方代理商、买方佣金还是卖方代理商、卖方佣金。所以第一步就是判断谁是买方，谁是卖方。尽管这个判断很复杂，但却是解决问题的一个很好的出发点。中介费也有可能需要计入完税价格。

协助。协助包含很多内容。它是指你得到了帮助，而且这种帮助是免费的。我做了一些事情，或者我免费给你一些东西以帮助你完成任务。协助是我们需要考虑的内容。协助可以包括很多内容，如材料、零部件、工具、模型以及工程设计。研究这些协助内容，以及判断是否有项目属于协助内容就显得非常重要。买家可以将协助直接提供给卖家，例如设计。同样也可以有第三方存在。买家可以指定第三方做设计，然后将设计交给卖家，由卖家使用这个设计去生产产品，最后产品被进口销售。所以你看到的就是一个各种服务和活动的流向图。协助可以是直接的，也可以是经由第三方完成的。协助的内容有明确的定义，多数情况下能够覆盖所有你能想象到的情形。

特许权使用费。本质上来说你可以拥有属于自己的一个特许权，去特许别人使用你的知识产权、专利、版权以及商标。别人必须要支付费用才能获得这个特许权。这笔费用是不是应计入完税价格呢？如果特许权是和商品的进口有关联或者作为交易条件的话，那么特许权使用费就应该计入完税价格。海关总署第148号令明确定义了什么是与商品有关联，以及什么是附带条件的交易。在中国，特许权使用费按照定义的话经常是作为交易条件出现。特许权使用费是不是与进口的商品有关联呢？多数情况下，答案是“肯定”，尤其是针对商标的情形。如果你看到已贴有商标的成品时，那么特许权使用费就与商品有关，Prada的手提包就是一个例子。如果你进口半成品，那情况就变得复杂了。你在中国生产这个产品，然后你在国内销售。这种情况就变得复杂了，因为你进口的可能是原材料，然后你在工厂里把它加工为成品。你出售了这个商品，而你所支付的特许权使用费与成品以及在中国使用的相关技术有关。这笔特许权使用费是不是与进口的原材料有关联呢？你要研究产品，查看特许权使用合同，了解使用的知识产权，以判断这是否和进口商品有关。

期后收益。期后收益与我们之前讨论的成交价格相关内容相似。买家出售商品，赚到钱，然后把部分钱交给海外的卖家，这就是所谓的期后收益。因为外汇管制政策，在中国很难看到期后收益这项。向国外汇款，需要进口报关单据，按单据上所列数额汇款。所以现在很难能看到商家存在期后收益并且许多商家缺乏相关机制。

现在让我们回到假设的情景之中。支付给卖家的专利特许权使用费是不是要计入完税价格呢？答案是肯定的。它属于征税范围，我们要做出相应的价格调整。这是因为它与进口的商品有关系。专利权是交易的一项条件，并且专利特许权需要购买。境外的制造商需要两者兼备才能投入生产，所以它是计入完税价格。

接下来的问题相对较难，是某一原版碟片的复制特许权费。有一张碟片进入中国，买家复制了这个碟片，接下来生产了更多碟片。就复制行为而言，买家支付了特许权费用，他有权复制。这种在中国发生的复制特许权费是否和商品进口有关呢？答案是“不需要对此做出调整”，也就是说你在中国复制碟片，而非进口碟片到中国。关税是针对商品进口，而这里的特许权使用费是为在中国复制而支付的。

在中国进行的专利加工程序的使用费。举个例子，同时存在一个买家和一个卖家，而进口原材料。买家使用一项专利来加工原材料并生产出成品在中国国内销售。专利特许使用费支付给了专利的拥有者。现在让我们回到两大原则上，即它是否与进口商品有关或者是否作为交易的条件而存在。每一个和专利权使用费有关的情形都是不同的。分析的时候，你的思考方法是一样的。答案是“不需要进行价格调整”。因为这项专利是和中国国内的生产有关，而和商品进口本身无关。这种情况主要出现在进口原材料时，如进口金属、塑料与纸浆。

接下来这个和协助有关。设计免费由买家送给卖家。我们还是回到手提包这个话题。买家将设计免费提供给卖家，卖家按此设计生产，然后再进口到中国。是否需要做出调整呢？答案是“不需要调整”。这关键是在进口国进行的设计和研发不需征税。上面这个例子中的设计是在中国进行，而中国正是进口国。但是如果设计发生在海外，如在新加坡呢？当然，在海外产生的设计费用是需要计入完税价格的。

在出口港至进口商工厂过程中产生的运费以及保险费。这种情况下是否需要调整完税价格呢？答案是肯定的，需要做出调整。在到达进口港的过程中的运费以及保险费必须被计入完税价格之中。海关总署第 148 号令中有“到岸价”这一条款。

延期支付货款所产生的利息。这也就是说，商品以 100 美元出售，买家 90 天后付款，因为这个延期付款的行为而产生了 5 美元的利息费。发票上显示的价格仅 100 美元，但是另一张发票上所支付的价格是 5 美元。这两张发票是互相独立的，所以只能说是“可能”需要对此做出调整。利息并不是支付的货款。货款是 100 美元，这才是成交价格。支付利息费是为了使支付货款这个行为得以成立，是为了让你在购买好商品的 90 天之后才付款，而不是在购买商品的当天付款。所以说这是一种金融手段，是为了支付货款这个行为的成立而不是为了购买商品这个事件本身。所以按照海关总署第 148 号令，只要能够满足相关条件，那么利息是可以不予征税的。当然针对利息应该有书面协议，而不能仅是口头协议。购买商品也可以不产生利息，买家可以在当天就付款，也可以在 90 天以后付款，他必须在这两者之间做出选择。由于延期付款而产生的利息率必须是合理的，否则就是欺瞒。因此如果商品的价格是 100 美元，而需要支付的利息也是 100 美元，那显然不是一个正常的商业行为，而且可能有人想走私或者低报商品价格。所以你必须确认这笔利息是正常的商业行为，并且你还要知晓银行的利率等。

进口商所拥有的工具被提供给卖家。这是一种协助行为，与设计非常类似。这种情况中，买家提供某些东西给卖家，而这些被提供的工具则被用于生产出口到中国的商品。你是否需要针对工具的价值而作出调整呢？答案是“需要调整”。“工具作业”是需要征税的，应当被计入完税价格，因此要做价格调整。你经常会在汽车产业看到“工具作业”这种现象。正如你在汽车工厂里看到大量的“工具作业”用于汽车制造领域。电子工业也和它有相似之处。在这两个产业里，需要有大量“工具作业”。这些工具可能是免费提供的，也可能是被算作成本而计入完税价格。

支付给代理商的佣金。除买方佣金外，支付给代理商的佣金是需要征税的。大多数进口商会告诉海关这其中涉及的代理商是买方代理商。之所以这么说，原因在于这笔佣金费用不必征税。作为一名关员，你必须对该佣金情况进行核实并且确保进口商对你所说属实。

总的来说，我们讨论了什么情况需计征入税，什么时候不需要。海关总署令第 148 号有详细列明。基本上发生在进口之后以及中国国内发生的行为不需要纳入海关征收关税的范畴，因为这些都与中国国内发生的活动有关。例如，在中国安装设备而产生的成本包括将设备放到工厂并使其运转。安装设备需要专业的工程和技术人员，该成本与海外设备制造无关，不能计入完税价格。针对这些不需要征收关税的项目，我们应该将其与商品的货款或应付款区别开来。有时商家会提供一个 200 美元的价格，说这其中包含了安装费用。但是进口商需要在发票上将其列出，否则海关就无法将其从完税价格中扣除。进口商也许很容易指出什么不需要征税，但其所提供的资料必须加以印证。如果进口商提供的材料不能够支持其观点，那就不能认定免税。应税与非应税的项目必须在发票上单独列出。

最后，海关总署令第 148 号对什么情况下存在关联方交易有 8 种明确的定义。50% 的跨境交易是关联方之间的交易。我们很容易判断出交易是否存在关联关系。通常你会看发票上的商家名字，它会告诉你交易双方是否有从属关系。如果商家名字互不相同的话，情况就变得复杂了。这时你需要去判断股权所有方及管理方等。那么如何去判断一个公平价格呢？这时你可以采用我们之前讨论的相同商品或者相似商品的办法，当然这些方法并不简单。你可以看看第 22 条和第 24 条中所说的倒扣价格方法以及计算价格方法。去核实大量的证据和材料，以及进行比较，这是一个相当复杂的过程。我想说的是在这些提供的场景中，需要你们有专业的知识，充分的耐心和大量的经验，同时也要求海关关员在与进口商打交道的过程中去获得信息以便作出正确的决定。

总结估价协定的目的，即我们需要的是一个公平、统一、同时被海关和纳税人理解的方法。归根结底，我们需要一个不受关联关系以及其他因素影响的成交行为。设想一下，如果关联关系影响到了价格或者其他方面，那情况就会变得复杂，这样就需要采用另一种估价方法来得到正确的完税价格。估价协定的目的并不是为了规定价格。我们不能简单地就说这个手提包值 150 美元而不是 50 美元。如果你采用了正确的估价方法，你就能得到正确的完税价格。只要你用了正确的估价方法，那你就不需要去担心一个手提包是 50 美元，是 100 美元，抑或是 150 美元。就全球而言，94% 的情况是运用成交价格方法的。我们对成交价格的定义就是：实付或应付的价格，该价格通常由发票给出，同时我们需要满足应用成交价格的 4 个前提条件。但我想说的是，在跨国公司的交易中第一个、第二个、第三个前提条件不常用。问题的关键是第四个前提条件，即关联关系是否影响价格。当你们遇到跨国关联交易的情况时，需要你们花费时间去思考。还有要做的是针对特许权使用费和佣金做出调整，以及将运费和保险费从中扣除等。

Customs Valuation

(Presented by Damon Paling, Partner at PWC)
(Transcribed and Translated by Song Jieyan and Liu Xinping, Bureau of Anti – Smuggling)

I think valuation is a very challenging topic. It is a very complex subject, which takes many years of learning, studying, practical experience.

On the agenda, I will give a general introduction of the evaluation history and the valuation principles. Then we will look at the six methods of valuation and make sure everyone will be familiar with them. Then we will look at mainly method one—transaction value. Lastly, we will look at the so – called adjustments to the transaction value. So as customs officials, this is what you will deal with most of the time on the valuation issues.

For section one, we will look at the general context. If we look at the history, we can say many years ago, there was the so – called BDV—Brussels' Definition of Valuation. That was the old system which was used all around the world. That system was quite difficult for everyone to use, because it was based on negotiations and uncertainty. Importers often found there was some fixed decision by the customs officers, and importers felt upset. They don't understand what the landed cost of the product they import is. So that is the old system and it was not very good. Then of course there is the GATT, the General Agreement on Tariffs and Trade. That was actually agreed way back on 1947, I think after the World War II. And then was the drafting of the GATT valuation agreement in 1979. In 1994, the WTO, the World Trade Organization was created. Then we do not really refer to GATT any more, but to WTO. Then we had WTO valuation agreement. Europe and the US adopted the WTO evaluation. In Asia, Indonesia used the valuation agreement in 1998 followed by Thailand, the Philippines and Malaysia. China joined the WTO on December 11, 2001. In January 2002, China adopted the WTO valuation agreement.

What is the objective of the agreement? For both the governments as well as the private enterprises, they want to move away from the so - called arbitrary values. For example, somebody would decide that the handbag is worth 100 US $, maybe somebody thinks it's 50 US $, but you could induce a debate without any basis, whether it is 50 or 100. We want to move away from that position, and have a fair, uniform and neutral system of valuation. Essentially that means commercial arrangements should be the basis of the value. So let's say I am the overseas seller of the handbag. I sell it to you here in China. That is the price we have agreed. That should be the basis of the customs value assuming everything is ok. We are not cheating and we do not have any special deals.

So the methods are not really to set a price. The rule of the valuation agreement is not to say whether the handbag is worth 50 US $, 100 US $ or 150 US $. The rules provide the methodology to determine whether the declared price is acceptable or not. If the declared price is acceptable, right, it is no problem. If the declared price is not acceptable, then the rules provide guidance on how to arrive at alternative value for the goods based on applying the methods of valuation. Nobody can say whether the bag is 50 US $, 100 US $ or 150 US $. You don't have to be the experts to know the cost of the production. The valuation agreement should arrive at a value in all circumstances. The rules would always offer a solution as long as the methods are applied correctly. Does that mean it is easy? No. Applying and interpreting rules are very difficult, but there will always be an answer. Sometimes you can get the answer very quickly, and sometimes it takes very long time. Sometimes you need a little bit information to get to the right answer and sometimes you need a lot of information from the tax payer to get the right answer. Customs value may not be the actual price paid for the goods. Maybe the tax payer comes to the customs officers and say, "I paid 100

US $. " But that does not mean 100 US $ is going to be the customs value. Most of the time it probably will be, but not always. 100 US $ for a handbag can only be acceptable as customs value subject to certain conditions or criteria.

Who is familiar with the 6 methods of valuation? They are: transaction value, identical goods, similar goods, deductive value, computed value and fallback value. The methods should be applied in sequences. It means you can not go and pick No. 3, similar goods. You have to start from No. 1, transaction value. If you can not use No. 1, you try No. 2. If you can not use No. 2, you try No. 3, 4, 5 and 6. That is very different from the old way under the BDV. That is also very different from what is used for transfer pricing purposes.

The key question is how often are each of these methods used. Why it is important? Because it tells us which method you are most likely to be using. We have usage rate from Asia, global and the global average. We can see that method one—transaction value is used almost 100 percent of the time. The global average is 94 percent. That means if you have 100 import transactions, 94 will be valued by way of the method one, and only 6 will be valued by way of other methods. Often people want to very quickly use alternative method of valuation to value the goods. That's not correct. The correct approach is that you must use transaction value unless the criteria are not met. Then you use the alternative methods. This research shows that 94 percent of the time you will use transaction value. We then see identical goods and similar goods. Why is that percentage so low? Because the definition of identical and similar goods is very specific. Let's take an example. There are two bottles of water, a bottle of water A, and a bottle of water B. We will probably say they are identical, made in the same country, from the same supplier, the same quantity, etc. Again let's take this example, the handbag and the other handbag. Would we say that the handbags are identical? No. Would we say they are similar? Well, to a person for shopping, maybe they are similar. But under the valuation rules, they are not similar, they are not commercially changeable. They are made in different countries, maybe, by different manufacturers. We cannot use one handbag to value other handbag.

Deductive value is used more often.

What is the price paid or payable? Price paid or payable is transaction value and it's the price when sold for export to the country of importation. So if I sell the handbag from Singapore to you here in China, that price is 100 US $. That is the price paid or payable. That is represented by commercial invoice. When the importers produce their documents, the invoice, the packing list, the bill of loading, airway bill, the invoice's amount is 100 US $. In simple term, it is the price paid or payable. The transaction value can only be met with these four conditions fulfilled. A is no restrictions on the sale of the goods. No restrictions means that the buyer is not restricted in terms of whom he sells to. If I sell it to you, you can only sell to this gentleman here. That would be a restriction. That may disable or prevent transaction value from being used. If you can sell the handbag to anyone in the room, you will say there's no restriction in terms of who you can sell to and where you can sell to. B is no conditions or considerations that cannot be valued. So let's say for an example, the example of the handbag. I sell you 100 handbags at 100 US $ each, but only on the condition you will buy another 1000 from me, that would be a condition which is affecting the price 100 US $. That condition may prevent the use of transition value. C is no further payment unless an adjustment can be made. So let's say for an example, I sell the handbag to you. You sell it to him. I've sold it to you for 100 US $. You sell it to him for 200 US $, but you and I agree that you will give me extra 10 US $ based on the sales income received. That extra 10 US $ is further payment which you make to me. That further payment would be dutiable. D is a relationship that does not influence the price. We could be related. I could be the mother company, and you could be the affiliate company. That's not a problem. That's legal so long as their relationship does not influence the price.

With regard to the definition of identical goods, it means that the goods must be exactly the same. It can be some adjustments for quantity, for commercial level, but every thing has to be perfectly the same. So let's say for example, a BMW 3 series, and we have a black one and a red one. They are both made in

Germany, both are exported to China. Would we say they are identical goods? We will say they are identical. Of course one is black, and the other is red, but all the terms of purpose, they are identical. Another example, let's say we have a shampoo imported by Johnson & Johnson, and we have a shampoo imported by P&G. Would those two bottles of shampoos be identical? No. If you go to the supermarket, you may think as a consumer, they are both bottles of shampoo, they are both looking after your hair. But for customs valuation purposes, they are not identical. They've been probably made in different manufacturers, in different countries, with different costs, maybe some different materials inside and different brand. When can you use identical goods? I suppose in practice when you have commodities, things like rice, sugar, flour, soybean, ore and aluminum. This tends to be where you have a product which is very basic, which has not been processed, which came from the same ocean or the same mine, that can be typically regarded identical or similar goods. You can not regard consumer products as identical or similar.

Here we look at method 3—value of similar goods. Method 3 is very similar to method 2. It just allows a little bit more flexibility. You can not say a BMW is the same as a Mercedes. Could you say the J&J shampoo is the same as the P&G shampoo? Yes or no? No, again they are maybe commercially interchangeable, but they have been made in different manufacturers, different countries, different brand value; you can not compare them based on those reasons. I think it is very difficult practices to use the method 2 or method 3, unless you have very basic goods.

Deductive value is method 4. Let's take the handbag example again. So the consumer purchased the bag for 200 US $. We would then deduct the in-country expenses and profit of the importer, the in-country taxes that have been paid, any in-country commission, freight, transportation to arrive backwards at a customs value. So it will be 200 minus, minus, once you minus all these items, then you have the deductive value. As customs, you need to ensure that tax payers present with complete, accurate and honest information. Unfortunately, some tax payers, some importers, they do not always tell the truth. However, the data for deductive value calculation comes from within China. Companies are requested to provide data and information to support the deductive calculation based on Chinese accounting standards and record keeping requirements.

Method 5, computed value is the opposite of method 4. Instead of looking at in – country sales price and in – country selling and distribution cost, you look what are happening overseas. If we come back to our handbag, for example, you would ask me how much it costs to manufacture the handbag. What is the material cost, labor cost, the other manufacturing cost? What is my profit? All the items together make up your computed value. The challenge for computed value is that you are here in China, I am overseas, I am in Singapore. How can you trust me? How can you verify what I am saying is true, correct, complete, accurate? I can just make up some numbers presenting to you in China. So computed value was once a good method. It is challenging for customs to verify that what I am receiving from overseas is true or accurate. It is much easier for you to verify information you receive in China rather than the information you receive overseas. For customs, you will always have to be mindful to say well, whatever I request overseas, can I rely on it to make a decision, and how can I verify what has presented to me is accurate and complete.

Fall back method is method 6. I do not think I have ever used this method of evaluation in over ten or twelve years. It is quite uncommon. I think if you apply methods 1, 2, 3, 4, 5, you are mostly likely to find the answer. You are mostly likely to be able to determine the dutiable value and agree it with tax payers. Method 6 is really when method 1 – 5 have failed to give an answer, then you use method 6. Method 6 does not mean you can make up the value. You can not say the handbag is nice, the stitching looks very professional. It's worth 200 US $. Method 6 requires you to go back and more flexibly apply methods 1, 2, 3, 4, 5. You should still follow general accounting principles. So there should be some logic, some basis for any quantification to determine the import price. Of course, you need to have discussion with the tax payer. Method

6 requires a lot of explanation, information exchange, so that you can reach agreement with tax payers.

In summery of the introduction, the key point is whereas you know transaction value is the main method, it is not always applied. Your alternative methods are used as the comparisons, like using identical and similar goods, but really it is very difficult to make it work unless you have something simple like iron, ore, aluminum, rice, fish, something like that. Deductive and computed methods tend to be used. Fall back method just gives you flexibility to go back and be more relaxed, in terms of how you apply other methods. Different methods of course can lead to delays in clearance which are lots of questions of tax payers. If you reject transaction value, you, of course, you have to have basis. It is very important that in your own mind you know why, why I have rejected method one, because tax payers will ask you and you need to be prepared to explain to tax payers why not method one. You also need to know it yourself, because you have to write a report, you need to document in the report why I do not use method 1. You then go through process, identical, similar, deductive, fallback. Competitive prices are often used as a reference point. Again it is very challenging to use the competitive prices unless you think you have got similar products, identical products. Let's say you have the golf club, is Callaway golf club the same as Mizuno golf club? It is not. Although they are competitors in the market place, they are not identical, similar goods for valuation purpose. Going down to shopping malls or going onto the internet, whereas you may gather information, it does not necessarily give you information which is perfect to apply method 2 or method 3 if you have to still use deductive method 4 or possibly method 5. So that's the end of section one. That provides a short overview of what is the history to transaction value, WTO valuation agreement, what is transaction value, and what are other methods of valuation. The key point of transaction value is used over 90 percent of the time. If you are going to reject method 1, you need to have reasons. If you use other methods, method 2 and method 3 are very hard to use in real life. Most likely you are looking at method 4. Deductive value is good for customs, because you can verify the data, because the data is coming from within China. Method 5 is hard for customs, because the data is coming from overseas, somebody may not tell you the truth. It's hard to verify whether it's true or not.

So let's move onto section two, which is use of transaction value. In this section, we will have some case studies and questions. As defined in GAC Order 148, the customs value of imported goods shall be the transaction value. That is the price actually paid or payable for the goods when sold for export to the country of importation. I think whenever I work on valuation cases, I always start by drawing some flow charts to understand what's happening, who is selling to who, who is paying whom, how much. When you receive a stack of documents, it is very difficult to work out what matters, and what does not matter. Whenever we do valuation, we always try to identify who is the seller overseas, who is shipping the goods to China, and we want to know who the buyer is. Transaction value, you would expect it to be an invoice. Let's say it is 100 US $, seller selling to the buyer for 100 US $, payment going back for 100 US $. That's the price paid or payable. Whenever you are working on valuation cases, it's the base place to start. We won't really discuss other methods anymore. We will focus on whether we will have transaction value or not. We will do case studies.

Question one: if you have a sale between related parties, can you use transaction value or not? Let's pick GE. This is GE in the US. This is GE in China, so related parties. So can you use transaction value in method one?

The answer is yes. But it is not that simple. We say yes in principle. What do we mean by in principle? We are assuming the relationship does not influence the price. If you check a company, and your conclusion is the relationship influences the price. Then you have no transaction value. You use the alternative methods of valuation. If you look at international trade, about 50 percent of all transactions you will see are related party transactions. About 50 percent! So, yes, you can still use transaction value so long as the relationship does not influence the price.

Question two: the price is dependent on other factors. We have a sale from overseas to China. The price is 100 US $, but there are some other factors which affected the price. Can we use transaction value or not? Let's say for an example, in this transaction, I am selling goods A for 100 US $, but this is only agreed upon if we separately sell goods B for 200 US $.

The answer is no. The reason is that transaction value can not be used if there is a condition or consideration on which value can not be placed. The obligation to buy other goods is such condition. In practice, the value of machinery is often discounted if there are tied sales. Another example, let's say a printer. A printer in the office is the printer plus the cartridge needed to fill the printer. Sometimes you will have the sale to say let me sell you the printer if you promise to keep buying the cartridge to refill.

Now question three: free of charge replacement parts. Let's say for an example, the seller sells to the buyer goods A for 100 US $. The buyer says A does not work, it is broken. So there is another one, goods A's replacement parts. The value is zero, because it's replacing the defective goods. So can transaction value be used?

The answer is no. Free of charge goods are not subject to sale. Therefore transaction value can not apply. Often what you may use is the early shipment to value the goods. Let's say for example. here the earlier shipment is goods A for 100 US $. We will use 100 US $ to value free of charge replacement.

Question four: consignment stocks. What happens is that the overseas supplier, the local buyer, the invoice, the goods of value for 100 US $, but there is no payment from the buyer to seller, because there is no transfer of title. The seller still holds the title. The buyer maybe has physical possession, but he does not have title.

We can not use transaction value. Stock is not subject to a sale. At the time of quotation, maybe you will use the deductive.

Ok, question five: invoice show quantity discounts. The seller sells to the buyer, the invoice says 100 US $, and did have 90 US $ after discount, the payment is 90 US $. So can transaction value be used?

Quantity discounts are normally allowed if they are freely given and applied to the specific shipment. Well, discounts do not mean rejection of transaction value.

Question six: goods that were purchased six month ago. Let's say the goods were purchased on 1st January, 2009, but the date of importation is 1st, July. Six months have gone by between the sale verses the importation. This scenario you may find a lot due to the current economic downturn. Goods may be purchased a long time ago, but are not being imported to China, because of the economic situation.

The answer is possible. It could be yes. It could be no. In terms of method 1, transaction value, there is no concept of time. If you use identical goods or similar goods, there is the concept of time, 45 days. You must choose comparisons which were imported within about 45 days. But in method 1 transaction value, there is no concept of time. What needs to be checked is whether the time has resulted in the change of value of the goods. You need to approve the original sale is a sale for export to China. If you could satisfy those, yes. If you could not, we will say no transaction value, use the alternative methods.

Question seven: a profit sharing arrangement. The profit sharing refers that seller sells to buyer for 100 US $, and buyer sells to the customer in China for 200 US $. Buyer gives further 10 US $ to the seller. The further 10 US $ comes from the profit made in selling the goods in China, the total price paid by the buyer to the seller is 110 US $. Can transaction value apply?

The answer is YES in principle. The profit sharing arrangement is acceptable. But to establish the dutiable value, you need to take transaction value of 100 US $, and add the 10 US $, so the dutiable value is 110 US $. So your method of valuation is still method 1. If you look at the method 1, there are four conditions. One condition is no subsequent proceeds like profit sharing. However, if you could quantify the profit sharing, you can still use method 1, say transaction value is Yes, but the value should be 110 US $. If the goods were not sold, there would be no profit sharing. So the transaction price would still be 100 US $.

Question eight: goods are bought at a very low price. When economy is bad, companies are trying to sell inventory. In the past, the customer had lots of money, and he could pay 200 US $. Now he has no money and could only pay 150 US $. The seller will reduce his price, so goods are now sold for 75 US $, instead of 100 US $. Can we use transaction value?

We would say possibly so long as the transaction value is real, so long as you still meet the four conditions for valuing the goods for method 1. Then we would say Yes.

Question nine: the buyer supplies the designs free of charge. Let's go back to the handbag. The buyer designs the handbag and the buyer provides the design to the seller. So they design the handbag, the stitching, the color, the fabric, and the look. The buyer has given the design and maybe E-mail the design to the seller. The seller uses the design to manufacture and sell the handbag to China. The design is given for zero because it's owned by buyer. Can we use transaction value?

In this example, we could assume that the design comes from China to overseas. So which case could we use the transaction value? What we have to do is to make an adjustment for the assists because we can still use transaction value so long as they quantify the design cost.

Question ten: adjustments to the transaction value. Here we forget about the transaction value, and this is what you see on the invoice. For the next section, we will talk about anything else that the buyer maybe pays overseas. We focus on what else has happened. Are something else happening? Should that be included in the dutiable value? So adjustments are required to ensure we have level playing field. Adjustments can be up or down. If our invoice price is 100 US $, we may adjust up to 110 US $, or we maybe adjust down to 90 US $. It depends on what we are making the adjustments for. You need to have legal basis for any adjustment or any deduction. If it is not in the law and if it is not in GAC Order

148, you can't adjust up and you can't really adjust down.

So let's review the list of outside the scope of transaction value.

Commissions and broker fees. Commissions are normally paid to an agent. For example, this is the agent, and he receives a commission of 10 US $. The question is "Is that dutiable or not dutiable?" Buyer commissions are non – dutiable and seller commissions are dutiable. Buying commission is what you call procurement commission. Why is buyer commission not dutiable? Essentially because the agent is acting on behalf of the buyer to purchase the goods. In order to work out whether an agent is a buyer agent or a seller agent, first, there should be a contract. There should be an agreement. You then need to say who sign that agreement, the agent to the buyer or the agent to the seller? You then need to say who does the agent represent? Who is its boss? Excellently worked out by who pays it. If I pay you, I am probably your boss. Who is paying the agent? That tends to be the boss. So commissions can be complex maybe because people cannot decide who is the buyer agent, the buyer commission or seller agent and seller commission. The first step is to work out who is the buyer and who is seller. It is very complex but that is a good place to start. Broker fees or intermediary can also be dutiable.

Assists. It is a long list of assists. Assists is where your kind of get help and it is a kind of free help. So I do something or I give you something for free and helping you out. I am assisting you. It is an assist that needs to be considered. Assists cover many things, materials, components, parts, tools, models and engineering designs. It is very important to study the list, to identify whether any things are on the list. Assists get complicated. The buyer may provide assists directly to the seller such as the designs. There could be a third party. The buyer may commission a third party to do the design, and then provide the design to the seller, and the seller uses the design to manufacture the product. The product is then imported. So what you have is like a circular flow of service and the activity taking place. It can be direct or with a third party. The list of assists is defined. Most of the time it can cover all of the scenarios that you could possibly imagine.

Royalties. Essentially you maybe have a license. License is someone to use your intellectual property, patent, copyright, and trademark. They have to pay a fee to use that. Should that fee be included in the dutiable value? Well it should be if the royalty is related to the import of goods or paid is a condition of sale. GAC Order 148 has a very good definition of what is related to the goods and what is conditional sale. I would say when you look at Order 148, it gives you a lot of good guidance to decide whether or not the royalty is related to the goods or paid as a conditional sale. In China, royalties are always paid as a conditional sale based on the definition. The question is that if it is related to the imported goods. Most of the time that probably is Yes especially for trademark. If you look at the finished products and the trademark is fixed, the royalties are related to the goods, for example the Prada handbag. It gets more complicated if you import a semi – finished product. You manufacture it in China, and then you sell it domestically. That is more complicated because what you import may be raw material, and you then have a factory to make the finished product. You sell it and the royalty is paid in relation to the finished product and for technology used in China. Is that related to the import of raw material? You have to look at the imported goods. You have to look at the royalty contract. You have to understand what intellectual property is being used.

Subsequent proceeds. Subsequent proceeds are very similar to what we discussed earlier on transaction value. The buyers sells, makes money and gives some of its money to the overseas seller. That is the subsequent proceed. In China, it is very difficult to have subsequent proceeds maybe because of the foreign exchange control. To remit overseas for trade payable, you need import declaration form. You could only remit up to the amount stated on the declaration form. So at the moment it is very difficult to see companies with subsequent proceeds and many companies do not have that structure in place.

Now we go back to our scenarios. Patent royalties paid to the seller. Is that dutiable or not? Yes, it is dutiable and adjustments are required. Why? It is probably related to the imported goods. Patent is a condition to sale, and patent royalties is required. The overseas manufacture process needs both of these conditions. Therefore, it's dutiable.

Next is a much harder scenario: reproduction royalties for a master disc. Just one disc comes into China. The buyer replicates the disc, so then produces many discs. For the replication, the buyer pays royalty fee. It is the right to reproduce that master disc. Does that royalty to replicate in China relate to imported goods? No adjustment required. What this means is that you reproduce it in China rather than import it to China. The customs duty should be assessed on imported goods. The royalty is paid for goods reproduced it in China, not imported into China. Therefore no adjustment required.

License fees paid for a patented process in China. Let me give you an example. You have the seller and the buyer. The imported goods are raw materials. The buyer uses a patent to manufacture the raw material and to finish the product which is sold in China. Patent royalty is paid to the license owner. We need to go back to two principles. Is that related to imported goods or is it paid as a conditional sale? Every royalty scenario is different. In terms of your analysis, your methodology should be the same. So the answer is No on the basis that the patent relates to manufacture in China, not to the imported product itself. That is especially the case where the imported material is very generic like metal, plastics and paper.

This one relates to assists. Designs sent free of charge from the buyer to the seller. We can go back to our handbag. The buyer gives the design free of charge to the seller. The seller uses that to make the handbag and the handbag is imported to China. Is any adjustment required? The answer is no adjustment required. The point is that the design and the development work undertaken in the country of import are not dutiable. The design work in this example was undertaken in China which is the country of import. So what if the design work is undertaken overseas, for example in Singapore? The cost incurred overseas should be included in dutiable value.

Freight & Insurance from port of export to importer's factory. Is the adjustment required or not? Yes. The adjustment is required. Freight and insurance to the port of entry must be included in the customs value. You read GAC Order 148 and clearly see CIF.

Interest charges for the delayed payment for the goods. This means the goods sold for 100 US $. The buyer pays maybe 90 days later. Because of that, there is an interest charge of 5 US $ due to the late payment. The price on the invoice is only 100 US $. There is another invoice of payment of 5 US $. So the two are separate. Adjustments may be required. The interest is not a payment to the goods. The payment for the goods is 100 US $. That's the transaction price. The payment for the interest is for the use of money. It is to be able to pay for the goods 90 days after you purchase that rather than the day you purchase that. It is financing, and it is the payment to use money rather than for the goods themselves. Under GAC Order 148, interest can be non – dutiable provided these criteria are satisfied. It is an agreement for the interest. The agreement must be underwriting, it can not be verbal. The goods could be purchased without interest. The importer could pay on the day he purchases that, or he could pay 90 days later. He must have the option. And the rate of interest must be reasonable. Otherwise, you are cheating. So if the goods are 100 US $, and the interest payment is 100 US $, clearly it is not commercial and somebody is trying to smuggle or undervalue the goods. You must make sure the interest is commercial, what the bank interest rate is and the similar.

A tool owned by the importer and given to the seller. So this is an assist and very similar to the concept of design. The buyer is giving something to the seller. In this case, the tool is used to manufacture the goods which are imported to China. Do you need to make an adjustment for the value of the tool? Yes, adjustments are required. Tooling is dutiable and should be included in the dutiable value. You often find tooling in the automotive sector, as you always see in the car factory, using a lot of tooling to manufacture the cars. Electronics is a little bit similar as well. The two sectors where a lot of tooling are required. Tooling may be provided free of charge, or a cost in which case is dutiable.

Commission paid to agency. Commission paid to an agency is dutiable except buyer agency. As customs officials, most importers would probably tell you the agent is a buyer agent. The importer would tell you that, so that the commission fee is treated as non – dutiable. As customs officers, you have to check it to make sure the importers are telling you the truth. He may not tell you the truth because I am sure you all have the experience.

In summary, we have talked about what is dutiable and what is non – dutiable. A long list comes directly from GAC Order 148. Essentially things which happened post importation and things which happened in China should not be subject to customs duty because that relate to the activities conducted inside China rather than to the imported goods coming to China. Installing equipment in China is a cost associated with putting equipment into a factory and making it work. That requires some expert engineers and technicians. The cost is not related to manufacturing machines overseas. For these to be non – dutiable, they should be distinguished from the price paid or payable for the goods. Sometimes the company will have a price for 200 US $, and they will say within that, it is the installation cost. But importer on the invoice has to distinguish it otherwise it is impossible for the customs to exclude that from the dutiable value. So importers maybe very quick to point out when it is not dutiable, but the documentation must support that. The importer's documentations do not support, and then you can not treat that as non – dutiable. The dutiable or non – dutiable items must be separately listed on the invoice.

So the last section is very brief. Under GAC Order 148, there are eight definitions of when a related party transaction exists. Fifty percent of all cross – border transactions are related party transactions. It is very easy to work out whether a transaction is related or unrelated. Normally you just look at the names on the invoice, it would tell you. You can see it is affiliated or not. It is more complicated one where the company names are different. Therefore, you need to look at who is the shareholder company and who is on the management board, etc. Generally this is not too difficult. How to test for an arm's length price? This is where you can compare to identical or similar goods as we discussed earlier. That is very hard. You can look at the deductive method or computed method which is article 22 and article 24. It is far more complicated to test a lot of evidence and a lot of documentation, and comparisons etc. what I say is that the scenarios where expertise is necessary, a lot of patience is necessary and a lot of experience and it requires a lot of work with the importer to get the information so you can make a decision as a customs officer.

To summarize the objective of valuation agreement, that is you want something which is fair, which is uniform, which customs understand and taxpayers understand. Ultimately you need the transaction which is not influenced by the relationship or any other factors. Suppose the relationship influences the price or other factors, and it is always complex, you are going to have to use another method of valuation to arrive at the correct dutiable value. The laws are not really there to set the price. You shouldn't say this handbag worth 150 US $ rather than 50 US $. If you apply the methodology, you arrive at the correct dutiable value. It shouldn't worry you whether it is 50 US $, 100 US $ or 150 US $ so long as you apply the right methodology to value the goods. The transaction value is used 94 percent of the time globally. That is our definition of transaction value, price paid or payable, generally represented, quite simply, the commercial invoice. Make sure these four conditions are fulfilled. I would say condition 1, 2 and 3 are generally not that applicable for multinational companies. The real issue is condition 4 "has the relationship influenced the price?" That is where you would spend most of your time when you have multinationals related party transactions, making adjustment for the royalties, commissions, making deductions for transportation freight, insurance and so on and so forth.

WCO归类知识简介

（普华永道合伙人 Damon Paling）
（缉私局　刘欣平　浦东海关　汪钰　根据录音整理翻译）

本次培训分成几个部分。首先谈一下归类的重要性，接下来讨论协调制度，随后再探讨协调制度在各国的应用，最后学习如何归类和归类总规则。

一、归类的重要性

归类的重要性显而易见，但多数人都只能想到前几点理由。一是很多人认为归类的重要性在于它决定了税率，但是归类也有很多其他重要作用；二是中国和很多国家签订了自由贸易区协定，这些协议也决定了商品的税则编码；三是贸易救济，如反倾销、反补贴及保护措施等。这些救济措施也是以商品归类为前提的。中国针对奢侈品等商品征收消费税，比如石油、烟草和酒类，这些都以商品编码为前提；四是非关税贸易壁垒，包括一些进口许可证，如由商检出具的进口通关单或者是卫生与农业部门出具的进口许可证。这些证件决定了进口商品的品质和安全。正确的协调制度对这些证件的签发有重要意义，它确保了进口商品的质量，对国内消费者负责。当然，从海关的角度看，某些企业可能为了逃避反倾销税等税款而瞒报编码，这就需要海关有足够的判断力识别错误归类。错误的归类是违规的，可能导致惩处。

二、协调制度介绍

协调制度的全称是《商品名称及编码协调制度》，我们一般称为HS编码。“协调”意味着寻求一致，而“制度”则是需要协调的内容。韩国或日本的税则和中国的税则很相似，因为这些国家都加入了协调制度公约。现在全世界有超过98%的国家使用协调制度，基本上每个国家都是世界海关组织的成员，并且都加入了协调制度公约。

（一）协调制度的历史

协调制度公约完成于1988年，分别在1996年、2002年、2007年进行了更新。为什么更新？举个简单的例子，我在新西兰海关工作的时候使用的是1988年版本的协调制度，当时的税则中只有黑白电视。而今，我们已经有了平板电视、液晶电视等。随着科技的进步，协调制度也需要相应的更新。又比如说现在办公室里常用的多功能打印机，具有打印、复印、传真等多功能，这个机器是传真机？打印机？还是复印机？可能在20年前，这样的机器根本不存在。因此更新协调制度是有意义的。截至2008年2月，协调制度公约共有132个的缔约方。位于布鲁塞尔的世界海关组织专门负责协调制度的更新，理论上每4年更新一次，但是由于工作量太大，所以实际上每5年至6年更新一次。对于一个国家来说，加入协调制度便利企业开展贸易往来。

（二）协调制度与税则

应该说税则书是一本颇具智慧的书。编写此书的作者是非常聪明的。税则共分为21类，97章，超过1200个四位品目和超过5000个六位子目，税则以第1章活动物开始，以第97章古董结束，包括第15章、第16章的加工食物、第32章的油和化妆品以及第46章的棉制T恤等。21类的分类方式使税则更易使用，97章的划分方式使其更具结构性。四位品目和六位子目提供更多细节。这种结构性降低了归类的复杂度。

关于归类总规则。我们通过税则书如何对一件商品进行归类？归类总规则共有6条，其中第一条用得最频繁，它确定了税则组成部分的法律地位，如品目、子目等。一是不能以目录，附则等作为归类依据；二是类、章及分章的标题，仅为查找方便而设；三是具有法律效力的归类，应按照品目条文和有关类注或章注确定。

什么是章注、类注和子目注释？税则有21类，每一类的开头都有本类的注释告诉你什么商品可以归入这一类，同样每一章的前面也有这样的注释告诉你什么商品能够归入这一章。子目注释则更加详细地对归类进行描述。章注和类注比较宏观，但子目注释等则非常详细且与需要归类的商品相关。但这并不意味着归类时需要通读所有注释，有时对一个商品归类需要一天的时间，而大部分商品只需5分钟就可以确定HS编码，某些商品可能略长。如果你熟悉税则就可以找到自己的方法，阅读章注及类注，做出正确的归类。

世界海关组织也将补充注释和说明编辑成册并提供协调制度的翻译。一共有5本补充注释的书，每本都对相关章节进行了注释。海关总署已将此译成了中文作为归类的辅助材料。某些商品在税则中有明确的归类，不需用到补充注释，但有时就需要查阅更多材料才能做出正确归类。最先需要的材料就是补充注释，它能帮助做出正确的归类。这些注释中有很多技术性细节。并非每个人都是工程师、医学家或是生物学家，但注释有助于商品归类。我们以第十一类《纺织原料及纺织制品》为例，本类中我们可以看到关于该类的注释，接下来是各章的名称，第50章蚕丝，第51章羊毛、动物细毛或粗毛、马毛纱线及其机织物，第52章棉花等。在归类时，可以根据这些名称来判断商品是否属于这一项下。以类注为例，类注十分重要，它常常告诉我们哪些商品不属于本章。第十一类的类注指出，本章不包括制刷用的动物鬃、毛（税号05.02）。如果你要归类的商品属于此类，则不能归入第十一类，而应该归到第五章的05.02税号下。注释告诉你哪些商品是被排除的。因此你在归类时应首先阅读注释，因为它会告诉商品是否被本章排除，如果被排除了，那么你应该归到其他类、章。类注也包含解释，解释和排除的作用刚好相反但同等重要。比如同样在第十一类就有对“高强力纱”的解释。如果进口商告诉你这个商品是“高强力纱”，那么你就可以对照类注来判断它到底是否属于“高强力纱”。如果商品和类注的描述一致，那么就可以归到相应章，如果不一致，那你就需要进一步了解商品。类注也有指引性描述，比如“除条文另有规定的以外，各种服装即使成套包装供零售用，也应按各自税号分别归类。”就是说如果有一套西装，西装是分成裤子和上衣分别归类的。总之，有时候指引性描述可以让你找到归类的答案。

关于章注。类有类注，章有章注。我们以第63章为例，一是第一分章仅适用于各种纺织物制成的物品。这就告诉你什么商品可归入这章。如商品不是由纺织物制成的，则不能归入第一分章。二是第一分章不包括的内容，这是排除项。如果商品符合排除项的描述，那就需要归入其他章。品目注释也是同样，品目注释与类注章注相似，对6位数编码注释，更加详尽。要阅读这些注释，如第63章是关于织物制品的，在4位编码层级有6302床上、餐桌、盥洗及厨房用的织物制品，其下的6位编码，有6302.10棉制针织或钩编的床上用织物制品，棉制的，化学纤维制的或其他纺织材料制。根据织物制品是以何种材料制成的，归入6302.21、6302.22或6302.29的不同编码。所以说对织物制品归类，重要的是知道其制成材料而不是其用途，棉制的、化学纤维制的或其他纺织材料。

含可可的糖食能否归入第17章？技术用途的传输带能否归入第十六类下的任何一章？门襟为左压右的裙子应为男装吗？这些都是稀奇古怪的问题，哪里可以找到答案呢？从类注、章注中可以找到。比如第一题，第17章的章注中就排除了这种商品。你不会也不需要背诵注释，但是在归类时要学会看注释。第二题，技术用途的传输带能否归入第十六类下的任何一章？第十六类类注一第5节也排除了这种商品。第三题，门襟为左压右的裙子应为男装吗？第61章章注表明：本章服装不适用于其样式已明显为男式或女式的服装，因此裙子不属于男装。没有人也不可能有人是所有商品的专家，你若要了解正确的归类方法就必须阅读这些注释。

三、协调制度与各国税则的联系

以上是归类的重要性并介绍了协调制度，现在讨论协调制度和各国税则之间的联系。

中国是协调制度的缔约方，中国的税则与协调制度具有统一性，中国要使用协调制度中所有的品目、子目及其对应编码，税则编码必须与协调制度相一致，不得改变，除非为适于本国法律而作文字调整。这意味着什么？从中国或任何一个缔约方的角度看，协调制度只能复制，粘贴，将其翻译成本国语言而不能做任何改变。对章注、类注、4 位或者 6 位编码都不得有任何改变，否则会影响国家在协调制度方面的信誉。不管在欧洲还是在美国，其税则书和中国的是相似的，因为它们都是协调制度的缔约方，税则不管是何种语言，其结构都相同，即 21 类 97 章。和其他国家一样，中国也有其职责，要征税、统计等，因此各国可以根据自己的情况制定后 4 位编码。完整的商品编码一共有 10 位，前 6 位与协调制度相同，后 4 位由各国自行制定。原因很多，包括征税、统计、进出口税率等，因此各国的后 4 位编码是不一样的。有些国家加入了区域性组织，比如欧盟或者东盟，它们可能有相同的税则结构，意大利、西班牙和法国的税则可能是相同的，也许在 10 位编码上会因为进口许可证等原因有细微的差别。

在国家法律法规和对海关归类的补充说明中可以找到各国归类指引。比如美国以颁布进口许可证而出名，你可以从网络上找到美国归类裁定。在中国，同样可以作出归类决定，这些决定在中国有效但在美国无效，反之亦然。中国可以依据税则作出归类决定，海关总署令第 158 号中明确规定了这一权力。协调制度是一项非常好的制度，让进口商和海关都能知道如何归类。因此，成为协调制度公约缔约国的益处在于包括中国在内的协调制度成员国使用全球通用的 6 位编码。最后一点原因很有趣，就是有关协调制度的争议可以提交世界海关组织协调制度委员会解决。如上海海关和某公司在归类问题上不能达成一致，口岸海关、直属海关甚至海关总署都无法解决，那么这个问题可以提交到位于布鲁塞尔的世界海关组织。世界海关组织会定期出版归类决定，将提交的争议结集刊印。企业也可随时向世界海关组织提交归类争议。

四、归类方法

我想在归类时你们会犯的最大的错误是在不了解商品的情况下急于归类。税则不会告诉你商品是什么，税则只告诉你商品怎么归类。我唯一的建议就是不要急于使用税则书，在打开税则书之前先弄清楚商品是什么。如果是一瓶水或者是一台笔记本电脑，那么归类可能很简单。但如果你从来没有见过，接触过或者用过这商品，你就需要找到该商品的技术数据了解它，然后进行归类，否则会归入错误的税号。一个归类高手要对一件商品归类时，他要问自己的第一个问题是“这是什么东西?”如果你不知道，那么就无法归类。要了解这是什么东西？有什么用？是用什么材料做成的？以什么形式进口？液体状还是粉末状？是分装进口还是整体进口？这几个问题都要在归类之前弄清楚。询问进出口商弄清楚这些问题，然后开始归类。如果你不知道这些问题的答案就打开税则书归类，只会让你很崩溃，最后放弃。从哪里可以获得这些信息呢？网络是很好的途径，我们利用网络休闲但也可以用网络来帮助工作。大多数公司会将自己的产品介绍放在自己的网站上，登录这些公司的网站可以看到这些产品的资料，了解这是什么样的产品，有什么用，构成成分或者制成材料，一般以什么形式进口等。当然也可以要求进出口商提供产品资料，包括发票、采购合同及装箱单等，这些资料能告诉你商品的进口形式、状态与包装方式。我认为，作为一名海关关员应该有一个问题清单，向进出口商咨询这些问题或者是通过网络自己解决这些问题，包括产品详细资料，如型号、材质或者颜色。商品进口形式不同可能导致税号不同。如果是橘子汁，那么它是浓缩的吗？如果是化学品，那么它是液体的还是片剂的？诸如这些问题都要弄清楚。根据商品的不同，你所要了解的信息也会不同，所以在归类前有一系列问题要了解清楚。假设现在有一瓶水，我们已知这是什么商品，接下来就要看该商品可归入哪一章，再看这章的品目及子目有没有对该商品的描述。比如商品是水杯，那么是用玻璃、纸张还是其他材料制成的呢？这仅是一个例子。当你了解了这一商品后，你就可以打开税则做归类准备，阅读可能的品目和子目，看何种描述更贴近要归类的商品。如果你没有找到符合要归类商品的描述，你可能需要返回到目录重新开始归类。为什么这样的流程在归类中十分重要？即使你工作很紧张，你也不希望做出错误的归类，根据这个流程归类就不会浪费你同事与上级的时间，也不会将时间浪费在向进出口商咨询无关的问题上。记住要问的问题都是有关商品的问题，比如商品的用途、材质等。按照这套方法归类，即使有人质疑你的结果，你也知道这归类结果是如何得来的，就有理由支持你的结果。最后，这套流程方法让你的思维更加缜密，更具逻辑性。归类本身就是一个逻辑性很强的过程。

五、商品归类总规则的应用

共有 6 条归类总规则。一是定义法律效力；二是拓展税目的范围；三是裁定方法；四是上述规则无法归类的情况；五是盒子、容器、包装材料和包装；六是子目的归类。前五条与 4 位编码及税目有关，而第六条与子目的归类有关。

绝大多数情况下，我们仅使用总规则一和总规则六。接下来我们会探讨这些归类总规则的细节内容。需要指出的是，这些归类总规则需要按照顺序依次使用，在这一点上与估价规则有类似之处。

（一）归类总规则一

它指出目录、按字母顺序的索引、类、章及分章的标题仅供参考。你并不能依据税则书中的目录对商品归类。总规则一着重说明的是，如果税目条文、章注、类注没有要求，则应按照其他归类总归则来确定。实际运用归类总规则一，首先找出一个或多个适用于该商品的税目。例如一瓶水，我们就会从第 14 章、第 15 章和第 16 章找到“水”。第二步，查看相应的类注以确定该商品是否被归入其中或在排除项内，以及是否有相对应的定义或者描述。第三步，查找相应的章注并找到特定的某一章，同样查看是否存在任何的例外、定义或者描述。第四步，我们会查阅那些拉丁文的表述，如“初步推定”“和其他的事物”“已作必要的修正”。因此从本质上来说这个过程是，打开税则书，找到某些合理的税目，查看类注、章注和拉丁文术语，逐渐接近正确答案。拉丁文的“初步推定”指第一印象，也就是说你乍看到某样东西，而这个东西是什么呢？你需要用这种方法来观察商品，而不应凭想象判断，或者不懂装懂。“和其他的事物”是指这个可能是某种商品，也可能是某种与此类似的商品。举例来说，可能是一小瓶水，也可能是一大瓶水。

当然这其中还牵涉到文章的标点符号。分号用于一长串内容中间的停顿。逗号则表示“或者”和“以及”。所以说英语是非常具有迷惑性的，甚至对以英语为母语人的来说也是如此。以下是一个英语名言，用来帮助你们理解这一点：

“女子，不依靠她先生，就一无所有。”

“女子，不依靠她，先生就一无所有。”

事实上这句英语名言告诉我们标点符号位置的不同，逗号是放在“先生”之前还是之后，从根本上改变了这句话的意思。

（二）归类总规则二

归类总规则二是由两个部分组成的。它从本质上拓展了归类的范围，从而将那些税则书中没有明确列明的商品纳入其中。

1. 归类总规则二（一）

一是不完整品或未制成品，但具有完整品或制成品的基本特征。“基本特征”这个术语并没有在协调制度中有所定义，因此不同商品的基本特征各有不同。我记得在几年前，当我们需要决定商品的基本特征时，有一个基于商品价值的所谓“60%”原则，即通过判断进口的商品是否代表了60%以上的价值，或者组成部分是否代表了60%以上的价值，以此来决定商品的基本特征。如，进口一辆不包含轮子的自行车，你会认为这辆车依旧具有完整自行车的基本特征，它只是由于不完整而缺少了两个轮子，所以你还是会把它归为自行车。

二是完整品或制成品，但以未组装件或拆散件的形式出现。这也许是出于包装、操作或运输的方便，或是由于国家法律法规要求必须通过此种方式进口商品。这里有个例子，有一辆自行车，它所有的部件都没有进行组装，而是装在一个箱子中。为什么呢？因为这样我们就能将它放入更小的空间之中。我们可以在现有尺寸的集装箱中放入更多的自行车，从而同时装载更多的商品。在这种情况下，这些自行车是制成品，只是拆成了众多的部件放在了运输容器之中，所以我们依然会将其归类为自行车。

首先分析未制成品或不完整品的状态，例如没有车轮的自行车。它是不是完整无缺？如果你认为不是，则分析它的不完整程度。它是否具有制成品的基本特征？一辆没有车轮的自行车仍然具有自行车的基本特征。如果你认为具有基本特征，则需要区分它是否完整或装配好。例如，如果我们要判断一辆自行车，我们只见到坐椅和把手，却没有见到车架，这种情况下是不是具有制成品的基本特征呢？我认为不具有。它们只是坐椅和把手，没有链条与车轮，因此我们将其归入其他税目。那这些商品是什么呢？我认为它们是一辆自行车的零部件，所以将其归入零部件而不是制成品。进出口商品的商业发票通常会写有商品是否未组装的说明，因此这条规则能够在此方面提供指引。但作为海关关员面对这种情况的时候，你可能会提出查验要求，通过开箱检查来确定集装箱内所装的商品，看它们是否组装或完整，然后决定接下来怎么做。就归类总规则二（一）而言，你必须要实实在在地看到商品。

2. 归类总规则二（二）

归类总规则二（二）拓展了税目的范围以满足不同材料或物质混合或组合的物品。一个比较恰当的例子是用作燃料的化学制品，它可能含有部分煤油与部分柴油。如何对它进行归类？我们初步判断，它可能被归入两个税目，即煤油或柴油。归类总规则二（二）为归类提供多项选择。如果你想获得准确的归类，就需要进一步参考归类总规则三。当然归类总规则二（二）只在税则没有对混合物或组成物具体列明的情况下才适用。当你在查阅类注与章注时，会发现有时税则中会提到应当归入此处的商品含有70%柴油等。因此即使是混合物，类注和章注也可能根据百分比给出一个确切的归类税目。

（三）归类总规则三

归类总规则三是一个裁定方法，它在商品可能被归入两个或两个以上税目时适用。考虑的依次顺序为：一是商品更为具体的列名。需要注意的就是那些对商品本质特征有着更为具体描述的税目；二是基本特征；三是按税则书中的税号顺序取最后一个税目。这里需要注意的是，归类总规则三只有在税目条文、类注和章注没有另行规定的情况下才使用，也就是说运用该规则时，仍需查阅类注和章注。

1. 归类总规则三（一）

列名具体的品目，优先于列名一般的品目。对这种情况作出判断需要个案分析，因为每天有成百上千的进出口商品，且缺乏一个快速有效的方法来判断到底哪个列名更具体。也许不同的人会给出不同的答案，并且每个答案都有其逻辑性。举例来说，名称列名比类别列名更为具体，税目“剃刀”要比“用手使用的工具”或“家用电子机械用品”更为具体，所以要记住找出最具体列名的税目。这里还有一个例子，用在汽车内的地毯并不归为“汽车装饰用品”，而是被归在更为具体的列名的税目“地毯”之中。如果每个可能的税目都仅述及混合物的某部分材料或物质，或零售成套货品中的部分物品，那么这些税目被认为列名同样具体，且货品不能按照归类总规则三（一）归类。此时需要查阅归类总规则三（二）和（三）。

2. 归类总规则三（二）

归类总规则三（二），即通过基本特征来归类。以下是 4 种可能出现的情况。一是混合物，例如酿造用混合物，其中含有 70% 小麦和 30% 大麦；二是不同材料构成的组合物。例如用塑料和橡胶做成的传送带；三是不同部件构成的组合物，如装在金属底座上的玻璃烟灰缸，应归为玻璃还是金属；四是成套零售的商品。在以上这些情况中，商品都是依据构成基本特征的材料或部件来进行归类的。影响到确定基本特征的因素包括材料、体积、数量、重量、价值以及商品使用过程中某种材料所起的作用。如前所述，中国在几年前曾广泛运用商品价格来确定其基本特征。如果某物品价值 100 元，那它每个部件的价值是多少？当其中一个部件的价值超过该物品价值的 60% 时，我们就能通过这个部件来确定其基本特征，从而找到适用的 HS 编码。关于归类总规则三（二），有几个定义需要注意。不同部件构成的组合物是指部件组装在一起形成不可分割的商品。如果商品的部件是可以分割的话，这些部件必须能够匹配适用。组成商品的部件通常不会单独零售。

3. **归类总规则三（三）**

当你走投无路的时候可以查阅归类总规则三（三），归入按税目顺序排列的最后一个税目。我想说的是，在现实生活中我们很少使用归类总规则三（三）。多数情况下，我们使用归类总规则一。

（四）归类总规则四

通常运用归类总规则一、二、三就能得出归类结论，但有时候在特定的情形下需要用到归类总规则四。或许你找不到任何一个匹配的税目，但是你可以找到一个与待归类的商品描述相类似的税目。也就是说，归类总规则四主要是运用于对市场上新出现的商品进行归类。具体来说，查看商品的描述、特征、目的、材料、用途以及商业价值，然后尝试找到合适的依据归类。

（五）归类总规则五

货物运抵边境时所用的外包装或容器不仅仅是指用来运输的容器，还包括贮存和销售时所用的容器。商品的外包装是否需要与其所装商品分离而单独归类呢？归类总规则五用于对某些长期使用的容器、包装材料以及包装容器进行归类。那些为一件或一套特定物品所设计的包装盒与其中的物品是一起归类的。例如，购买照相机时就会得到一个相机套，购买吉他之类的乐器时就会得到一件乐器套，因而你会将它们一同归类。这些外包装必须长期使用，并且与它们的包装对象搭配。因此外包装与商品必须同时进口，使用同一张发票、提运单，放置在同一个容器之中。但如果容器或外包装构成了商品的基本特征则另当别论。归类总规则五还包括常用包装材料或包装容器与商品同时进口的情况，其中包装材料或容器显然可重复使用的不受本规则限制。你可能会遇到桶、板箱以及托盘，海关能对这些物品单独归类。可再利用的包装在进口之后可能会被重复使用，因此入境时可视作单独进口的商品。

（六）归类总规则六

作为最后一条总规则，其内容与子目有关。多数情况下，我们是用到总规则一中提到的税目、类注、章注，另外加上总规则六所提到的子目。因此，税目与4位编码有关，而子目则与6位、8位和10位编码有关。可以说总规则一与总规则六是商品归类的基础所在。首先你解决税目的问题，然后再运用子目，并查阅税目注释和子目注释，最终得出准确的商品归类。

Customs Classification

(Presented by Damon Paling, Partner at PWC)
(Transcribed and Translated by Liu Xinping, Bureau of Anti – Smuggling, and Wang Yu, Pudong Customs House)

I think for this training we have the following several sections. Why is it important to classification? Then we will talk about the harmonized system. And we will talk about how the harmonized system relate to national rules and lastly, the General Rules of Interpretation (GRI).

1. Importance of classification

This may seem very obvious but I can tell you many people may think about the first few points. Many people think that classification is there only to determine how much duty payable. However as we can see tariff classification has many other important principles. For example as we know China negotiates many free trade agreements with foreign countries. Under free trade agreement to determine whether there is substantial transportation, we may look at the HS code of the product. Of course there are trade remedies, such as anti – dumping, countervailing and safeguard measures. For these trade remedies you also need to know what the HS code of the product is. In China we also have some consumption tax on some product. Luxury taxes may be exercised on some products, like petrol, tobacco or cigarette, alcohol. It is very important to determine the products to know the right consumption rate on the products. The last point is non – tariff barriers like the import license issued by the CIQ or the import license from the ministry of health or ministry of agriculture. So these licensees are very important because they determine the quality, the health and safety of the products. It is important that the correct HS code is used that the correct license is issued in order to protect the consumer in China and make sure the products are high standard. Of course from a Customs official point of view, clients usually use the wrong HS code to avoid some of these requirements, the import license, and the anti – dumping duties. So this is where the customs official need to be diligent to make sure the correct HS code is used. Incorrect classification is a compliance violation and may result in penalties.

2. Introduction to the HS

The full name of HS is The Harmonized Commodity Description and Coding Systems, so we just called it the HS code. "Harmonize" means trying to do the same, everything is the same. "System" just tries to describe the thing you are going to harmonize. What it means is that if you ever picked up a tariff book from South Korea or Japan, it will look similar to China's tariff book, because these countries use the HS system to classify all the commodities. Now we see that about 98% of world trade is covered by the HS system. It means nearly all the countries are members of the World Customs Organization. Every country has signed the HS system, and therefore they follows.

(1) History

Internationally, the HS convention was implemented in 1988, and then was updated in 1996, 2002, and 2007. Why is it needed to update? When I was working at the New Zealand Customs, in the tariff book, the original 1988 version only referred to the black and white television. In fact now we have flat screen, liquid plasma and LED television. So as the technology advances, the HS has to update to reflect the new technology. Another good example would be in the office. You may have a multifunctional printer which can fax, print and copy. So what is it? Is it a fax machine, a printer or a copying? Maybe 20 years ago, the multifunctional device didn't exist. This means update is a good job. As at Feb 2008, we see 132 Contracting Parties to the HS Convention. And we all know the WCO in Brussels is responsible for updating the HS code. And the HS should be updated in every four years in theory, but it is too much work for WCO. Maybe they update it very five or six years. For a country, you must join the international trade and use the HS code, because it is easier for companies to understand.

(2) HS system and tariff book

Now we move into the detail, to the tariff book. The tariff book is a very clever book. The person who designs it is very clever. If we look at the book, there are 21 Sections, 97 Chapters, over 1200 4 – digit Headings, and over 5, 000 6 – digit Subheadings. If you pick up a tariff book you will start with live animals in chapter 1 and in chapter 97 you have antiques. So the book starts with something live, and you process them to food which is chapter 15, 16. May be you will have some car oils, cosmetics in chapter 32 and so on so forth. You may grow cotton into a T – shirt that would be in chapter 46. The 21 sections are making the tariff book easier to use. And then we have the 4 – digit and 6 digit headings and subheadings which we will look at in more detail. So I guess the point is a book with 21 Sections, 97 Chapters is too difficult to use but the structure makes it easy to classify a product.

Next we have the GRI (General Rules of Interpretation). GRI tells us how to classify the product. There are 6 GRIs. The GRI 1, I guess is the rule you will use most of the time. GRI 1 defines the legal status of the various components which heading and subheading. Most important to know is that if you look at the table of contents, the alphabetical index, or the titles of sections, chapters and sub – chapters, those are for reference only. You can't classify based on the title of a chapter, or the alphabetical index. To classify goods you can refer to the terms of headings, the terms of relative sections or chapter notes.

What are the Section Notes, Chapter Notes, and Subheading Notes? As we said there are 21 sections, and each section has the notes of what products fits into the section. And each chapter also has similar notes that would guide you whether the product can fit into the chapter. Terms of headings or terms of sub-headings got into a very specific level to identify the classification question. If you look at the chapter notes or sections notes, they may be very high level, and not that specific. But when you get into the subheadings, it is vey specific and may relate to the product you are trying to classify. What is most important for classification is that you read the Section Notes, Chapter Notes, and Subheading Notes as well as Terms of a Heading or Terms of a Subheading. That doesn't mean it takes you one day to classify a product. Maybe most of the products take 5 minutes to work out a HS code. Some products will take longer, but when you are very familiar with the book you can work your way around and read the chapter notes, section notes and make the right decision.

There are also additional reference texts, the explanatory notes. The explanatory notes are also published by theWorld Customs Organization, and they offer official interpretation to the tariff book of the HS system. If you look at the explanatory book, there are five explanatory notes. Each book covers the corresponding details of the chapters and sections in the tariff book. In China these has been translated into Chinese and published by the GAC, and served as official documents to assist with the HS. When you classify the product, you don't always use the explanatory notes. Some products are very clear in the tariff book, while others you need to do further research. The first documents you need to look at will be the explanatory notes, and it may help you to get to the right answer. They contain really details, especially on the technical descriptions of the products. We are not all engineers, chemists, or biologists. Yet you have to classify these products. In order to help and to guide he normal person, the explanatory notes help you to classify. Here we can see an example of a section. The section we choose is section XI – Textiles and Textile Articles. So we can see we have the title of the section. Then we have the section notes beginning at the section, and then we have the title of the chapters. Chapter 50 is silk. Chapter 51 is wool, fine or coarse animal hair; horsehair yarn and woven fabric. Chapter 52 is Cotton, etc. You will see this label, work through and classify where you think your product falls. This is very important because often the section notes tell of the exclusions. For example, the section XI shows that this Section does not cover animal brush – making bristles or hair. If that's the product you have, when you read the section notes, you straight your way and tell that in section XI if you have Animal brush – making bristles or hair, you should be using heading 05. 02 which is in chapter 5. The first point is that section notes often list out exclusions. That's why you have to read it because if your product is listed out as exclusion, you must go somewhere else in the tariff book. The section notes also have definitions. Let's see the example, for the purpose of Section 11, the expression "high tenacity yarn" has certain definition. If an importer tells you that this is high tenacity yarn, you can read the section note and check whether they are the same or not. If they are the same, it's great. If they are different, may be you need to do a little more research. The section notes also have some instructions. For example we see here "Unless the context otherwise requires, textile garments of different headings are to be classified in their own headings even if put up in sets for retails sale." You are going to buy a suite, a suite is classified separately to pants and jacket. Anyway, the section notes can give you instructions, and they're trying to help you to solve the problem.

Now let's look at chapter note. We have the section note for the section and we have the chapter note for the chapter. For example, we look at chapter 63. Note 1, Sub – Chapter I applies only to made up articles, of any textile fabric. Again, it's telling you what's covered in this chapter. Maybe the article is not made up of cloth. You may not use chapter 63. Note 2, Sub – Chapter I does not cover certain things. Again, it has given you exclusion. If your products go into that exclusion, you may not use chapter 63. Another chapter might apply. And there is also subheading note. Subheading notes are just the same as the chapter note and section note. It just refers to subheading which is in the 6 – digit level in more details. All these notes need to be read. So here in chapter 63, we can see linen. Heading 63.02 defines bed linen, table linen, toilet linen and kitchen linen at the 4 – digit level. And then subheadings 6302.10 defines bed linen, knitted or crocheted, of cotton, of man – made fibers, of other textile materials. Depending on what your linen is made of, you can follow the 6302.21, 6302.22, or 6302.29. If you classify linen, you need to know what it is made of rather than what it is used for, cotton, man – made fibers or other textile materials.

Can sugar confectionary containing coca be classified in Chapter 17? Can straining cloth be used for a technical purpose be classified in any chapters under Section XVI? Should dresses with left over right closure at the front be regarded as men's or boys' garments?

Very odd and strange questions, but where to get the answers? We can find them in some chapter notes and section notes. For example, question 1, can sugar confectionary containing coca be classified in Chapter 17? No. Note 1 in chapter 17 excludes the products from chapter 17. You will never memorize this. The point is when you classify product, when you go and read the section notes, the chapter notes, you will get answers to these questions. Question 2, can straining cloth used for a technical purpose be classified in any chapters under Section XVI? We go to our section notes to see note 1. The section XVI excludes such kind of cloth. Question 3, should a dress with left over right closure at the front be regarded as men's or boys' garments? No, the note in section 11 does not apply where the cut of the garment clearly indicates that it is designed for one gender. You are not expert in every product, you never will be. In methodology, you need to read the section notes and the chapter notes.

3. HS system and national Customs tariff

We've covered the first two sections which was the importance of classification and introduction to the HS, and now we will look at how that is related to the national tariff book.

Because China is a contracting party, China HS has uniformity to the HS. China should use all headings and subheadings together with their related numerical codes. China tariff should have all the general rules of interpretation, all section notes, chapter notes and subheading notes. China tariff code should follow the numerical sequence of the HS and no modifications are permitted except textual adaptations for the purposes of domestic law. So what does that mean? From China's point of view, or all the other country's for that matter, for the HS, you basically copy and paste them to the China tariff book and translate them to Chinese. You can not make changes of the 6 digit level or the section notes, because that will violate the credit on your HS code. As a Customs officer, if you ever go overseas or work overseas, you pick up a tariff book in Europe, America, basically they look like China's tariff book, because they are all contracting parties to HS System Convention. Tariff books are either in Chinese or in English but they all have 21 sections, 97 chapters. Like any other countries, China wants to collect certain duties, collect certain statistics, to encourage or discourage certain industries. So what China and other country can do is to design 7th and 8th digit and also the 9th and 10th digit. In total, to classify the product, it will be 10 digits. The first 6 are based on the HS. China decides by itself what that the other 4 digits should be. We can see it is important for many reasons, such as duty collection, statistic collection and import/export duty. Some countries are part of regional groups like EU, or ASEAN in south East Asia. They may have the common tariff structure. If you go to Italy, Spain, or France, the tariff book should be the same. Maybe at 10 – digit level, there will be some miner differences because of import license reason or something.

Guidance to national classification can be found in law, national regulations, explanatory notes to national customs tariff. For example, I think the country most famous for issuing the import license is America. Some of you may go on the web site to search tariff rulings. Here in China, you also make tariff classification decisions. Those decisions are binding in China but not in the US and vice versa. China can make classification decisions based on the tariff book which is regulated in the GAC order 158, 2007. HS System is a very good system, and would help the company and Customs to figure out the classification. The implications of being a Contracting Party to the HS Convention are that, all contracting parties to the HS System Convention including China all have the same 6 digits, The last point is interesting. International HS disputes can be highlighted by the WCO HS committee. If there is a dispute between the company and China Customs, and from the port Customs to the regional Customs and even to the GAC, the dispute cannot solved. It could be elevated to the WCO in Brussels where there is a HS committee. They will make the decision to the classification of the commodity and publish it. And company can always take dispute to Brussels to the WCO for resolution.

4. How to classify

I think the biggest mistake you can make is that you pick up the tariff book before you know what the product is. The tariff book does not tell you what the product is. The tariff book tells you where to classify the goods. My only advice to the classification is that do not rush to pick up a tariff book. Before you pick up a tariff book, know what the product is. If it is a bottle of water or a laptop, it is very simple. I think the biggest mistake for most people is that they are too quick and rush to a tariff book before understanding what the product is. If you never see the product, touch it, or use it, you will see the technical data and try to classify the product. If people are very well in classification, and want to know the product, you should always ask the question. What is the good? If you don't know that, you can't even start to classify. What is the product? What is it used for? What materials or substances does it comprise? In what form/format will it be imported, as liquid or as powder? Will it be imported unassembled or assembled? You should ask yourself before you even pick up a tariff book. Ask the importer and the exporter these questions. You get the answers and then pick up a tariff book. If you don't know the answer to these questions, you will be frustrated in classification and throw the tariff book away. Where do you get these information? We can use the Internet. We can use Internet for pleasure and we can also use Internet for work. And most of the companies' products are probably on their websites. Go on the website, download the information and find out what the product is, what it is used for, what it is made of, what form it will be imported, and then you will find out the answers. Of course you should ask the importer or the exporter for the documents. You can ask for any invoices, purchase order or packing list, because that will tell you in what form it is imported, in liquid, in powder, assembled, or unassembled. I think as a customs officer you need to formalize a list of questions that you want to ask the importer or customs broker. Or even you can work on your desk and study the information you find from the internet. Key questions should cover: product specification. What's the size? What's it made of? What's the color? Is it the concentrated if it is orange juice? If it is chemical, is it liquid? Is it imported in palate form? You need to know these things. You obviously need to modify your questions case by case. You can see there are still a few questions that you should ask to confirm the facts before you classify the product. Assuming we know what the product is, for example a bottle of water, we need to look at the chapters and find a likely chapter. And then you will probably look at the headings and subheadings to see if you are right at your analysis. Now, here is the example, we have a drinking cup. If it is a drinking cup, is it made of glass, made of paper? This is just an example. But once you establish a product, you can open the tariff book. That is to say if you need to read possible headings and possible subheadings, you should see the descriptions that closely match the product you are going to classify. If you don't find something, then you will probably be looking at the wrong part of the tariff book. You should probably go back to the table of content, and start again. So why is this process important to work out what the classification is? If you follow the process, it will help you to avoid premature, incorrect conclusions. Even if you are under pressure and you don't want to make the wrong decision, take your time and follow the process. Do not waste you colleagues' time or your boss's time or the importer's time by asking irrelevant questions. Make sure you ask these basic questions. What is it? What is it used for and how it will be imported? What's it made of? Of course if you follow the methodologies and somebody challenge and disagree your opinion, you want to make sure that you have the answer to support your opinion. Therefore if you follow the proper methodology, and through that methodology they will understand how you get your answer. They will probably agree with you. Lastly, it helps you to think in a structured and logical way. So it is a logical, analogical process.

5. Application of GRI, the General Rules of Interpretation

We have six GRIs. First five rules are related to four digits and headings, and the sixth is related to classification at subheading level. Rule one defines the legal elements. Rule two broadens the scope of headings. Rule three is the referee. Rule four is when all else truly fails. Rule five is boxes, cases, packaging and packing. Rule six is Classification in subheadings.

Most of the time you will just be using Rule one plus Rule six. We will look at each of these rules in more detail. One point to add is that rules should be applied in sequence. It's a little bit like Customs valuation.

(1) Rule 1

It simply says that the table of contents, the alphabetical index, and the titles of sections, chapters and sub - chapters are for reference only. You can't classify products based on table of contents in the tariff book. What it does say is that for legal purposes classification is determined according to the terms of headings, the section notes, and the chapter notes, provided that those headings or notes do not require classifying somewhere else. Firstly you find one or more headings that apply to the goods. For example, we have a bottle of water. We go to chapter 14, 15 or 16, and we may find water. Secondly we would look around the section notes to see if articles are excluded or included, defined or described. Thirdly we would look at the chapter notes to see the specific chapter, exclusions, definitions or descriptions. Fourthly, we look at these Latin expressions, Prima Facie, Inter Alia, and Mutatis Mutandis. So essentially you open up the tariff book, find some headings that are reasonable, check the section notes, the chapter notes and the Latin terms, and then you should be close to the right answer. Prima Facie simply means at first view or on the first appearance. So you look at it, and what is it? That's how you should look at the product. You shouldn't imagine it is something else. Look at it at first glance and what is it. Inter Alia, among other things, means it could be this or something like this. For example, it could be a small bottle of water or a big bottle of water. Mutatis Mutandis means with the necessary changes having been made.

And of course you have text punctuation. Semi – colons means a break in a listing. And you have commas, which could mean "or" and "and" . English language is very confusing, even for English speakers. Here is a saying to help you remember this.

"Woman, without her man, is nothing."

"Woman, without her, man is nothing."

Essentially it's a saying just to show the difference in terms of where the comma is and how that changes the expressions or the meanings of the same sentence. So simply by putting the comma after "man" or before "man", it completely changes the meaning of the sentence.

(2) Rule 2

There are two parts of GRI 2, part A and part B. It essentially extends the scope of classification to include goods imported in a condition not specifically recognized in the tariff.

i. Rule 2 (a)

The first is incomplete or unfinished provided that they have the essential character of the complete or finished articles. So the term essential character is not defined in the HS. Thus, the factor that determines essential character will vary between goods. I know several years ago, in China there is so called "60 percent" when you try to determine the essential character based on the value of goods. So the imported goods represent more than 60 percent of the value. What if the components represent more than 60 percent of the value? That will be the way to determine the essential character. For example, you import a bicycle without the wheels. You will probably say that bicycle still has the essential character of a finished bicycle. It's just incomplete and missing two wheels. You will still classify it as a bicycle.

The second is completed or finished but presented unassembled or disassembled. So maybe shipped for the convenience of packaging, handling or transport, or the unassembled parts must typically have to be presented for entry at the same time unless otherwise provided in the national legislations. This is another example. It's a bicycle with all of the parts there. But it is disassembled and in a cargo box. Why? Because you can pack into smaller space, therefore you know the shipping container and fit more bicycles in so that you can ship more products at the same time. In this case, your bicycles are finished, and it's just into pieces in a cargo box. You will still classify it as a bicycle.

First, analyze the state of unassembled or incomplete item. For example, bicycles without wheels. Is it complete with no parts missing? If you say no, analyze how incomplete it is. Does it have the essential character of the finished goods? A bicycle without wheels still has the essential character of bicycle. If you say yes, classify as if it was complete and assembled. If, for example, we have a bicycle, and we have seat and some handles but we don't have the frame, does it have the essential character of the finished goods? I probably will say no. It's just seat and handle, without frame, without chain, without wheels and you will classify it elsewhere for what it actually is. What is it? I would say parts, the parts of a bicycle. So you will classify it as parts rather than finished article. You see the commercial invoice for import and export. Normally it would say disassembled, unassembled or something like this. So it helps to guide you. But at these situations as a customs officer, maybe you will have to request for an inspection, open up the container, see what's physically in the container, and then decide if it is assembled, unassembled, complete and incomplete. You have to physically see the products in the case of Rule 2 (a).

ii. Rule 2 (b)

Rule 2 (b) expands the heading to cater for mixtures or combinations of materials or substances, and materials in composite goods. The result is that goods composed of more than one material or goods are prima facie classifiable in two or more headings corresponding to each one of the constituent materials or goods. I think the example here could be a chemical. A chemical may be used in biofuel, and maybe it has part coil oil, part diesel. What would you regard it as? So prima facie, at first glance, it could be classified in two headings, it could be coil oil and it could be diesel. So essentially it is about the choices to classify. To determine the appropriate classification, you go to Rule 3. Of course Rule 2 (b) only applies in the absence of specific provisions in the nomenclature covering mixed products or combination articles. So when you read your section notes and chapter notes, sometimes they will say product classified here provided that it has 70 percent diesel. You may find that even you have a mixture, the chapter notes or section notes will give you the answer based on the percentage content.

(3) Rule 3

So Rule 3 is the Referee. It applies when goods appear classifiable in two or more headings. The considerations in descending order of application are firstly more specific description of the goods. So you always look at the heading which has the most description relative to the nature of the product. The second is essential character. The third is the heading appearing last in the tariff among those that equally merit consideration. So when you absolutely stuck, just work out the last heading. The important note is that GRI 3 only applies if the terms of the headings or section or chapter notes do not otherwise require. So when you apply GRI, still remember to read chapter notes and section notes.

i. Rule 3 (a)

Specific description preferred over general description. I think here is case by case. There are thousands of products, the imported and exported everyday. There is no hard and fast rule by which to determine which heading is more specific. Maybe three people have three answers, and they all have strong basis or logic for their answers. I give you an example here. A description by name is more specific than a description by class. For example, the heading "Shavers" is more specific than "Tools for working in hand" or "Electro – mechanical domestics appliances". So you always look for the heading which is more descriptive. A description which more clearly identifies goods is more specific than one whose identification is less complete. We have another example. Carpet for use in motor cars not classified as "Accessories for motor cars" but where it is more specifically described as "Carpets". When each of the potential headings refers to only a part of the materials or substances contained in mixed or composite goods or to only part of the items in a set up for retail, those headings are to be regarded as equally specific and GRI 3 (a) can not be applied. So if you get two headings which are very similar, it doesn't solve the problem and you wouldn't use GRI 3 (a), you will then start to look at 3 (b) or 3 (c).

ii. Rule 3 (b)

Classification based on essential character. Here are the examples of 4 possible situations. The first is mixtures, for example, mixture for brewing. Let's say you get 70 percent wheat and 30 percent barley. The second is composite goods consisting of different materials. For example, conveyor belt of plastic and rubber. The fourth is composite goods of different components. What happens to glass ashtray on a metal stand? Is that an article of glass or an article of metal? The fourth is goods in sets for retail sales. So in all these cases, the goods are to be classified according to materials or component which gives essential character. Some factors that determine essential character are material, bulk, quantity, weight, value, role of material. As I mentioned before, a few years ago, China used to use value a lot to determine the essential character. If the item worth 100

RMB, what is the value of different components? When one component represents more 60 percent of the value of goods, that component will determine the essential character. Based on that, you will use the applicable GRI 3 (b). There are some definitions to note. Composite goods consisting of different components means goods in which components are attached to each other to form an inseparable whole, and goods with separable components provided that the components are adapted to the other, and mutually complementary. Together the components form a whole which is normally not offered for sale in separate parts.

iii. Rule 3 (c)

You can move to GRI 3 (c) when you are really stuck. You take the heading which occurs last in numerical order. I would say in reality, very rarely do we use Rule 3 (c). Most of the time, we use Rule 1 to classify products.

(4) Rule 4

When all else truly fails. Normally Rule1, 2, and 3 are enough, but one day in interesting cases you may use Rule 4, in which you look for the heading most similar. You can't find any heading, but you can find a heading which is close in terms of description to the goods classified. As I said, Rule 4 is mainly applied for the goods newly appeared on the market. Again how would we do it? We look at description, character, purpose, material, use, and commercial value, and try to work out the appropriate basis to move forward.

(5) Rule 5

You will come across Rule 5 from time to time. So goods arrive at the border packed or in cartons refer not only to containers suitable for transporting but also for storing and marketing the goods. Is the packaging considered as separate goods that have to be classified separately from the article it contains? So this Rule governs the classification of certain long – term use containers and certain packaging materials and packing containers. Containers to be classified with the articles for which they are intended are those which are specially shaped or fitted to contain a specific article or set of articles. For example, if you buy a camera, the camera will come in a case. If you buy a musical instrument like a guitar, the guitar will come with a case. You will classify those together. They must be suitable for long - term use, and must be presented with the articles for which they are intended. So the items must come together, have same invoice, same bill of lading, and packed in the same container. An exception is containers which give the goods their essential character. GRI 5 (b) talks about the packing materials and packing containers entered with the goods normally used for packing. The exception is that when material or containers are clearly suitable for repetitive use. Here you get barrels, crates and pallets. You know customs can require separate classification of those items. So reusable packing is likely to be used again after importation. Hence, governments can treat it at the border in the same way as if it is imported separately.

(6) Rule 6

Rule 6 is the sub - headings, the last rule. Most of the time, you will classify using Rule 1 about headings, chapter notes, section notes, plus Rule 6 which is the sub - headings. So heading is about 4 digit level. Sub - heading is about 6 digit, 8 digit and 10 digit level. So when you give your opinions to your colleagues, the importer, or customs broker, you will say Rule 1 and Rule 6 is the basis for classifying products. You put out the heading level, use subheading, and in terms of subheading and subheading notes, you will arrive at the right answer.

FTA 原产地知识简介

（普华永道合伙人 Damon Paling）
（浦东机场海关　施旼　根据录音整理翻译）

随着中国经济的不断发展，中国也非常愿意与其他重要睦邻国家建立紧密的贸易伙伴关系。中国目前正与亚洲、欧洲等多个国家间磋商签订自由贸易协定。所以这一新领域对中国海关越来越重要。我认为我们有许多地方需要加以研究和学习，包括许多重要的专业术语。

我们先来探讨构成自由贸易协定的法律基础。这些法律的渊源是什么？首先应当明确订立协议时那些应当遵循的原则。接到进出口商呈递的货物原产地证明后，海关必须要按照恰当的程序处理。当然，并不是所有贸易都能享受自由贸易优惠（优惠税率），它必须要符合一系列严格的标准。从海关监管角度来看，辨别进出口货物是否符合享受自由贸易优惠（优惠税率）非常重要。海关不能让那些本不符合标准的公司得到关税优惠。

培训分成两部分，第一部分是基本概念，第二部分是关于原产地规则的详细内容。在第一部分中，主要讲述三个部分：法律框架、自由贸易协定和优惠关税的税率。然后探讨原产地规则。

从海关的角度看，原产地规则和商品估价、税则归类、基础架构、通关程序一样都很重要。所有的这些工作都是相关的。虽然我们今天的主要话题是原产地规则，但是当我们在确认某商品的原产地时，必须考虑商品的 HS 编码和商品的估价。这些都相互关联，我们不能只顾其一而忽略其余。

当我们在研究国际贸易的法律框架和 WTO 协议中的某些法律文本时，常会碰到两个概念：优惠性原产地规则和非优惠性原产地规则。什么是

“优惠”？简单来说，优惠就是指（一方）给予特定群体特别的优待。举个例子，当你在排队购物时，如果获得优惠，你就可以越过长龙，直接走到队伍前面购买。同样道理，优惠性原产地规则就是指能让商家在国际市场上获得特别待遇的规则。站在中国的出口贸易公司和生产商的角度来看，当他们把商品出口到国外，希望得到出口优惠，可以少缴关税。反之，从出口到中国国内市场的国外的生产商的角度看，他们也希望得到关税优惠。因此中央政府认为这种优惠性政策可以发挥作用，所以就引进了这种优惠性原产地协定。

非优惠性原产地规则和反倾销、反补贴相关。但今天不讲此类话题。这属于不同的学科领域。

每谈到一份自由贸易协定，都不得不说到它产生的特定的历史背景。在WTO框架下的国际贸易关系中，有三种重要的贸易形式。第一种是多边贸易，多边指的是很多个国家，WTO就像一个大型俱乐部，有许多成员国参与其中。中国是成员国之一，日本和韩国也是。亚洲很多国家都已经加入了世贸组织。

第二种是包含两个以上国家的区域性贸易关系。例如，中国与东南亚的东盟国家之间建立了自由贸易区（FTA）的关系。在北美洲，加拿大、美国和墨西哥之间就签订了北美自由贸易协议（NAFTA）。

国家间也可以同样签订双边自由贸易协定。例如中国最近刚与新西兰签订了双边自由贸易协定。中国至目前已分别和智利、新加坡、巴基斯坦等国分别签订了双边自由贸易协定。中国关注发展区域性的和双边的自由贸易关系。

WTO文本协议的渊源是关贸总协定（简称为GATT）。WTO成立于1995年，是致力于促进各国间贸易的国际组织。你们当中有人可能从报纸上看到过有关“多哈回合”的报道。多哈回合就是致力于剔除各国间贸易壁垒的谈判，但它的谈判进程相当缓慢，各国为了各自的利益谈判，难以达成一致意见。所以，像中国这样的国家，就不愿意无限期地等待多哈回合的结束，其间他们会努力推行自己的消除贸易壁垒的战略。

各缔约方在自由贸易协定中的地位都是平等的，任何缔约国都不能将其他国家拒之门外。首先，我们可以举例进行比较。假如我们都是世贸组织的成员国。假设 A 国和 B 国想建立自由贸易协定（FTA）关系，其中 A 国与 B 国签订了自由贸易协定，我就不能借此对中国设置贸易壁垒，大家的地位都是一样的。双方只能建立互相降低贸易壁垒或者无贸易壁垒关系。自由贸易协定不能产生排他作用。自由贸易协定就是指缔约双方特殊的贸易关系。

如果你想了解 WTO，你可以登录 WTO 网站查询各类协议文本。你可以阅读关于自由贸易协定概念的第 24 条。假如和中国一样的国家想和其他国家建立 FTA 关系，就必须遵守 WTO 协定中的第 24 条。另外，自由贸易协定的效力必须适用于所有的商品交易。关税税率不应提高并且缔约国必须具有相似的经济和战略利益。

从国家间不同程度的融合关系来看，有自由贸易区、共同市场、关税联盟等。以欧洲为例，它们最初建立了自由贸易区，后来变成关税联盟，然后形成共同市场，现在它们是一个经济联盟。现在这 25 个国家建立了一个稳定的经济一体化关系。到下一阶段就是政治联盟了。到那时，25 个欧洲国家将成为一个国家。但这不太可能实现。因为即使它们联合组成经济联盟，相互之间也难以形成真正的融洽，因为激烈的利益冲突依然存在。如果让我们看中国会以什么样的贸易优惠形式签订自由贸易协议，你会发现中国不大可能去建立一个关税联盟、共同市场或其他相类似的形式。

所以，FTA 包括哪些方面呢？FTA 包括服务贸易、投资贸易、知识产权、人员流动、政府采购业务和促进自由贸易的发展。当然，你可能会对人员流动比较感兴趣，当人们想来中国时，需要申请签证，而在 FTA 里，缔约国之间可以简化申请程序。有时候人们还需要停留较长的时间。但这次探讨的核心内容是促进自由贸易的发展，也就是促进商品在国际市场上的流通。要看到 FTA 涵盖了很多不同方面内容，但最重要的还在于推动国际自由贸易和商品进出境。

FTA 的目的是为了降低关税税率。按照 FTA 中议定的关税税率，一开始不会从 10% 就马上降低到零关税，但是会逐步降低，可能从 10 降到 8，再降至 6、4、2，最后到 0。若干年后实现自由贸易。

在自由贸易协定中，也有一些例外规定。每个国家都有敏感领域，如国家安全、国内支柱产业等。举个例子，如军工业。我们都不希望看到武器在世界上自由交易。因此，自由贸易协定中都排除军火交易。一些自由贸易协定同样也会排除酒类与烟类产品，即便为部分人所喜爱，但还是会因对人体有害而被排除。但总的来说，绝大多数商品（约95%）被包括在内。

综上所述，所有商品可分成三级：普通物品、敏感物品、高度敏感的物品。如果某一商品被划分为高度敏感物品，那会带来什么结果呢？相关FTA会对此作出规定，普通物品的关税税率会从10、8、6降到4、2、0，而这些物品的降税时间将会需要更长的时间，如从10到9、8、7……对一些农业国家来说，农产品常会被划分为敏感商品。农民种植如玉米、小麦、稻谷等农作物需要得到贸易保护。所以这些农作物的关税税率的减缓过程会相当缓慢。如电脑、椅子与桌子则属并不太“敏感”的商品。但在自由贸易协定中，你需要根据HS编码鉴别商品并划分是否属敏感类。

多数企业会对关税的优惠税率感兴趣。它们也会为此提出建议或咨询。优惠税率是指一家企业能在自由贸易协定中受益多少。站在海关的角度，就是指海关会从自由贸易协定中损失了多少税收。因此站在不同角度能得出不同定义。当各国政府间谈判协商自由贸易协定时，它们会通过制作一些金融数据模型计算出它们在一段时间内会损失的关税。当中国政府与其他国家协商签订自由贸易协定时，会计算出在它们作出关税让步后所遭受损失的税收损失或会有哪些货物会因此大量进口到中国。与此同时，中国商品也能在其他国家作出最小的关税牺牲下更容易地进入到海外市场。

即使中国与其他国家如智利签有自由贸易协定，但这并不意味着所有中国和智利的货物就有资格自由贸易。它们必须符合原产地规则。关键就在这里，从一国的出口并不意味着原产地是该国。举个例子，在印度生产的商品，然后经新加坡运往中国。这个出口企业可能会以新加坡为货物原产地来申报。这里有一个基本的概念就是完全获得或实质内容上的改变。符合实质内容上的改变必须是在最后一个经运国所作的改变。举个例子，印度生产衬衫，在新加坡贴上标签。然后这些衬衫卖到中国来。但并不意味着贴上了标签就是实质内容上的改变。因此这里有两条规则：完全获得和非完全获得。而非完全获得又有3个标准：以商品归类划分、附加值划分、经过特别的生产工序划分。当然，也有些额外标准，例如累计规则、直接运输规则和其他特例规则。

完全获得是个简单概念。一些来自海洋的或者农村自己的产品，例如水果、蔬菜、鲜活的动物，都属于完全获得。如果你看税则的第 1 至第 8 章，这些大多是完全获得商品。八章之外的可能就不是完全获得的商品。因此，你要关注和学习的重点规则是实质内容上的改变，主要有以下 3 个标准：是否改变了 HS 编码、是否在供应链上有足够的附加值，是否在生产过程中经过了特定工序。

对于附加值，你除了需要辨别产品原产地，还需要知道产品的价值。举关税税目变更的例子，这个例子发生在美国和新加坡之间的自由贸易协定中。商品从马来西亚运往新加坡，然后到美国。马来西亚把生产出来的 HS 编码为 1207. 10 的棕榈果运往新加坡，在那里，新加坡把棕榈果加工成 HS 编码为 1511. 90 的棕榈油，然后再运往美国。这里，HS 编码的前 4 位 1511 已经改变。我们再来看第二种情况，这次，马来西亚把未加工过的 HS 编码为 1511 的棕榈油运往新加坡，而新加坡只是简单地将其提炼成棕榈油，在这种情况下，两边的 HS 编码是一样的，所以第二个情景中的产品就不具备“关税税目改变”的条件，因此不具备获得 FTA 中的原产地优惠的资格。

现在我们再来看一个经过特别加工生产程序的例子，发生在中国内地和香港之间签订的 CEPA 协议中，里面第 5208 节是关于棉质衣物的规定。其定义的主要制造工序为：煮炼、漂白、丝光处理、印花、染色、光白漂染，等等。所有这些程序都需要你去确认，如果没有经过这些工序，就不能获得原产地证明。这是个很有效的规则。为什么？在香港，这一商品的附加值很低。若想对一件棉布漂白，花费成本并不高，不需要很多人工、材料或管理成本。所以，可能产品的附加值只有 5%，但仍可获得原产地优惠。

确认附加值其实是个相当复杂的程序，需要确认一些标准，包括材料成本、劳动成本、营业费用和商品利润，这些标准决定了该商品是否能获得原产地优惠。附加值规则是个通用规则。中国目前签订的所有的自由贸易协定中，附加值规则大多基于离岸价格。再举个例子，很多 FTA 协议中有关于40%或60%附加值标准的规定。前面香港的例子可见，如果生产商只是漂白衣服的棉质纤维，那么决不能达到40%的附加值，所以不构成原产地资格。

再举一个需要计算的例子。这是个关于东盟的自由贸易协定。在原产地规则里，基本上都需要40%的当地附加值条件。在新加坡，有一个专门制造印刷电路板的公司，离岸价格为10美元。看一下商品的材料清单，里面包括有价值2美元的铜箔，来自新加坡以外的地方；有1美元的电阻器，非新加坡本地产；2美元的晶体管、2美元的电容器、1美元的镀锡板是在新加坡制造的。当我们计算这个产品的附加值率的时候，我们要把晶体管、电容器、镀锡板的价值加起来，因为这些都是新加坡制造的，所以一共是2美元+2美元+1美元，然后再加上2美元的安装和调试费，这也属于人工、管理费用和利润的一部分。现在这个价值10美元的产品里面，一共有7美元附加值，一共是70%。这样，这个商品在新加坡本地的附加值率就高于40%了。海关关员最重要的是要熟悉商品，由什么材料组成、这些材料从哪里来，从新加坡以外还是新加坡本地产。其次，还必须知道商品的制作工序，付出的成本。这样，才可计算出具体的附加值，最终判断是否符合原产地规则。

累计规则。累计规则是一个比较复杂的概念。举东盟和中国之间FTA的例子。假设有货物从新加坡进口到中国。在新加坡有生产厂，而生产的原料来自印度尼西亚。在东盟和中国之间，印尼处于该协议范围。在印尼有另外一家工厂，以15美元的价格从印度买进零件，制成产品后以100美元的价格卖给新加坡，而印尼和新加坡之间的贸易可以看成是东盟国之间的贸易，所以从15美元到100美元的差额可以看成是附加值，而这个附加值率高于50%。然后产品从新加坡卖到中国后，价格从100美元升到200美元。在累计规则下，从印尼到新加坡的100美元，可以纳入东盟国之间的优惠贸易范围，因为在印尼的附加值高于50%。因为印尼从印度进口的材料做成产品出口给新加坡东盟国，所以这个差额可以看成是优惠的条件。而从新加坡到中国，价格上升了100%，也符合优惠的条件。你也许会问，这两者怎么联系起来呢？因为最原始的材料是在印度进口，但经过累计规则，15美元就是计算的基础了。

特别规则。当然最重要的还是最后一点，你必须持有一张有效原产地证明。当商品从印尼运抵中国时，它必须具有印尼的原产地证明，证明是印尼生产的，附加值可以累加。但是假如没有这张原产地证明，海关就会以（100+0）/200 的公式来计算，达到 50%，这样就不符合原产地证明了。

微小加工及处理。因此，在所有的 FTA 协议里面，对于这种加工都有明确的规定。什么是微小加工及处理？就是一些很基本的如包装之类的工序，这些工序是不足以获得原产地资格的。这些工序太简单、太细微了，不能获得 FTA 优惠。

另外一个重要的规则称为直接运输规则。商品从新加坡运到日本，再运到中国，这样能享受 FTA 的优惠吗？是或否？要回答这个问题，首先要看货物移动路线。如果货物是从新加坡直接运往中国的话，这是最基础的路线。然而在一定条件下，有时候会出现间接性运输。举个例子，从新加坡运往中国途中经过日本，在日本不进行任何制造加工活动，这个是会被允许的。再拿香港举例子，香港是一个很大的贸易中转站，它不属于中国和东盟国之间的 FTA 优惠范围，但是中国一般都会允许来自东盟国的货物经过香港，所以这个间接运输也没问题。

总之，首先必须要了解自由贸易协定必须在 WTO 法律框架内制定。对于原产地规则，则每一个都有所不同。商品分为完全获得和不完全获得。对于不完全获得的商品，必须要注意 HS 编码、附加值和特别的生产工序。而且要谨慎注意细微加工及处理的程序、直接运输的规则，这些都会影响商品优惠税率的资格。

自由贸易协定现在越来越重要了。正如大家所知，中国近几年的平均关税率为 9.8%。越来越多企业要求得到原产地进出口优惠。

我们看看关于原产地管理规则的具体实施。

A 生产商在马来西亚，获得了一个原产地证明，先把货物销售给新加坡的 B 进口商。新加坡的 B 公司又转手卖给韩国的 C 公司。他们都从销售中获利。现在的问题是该批货物能否获得马来西亚和韩国的 FTA 优惠？货物从马来西亚直接运到韩国，但发票地址写韩国，这是一个非常普遍的问题。很多原产地规则都希望物流过程和发票显示的一致。因此，货物从马来西亚到韩国，发票上显示的也应该是从马来西亚到韩国，不能够经过新加坡。这是个问题。

再举一例，假如货物在中国生产，然后卖到香港，但是船运到泰国，因为从香港又卖到泰国。即使有 Form A 证书，泰国海关也会拒绝这原产地证明。为什么呢？因为你即使在香港交付款，但是泰方不认为香港受中国与东盟 FTA 协议的管辖。所以这是一个实际又棘手的问题。如果单是发票经过新加坡，而原产地没有改变，货物在马来西亚生产，最终加工地也在马来西亚。有一些自由贸易协定就为此问题作出相关规定。如在 2004 年签署的东盟自由贸易协定中第 20 条规定，在以往的销售国和开发票的国家中，有任何一个不属于东盟成员国，或是东盟的出口商，都符合资格。所以，这里 FTA 第 20 条特别条款很好地解决了关于第三方发票的问题。

再例如，马来西亚卖给新加坡 100 元，新加坡卖给中国 150 元，原产地证明上标明产品价值 100 元，但是发票却标明 150 元。企业常常会这样向海关提出请求："我仅是在瑞士开了进口发票而已，货物仍然是在马来西亚生产，然后从马来西亚运往中国，所以应该享受 FTA 优惠。"这里，我们可以参考日本海关的处理方法。日本虽然原产地规则没有规定，但日本海关经常接受第三方发票。当我们在处理原产地问题的时候，必须研究 FTA，研究原产地规则。

关于"背对背规定"。举个例子，新加坡是个重要的中转枢纽。在马来西亚有家生产商，出口货物到新加坡，然后再运往中国。在一些原产地规则里有另外一个规定，就是新加坡也提供 Form A，我们称为"背对背"。因此，在新加坡没有经过加工，没有附加价值产生，只是简单的货物中转，然后运往中国。所以，"背对背"的原产地证明在原始原产地证明的基础上，在中间出口国中产生。所以作为中间出口国新加坡，其政府制造了同样的一份 Form A 出来，送往中国。海关可以从这些材料上作出判断。如果观察供应链，你总会发现一些像新加坡、香港等的中转地。你可能无法把货物从一个地方直接运输到另一个地方。所以"背对背规定"使得这样的操作有弹性。对于企业有好处，而对政府来说可能多了一些难处。但如果政府鼓励贸易，就需要出台有弹性的政策使交易过程灵活。

接着讨论申诉。申诉是很重要的，不是所有货物或公司都符合 FTA 的条件。你必须符合原产地规则的要求。在不同的国家，有不同的制定部门负责原产地证明。出口商或者生产者需要申请这些证明并交给进口商。进口商向进口地海关递交，还有发票和装箱清单等。

如何获得原产地证明呢？在很多国家分两个程序。第一个是生产商必须注册，政府去查看并确认生产商情况。企业必须进行年审，必须递交文件申请原产地优惠。每一次货运都必须有一份原产地证明。所以每一次出口商出口货物，都必须向政府部门申请原产地证明。

原产地证书都是大同小异的。WTO 协议提供了简化的版本和基本的海关程序，还提供了原产地证书的标准格式。因此，虽然分为 Form A，Form D 或 Form E，但基本相同。

一些自由贸易协定不需要原产地证书。例如，美国－新加坡、美国－澳大利亚。如果海关认为有问题，会自行向进口商索取原产地证书。企业必须保存至少 3 年的记录。海关可随时要求审查记录。若企业不能提供证据的，甚至可以被判为犯罪。

出口后原产地核查。例如，在上海，海关接到之前批准过的申请，但是现在认为有问题，海关可通过一定程序询问出口商，要求其配合核查。这种情况确实存在，但不常见。

预裁定。显然，海关和企业都不希望有争议。但如果确实发生了，在 FTA 里企业可以寻求预裁定。在中国，现在关于原产地证明的裁决可能还不是很普遍，但以后会增加。

关于争议。工作之中常常出现争议。怎么去解决争议？当一个争议发生，常常会和政治相联系。例如，你拒绝给予从巴基斯坦进口的货物原产地优惠，巴基斯坦出口商会向其政府抱怨，而巴基斯坦政府就会转来向中国政府了解，尽力解决问题。所以当你在执法时，海关和申请企业之间的原产地争议，可以变成政府和政府间的协商谈判。

第二部分谈了关于三方发票的问题。当你收到一份文件，你经常会见到从瑞士出口商的发票，和马来西亚政府的 Form A 证明文件，怎么去把这两份文件联系到一起呢？也许公司名称不一样，但是货物描述等是一样的，也许货物的价值不等。文件之间总会有一些差异，这些差异需要解决。另外，HS 编码也可能会出现不同。另外，原产地证明上都会有 HS 编码，但这个编码可能和进口报关单上的不同。也许其中的前 6 到第 8 个数字是一样的，但是第 9 位或第 10 位就不同。是接受还是拒绝？这是一个实际的问题。

前面，未述及贴商标标签。你也许会遇见从某国进口的商品，上贴的标签是该国产，但这不等于原产地就是该国。以威士忌为例，在新加坡混合和装瓶后，瓶子被贴上了“新加坡制造”的标签，但根据原产地规则，这并不符合新加坡原产的要求。

申请。海关要问清楚什么是充分的加工工序？在哪里制造？加工程序是否复杂？你必须要有原产地证明。

中国已经开始实施一些 FTA。原产地证明的规则将很有用。

注：本编三篇文章的原文是上海海关关员根据普华永道国际贸易咨询（上海）有限公司合伙人 Damon Paling 先生讲座录音整理而成，经 Damon Paling 先生确认授权使用。

Free Trade Agreements (FTA)

(Presented by Damon Paling, Partner at PWC)
(Transcribed and Translated by Shi Min, Pudong International Airport Customs House)

Now as the economy has moved on, China is very anxious to develop closer trading relationships with key countries. So China is very busy with pursuing free trade agreements with neighbours in Asia, neighbours in Europe etc. So this is a new topic which I think will become more and more important for the China Customs in the years ahead. So I think it has a lot for you to learn. There are a lot of jargons or, what we say, terminology here, which means very important thing.

We first want to look at some legal basis for free trade agreements. Where do they come from? We just don't make them up there are certain protocol that should be followed. Companies present you a certificate of origin, it's very important that is processed in the right way. Not everyone qualifies for free trade, you must meet certain criteria. So it's very important from the customs' point of view that you know the company has met the criteria. If they don't qualify, you are obviously to make sure they don't get any preferential treatment.

The training is split into two parts, part one is a basic concept, then we will take a break. Part two is looking at some more detailed concepts around rules of origin. In part one, we have three sections: legal framework, free trade agreements and preference. And then we start to look at rules of origin.

Firstly, when we look at the Customs world, valuation is very important, classification is very important, general structures and procedures are important, so is origin. All of these issues are connected. So today we focus on origin, that's true. But as you will see, when you are determining the origin of the product, you also look at what is the HS code of that product; you also need to look at what is the value of that product. So this topic relates very closely to these two topics as well. So you cannot be just an expert in one, you have to learn about all of these topics together.

So I think if we look at the legal framework, essentially, in trade, in WTO terms, we have two concepts: preferential and non – preferential rules of origin. Today we are going to focus on the preferential rules of origin. What does preference mean? Preference means just like special favor, it means somebody gets preferential treatments. So let's say for example. You go shopping and you want to buy a product, and there is a long queue. Preference would mean you go to the head of the queue. You don't have to wait. Preferential rules of origin means special rules which give you special access to the market. For Chinese companies and manufacturers exporting overseas, they want to access foreign markets with preference and they want to pay fewer customs duties. Foreign companies that manufacture goods overseas export to China, they want to access China market with fewer customs duties. Central government in Beijing thinks it a good idea and hence they introduce preferential arrangements.

Non – preferential rules of origin deal with anti – dumping, countervailing. Today we don't discuss that topic. It's a very different subject area.

Whenever there is a free trade agreement, there are background and history to add. We can see that in the international trade, relation to the WTO, there is a "three scenarios". Number one is what we call multilateral; "multi –" means many, so the WTO is like a club, with many members. China is a member, Japan、Korea. Many countries in Asia are members.

Regional is where more than two countries to create a special club. So China, for example, has a FTA with ASEAN, which is 8 countries in Southeast Asia. In North America, Canada, US, Mexico have this special club called NAFTA.

You can also have bilateral FTA. For example, China just recently entered into a bilateral FTA with New Zealand. China has bilateral FTA with Chili, Singapore, Pakistan etc. China is focusing on regional and bilateral relations at the moment.

There is a WTO agreement on rules of origin; WTO used to be called GATT, General Agreement on Tariffs and Trade. WTO is formed in 1995, and we know that WTO should do these things. Some of you may have read the newspaper about the Doha Round. The Doha Round is another round of negotiations to remove trade barriers. The Doha Round is moving very slowly. Everyone is fighting. Therefore, countries including China don't want to wait for the Doha Round to be complete. They want to continue a strategy of reducing trade barriers with other countries.

When you have the FTA, of course, you should not discriminate. Everyone should receive an equal treatment. You can not block other countries. At firstly, compare to what those countries have today. For example, let's say three of us, are in the WTO. Let's say I wanted to enter into a FTA with country A. We can enter into the FTA, but I can not increase the barriers to you. The barriers should stay the same. We just have lower barriers or no barriers. A FTA doesn't mean blocking others. All this means give special trade between two of us.

If you want to go to the WTO, agreements you can go online, you can read the article 24, introduces the concept of Free Trade Agreement. Whenever countries like China want to into FTA, they have to follow the terms of article 24 of the WTO agreement. What it means is that the FTA should cover all products trade basically. As I said, no increase in tariff rates, and countries really want to have similar economic or strategic interests.

In terms of agreement, there are different levels of integration, such as Free Trade Area, Common Market, Customs Union etc. Let's pick Europe as an example. Europe, several years ago, first, they put in place a FTA, then they expanded it to create a Customs Union, then they expanded it to create a Common Market, now they have economic union in Europe. Currently there are 25 countries who have this level of economic integration. The next step will be political union where more than 20 countries of Europe will become one country. That is not going to happen, because even though they have economic union, they don't always like each other, they still fight with each other. But if we look at free trade agreements, just in this box, what China is doing and what you will deal with are these free trade areas. China will not create customs union, or common market, or something like that.

So what is covered in FTA? This is very important. Because for customs, something you are interested in, but something you are not. You can see that FTA covers trade in services, investments, intellectual property, and movement of people, government procurements, and trading of goods. Certainly, you will be interested in the movement of people, people coming into or out of China must have proper visa, etc. Under a FTA, they maybe simplify the visa procedures. People maybe have to stay here for longer. But the key one is promoting free trade, and this is the movement of goods. But it is also important to recognize that many different things are covered in FTAs. That is a key point but for Customs, most of your focus really is on free trade, movement of goods into or out of China.

What's the objective? The objective is of course is to reduce tariff rates. What you tend to see is that tariff rate on day one when the FTA takes effect. Tariff rate does not go from 10 percent to 0 percent. There will be a gradual reduction, maybe 10 to 8, 6, 4, 2, 0. Maybe after several years, there is free trade.

In FTA, there are certain exclusions. Countries always have sensitive areas, sensitive areas for national security, for domestic industries. For example, fire arms and guns. We don't want people trading guns around the world, that's not good. So are you looking at a FTA, fire arms are typically excluded. Some FTAs may also exclude alcohol products or tobacco products, because these are also bad for us, even if you like them. But generally, most products should be included by almost as we are talking almost 100 percent or 95 percent.

For the inclusion, you tend to see three tracks: normal, sensitive and highly – sensitive. What's the difference if you put a product in highly – sensitive? What that means is still covered by the FTA, but tariff rate would reduce much slower or much later. For example, consider the tariff rate is going from 10, 8, 6 to 4, 2, 0, then it may go 10, 9, 8, 7, 6 over longer period of time. For lots of the countries, what is sensitive is often the agriculture sector. Farmers grow crops like corn, wheat or rice, which means they like protection. So often the government will put sensitive agricultural products on this track to slowly reduce the tariff rates. Most products are for normal track. Computers, chairs and tables etc, they are not very sensitive now. When you look at FTA, it's important for you to identify the products classified with HS code and then establish which track is on, normal, sensitive or highly sensitive.

Margins of preference is what companies are interested in. Companies may come to you for advice or seek some questions on this. Margins of preference is, in simple term, how much can a company save from using a free trade agreement. From a customs' point of view, we can say how much customs revenue we lose because of the free trade agreement. You can see it from different perspectives. When the government is negotiating a FTA, they will normally do some financial modeling to work out how much revenue they would lose over a certain period of time. But at the same time, China government will also try to make sure that foreign countries make minimal sacrifice so that products made in China can have good access to overseas market.

Even if China has an FTA with a country like Chile, that is not mean that all products between Chile and China qualifies for free trade. The products must satisfy for the rules of origin. Key issue is here, Country's export is not necessarily country's origin. For example, a company makes a product in India, it is transshipped through Singapore and then to China. If no processing in Singapore, that product is not Singapore origin. That company may try to claim Singapore origin. The basic concept is wholly produced or obtained or substantial transformation. Substantial transformation has to take place in the last country. For example, from India I make T – shirts, and in Singapore I put labels on them and then I send them to China. But it doesn't mean that affixing the label is substantial transformation. So there are two rules: wholly produced or obtained, not wholly produced or obtained. For not wholly produced or obtained, there are three rules: change in tariff classification, value added, and specified manufacturing process. There are also some additional rules, such as cumulation, direct shipments, exceptions and product specific rules.

Wholly produced or obtained is very simple. Something which is coming out of the ocean, in the country, something which is growing as some fruits, some vegetables, some live animals, that is wholly produced or obtained. If you look at the Tariff book, it's probably anything in the Chapter 1 to Chapter 8. If it is beyond the Chapter 8, it is probably not be wholly produced or obtained. So the key area where you will spend most of your time is substantial transformation, we will look at these issues. Has it been changed in HS code? Has it been sufficient value add in the manufacturing supply chain? Has a specified process manufacturing taken place?

Values added, you need to know about the valuation, not just about the origin. Let's take a look at the example of change in tariff classification. This example comes from the FTA between United States and Singapore. The products are shipped from Malaysia to Singapore to USA. Malaysia makes palm nuts which is on the HS code 1207. 10, and sends the palm nuts to Singapore, and Singapore refines them into palm oil, that changes the HS code to 1511. 90. And they continue to go to USA. According to this rule, you need to change to heading 1511 from other chapter, so it changes the heading of HS code. Let's look at the second scenario. This time Malaysia sends the crude palm oil which is classified under 1511, and Singapore simply makes the crude oil into the refined palm oil, which has the same HS code as the crude palm oil, so the product disqualified for Singapore origin under the FTA based on this rule of change in tariff classification.

Now let's look at an example for specified process of manufacturing. Here we are talking about CEPA between Hong Kong and Mainland China. What rules is here on the 5208, which is about some basic cotton clothing. The processes which you need to undergo are scouring, bleaching, or mercerizing, printing, dyeing, or optical whitening and etc. About these types of activities which require you to confirm the original products. If you don't undergo these types of activities, you won't qualify for origin. This is a good rule. Why? In Hong Kong, maybe this is a very low value added. If I want to do some bleaching of a cotton fabric, it does not cost much money, not too much labor and materials overhead. Therefore, if I do bleaching, there maybe only 5 percent value – added to the product, I can still qualify for the preference of origin. So for this, product is in a good situation, not bad situation, because it makes it easier to qualify.

Value added is a very complex exercise. It has to be certainly mounted to the activities taking place, in terms of materials, labor cost, overhead cost and profit for the product to qualify for preferential origin. The values add is a common rule. So if you read all of the China FTAs, this is the most common rule in most of China FTAs. The value add is normally major based on FOB value. So let's give an example, here we have some free trade agreements around the origin. So you can see that a lot of FTAs have 40 percent or maybe 60 percent value – add. So if we go back to our clothing example in Hong Kong CEPA, if you just bleach the cotton fabrics, it is no way you have 40 percent value add, so you could not be in the value – added rule.

Let's have a look at the numerical example. Here we look at the ASEAN FTA. In the rules of origin, you must have 40 percent local content, so 40 percent of activities must take place. In Singapore, this company is making printed circuit board (PCB) with FOB value of 10 US \$. What you have to do is to say what making up the product, so we look at the materials. We can see there is Copper Foil which was worth 2 US \$. And the resource is from outside Singapore. They have resistors with 1 US \$, also outsourced from outside Singapore. The transistors 2 US \$, capacitors 2 US \$ and plating 1 US \$ are from Singapore. So these materials are going into the manufacturing process. The manufacturing process is value add with assembly and testing taking place. Because the values add is 2 US $. So let's work out what is the qualified percentage. We should add the capacitors, the transistors and the tin plating, because they all come from Singapore, so 2, 2, 1. We should add more 2 US $ for assembly and testing value, because it is also from some of labor, because some overheads and profits. Now total is 7 of the 10 US $ dollars, 70 percent. So this product is more than 40 percent value added in Singapore origin. What is important to the customs' point of view, you need to understand what is the product, you need to understand what materials have been consumed in the product where they come from, outside Singapore or inside Singapore, you need to know what manufacturing process took place, and what kind of cost is paid. With all these you can determine whether or not the product qualifies.

There is another concept – cumulation. Cumulation is a little bit more complex. And next example we will talk about ASEAN – China FTA. So, here we are in China. Products are coming from Singapore. And in Singapore we have a factory. In the factory you got materials from Indonesia. For the ASEAN and China, Indonesia is included. So in Indonesia, it is another factory. Indonesia sources the products from India. This product worth 15 US $, in the factory of Indonesia, they make a component. The item imported into Indonesia with 15 US $ now worth 100 US $. When the product moves from Indonesia to Singapore, they want to trade that as ASEAN, so they have to take the certificate of origin from 15 to 100, which is more than 50 percent local content. The product moves from Singapore to China with from 100 US $ to 200 US $. Under the cumulation rule, what you can do is to put this 100 US $ for Indonesia to Singapore, you can treat all that 100 US $ as qualifies ASEAN, because more than 50 percent of that are produced in Indonesia. So what is originally Indian material is made into the component which is imported to the ASEAN. So the margin of 100 value added can be treated as Singapore – ASEAN origin. And the 100 to 200 from Singapore to China is 100 percent to qualify the content. You may think how can that be, because 15 come from India, but under the cumulation rule, you can treat that 15 as qualified content.

Special rule. Of course the key point is on the last one, you must have a certificate of origin, so when that component moves from Indonesia into China, it must have a certificate of origin to certify this product is in Indonesia origin. If it did not have this certificate of origin, the customs may qualify your product from 100 plus 0 to divide 200, 50 percent qualified the content, if you did not have the certificate of origin.

Minimum processing. You can not move products through countries in claim origin without doing something. In all of the FTAs, there are restrictions. And what they say is minimum processing. In a few of basic things like packaging operation, simply that may be insufficient to qualify the origin. Too minimum, too simple, therefore you can not take the advantage of FTA. It is very important to understand the goods how they make.

It is another important rule called direct transport. The products are shipped from Singapore to Japan then to China. Should the products are qualified for preference under the FTA? This question should be answered by the direction rule. Direct shipment rules says the goods basically should be from Singapore to China that is the basic concept. However, in certain situations, indirect transport may be allowed. So let's say for example, there is no direct shipment from Singapore to China, it should via Japan, so long as no manufacturing takes place in Japan that will be allowed. Now let's take Hong Kong for example, Hong Kong is a very large transshipment area. Hong Kong is not part of China – Singapore FTA. China would normally allow that will be OK so long as there is no further processing in Hong Kong and so long as there is no other direct means from Singapore to China.

Let's review the points of part I. Just to summarize free trade agreements must follow a particular framework or structure that must comply with WTO rules. Wholly produced, not wholly produced, for the not wholly produced, you may notice the change in HS code, the value add or the specific process of manufacture taking place. You should also watch out for minimum processing, direct shipment rule to validate the product qualified. So now I don't have an example but you would find and read the rules of origin, they may basically cover everything on these lines.

FTA is becoming more and more important. You know, the average duty rate these years in China is 9. 8 percent. More and more companies will be claiming preferential origin as China negotiates more FTAs.

Here we go into a more sophisticated application of rules of origin.

Let's look at a scenario. Company A is in Malaysia, a manufactory. A certificate of origin is obtained into product, and sent to company C. Company A, as a manufacturer, however, first sells its product to the regional importers in Singapore, Company B. Company B in Singapore then sells to Company C, in Korea. When they sell, they take some profit out of it. They sell for 150 US $. From 100 US $, to 150 US $, we call it margin. So the question is whether this product still qualify under the Malaysia – Korea FTA. About the origin, the goods being directly shipped from Malaysia to Korea, but the invoicing is taking place in Korea. This is a very common scenario. So what do the rules of origin tell us? A lot of rules of origin will expect that the goods flow to match the invoice flow. So the goods go from Malaysia to Korea, the invoice should be from the Malaysian company to the Korea company, can not go via Singapore. So this is a problem.

If we take another example right now, if you are manufacturing in China, and you sell to Hong Kong, but ship directly to Thailand, since Hong Kong sells to Thailand. Thai customers will reject the claim for preferential origin, even if you have the Form A. Why did they reject? Because its sell took place in Hong Kong, and Hong Kong is not the part of ASEAN – China FTA. It's a practical and problematic issue. Simply because the product was invoiced through Singapore, in this example doesn't change the origin of the product, but still it's manufactured in Malaysia, the last processing of this manufacture took place in Malaysia. Some FTAs have made specific provision in the rules of origin to solve the situation. Here in ASEAN FTA in 2004, they introduced Article 20, in which it says in cases where the sales and voice is issued by either the company located in a non – member state, or by ASEAN exporter, you can qualify. So here in FTA, they eventually created a specific provision, Article 20, which says you can do some third – party invoicing.

I had a case, Malaysia sells to Singapore for 100 US $, Singapore to China for 150 US $. The certificate of origin of the product would say the product valued at 100 US $, but the commercial invoice would say 150 US $. Companies will come to you and say, "I only invoiced with Switzerland and I still made the product in Malaysia. I shipped the product from Malaysia to Shanghai. Therefore you should still grant me FTA preference." In Japan, even the rules of origin is silent, the practice of customs is to allow third – part invoicing. Again, when you are working with the origin issues, you have to study the FTA, study the rules of origin.

There is another scenario which is called the "back to back" provision. In Singapore, again, there is a key hub for transshipment. In a manufacture in Malaysia, we ship the product from Malaysia to Singapore, then from Singapore to China. Under some of the rules of origin, there is a provision where Singapore will issue another Form A, which we call "back to back" . There is no manufacturing in Singapore, there is no value added in Singapore, just purely the transshipment, may be consolidation in a new container, then shipped to China. "Back to back", certificate of origin was issued by the intermediate exporting country based on the first certificate of origin. The intermediate exporting country Singapore, Singapore government issues an identical Form A, which goes to China. China Customs will see that and then make a decision. If you look at supply chains, you'll always to have some transshipment through somewhere like Singapore and Hong Kong. You can't always ship directly from one place to another. So "Back to Back" makes everything more flexible. Good for companies. Maybe it makes hard for the government, but the government wants to encourage business. It needs to have a flexible rule to suitable for extra business operations.

Now we'll talk about complaints. Complaints are very important. As I said at first, not all the goods or companies qualify for an FTA. You have to meet the requirements of the rules of origin. Different countries have appointed different government departments to be responsible for issuing certificates of origin. The exporter, or the manufacturer, will maintain that, and give that to the importer. The importer will submit certificate of origin, along with the invoice, the packing list to Customs.

How to get a certificate of origin? Most countries have a two – step process I think. First is the manufactory should be registered and the government may go visit the factory to just confirm what's taking place. Companies may have to submit certain court statement to support the claim for preferential origin. Once that's proved, they would be issued the certificate of origin. Every shipment must have a certificate of origin. So every time the exporter export a product, must be a new certificate of origin to match that product.

Certificates of origin basically are all of the same. WTO agreement provides the revised version for simplification and harmonization of custom procedures. It also provides a standard format for the certificate of origin. So, it might be called form A, form D, or form E etc, but basically the same.

Some FTAs do not require a certificate of origin. For example, US – Singapore, US – Australia, you can ship the goods, make your claim. If the Customs questions, then the company has to produce the documentation. Companies have to keep their records for certain period of time, may be three years. Custom officials need to audit the companies, they should produce the records so you can complete your orders. If there is no document as evidence for you to review, maybe it indicates that the company is cheating. If they can not produce the evidence, they must be guilty of some crime.

Post – exportation origin verification. Let's say you are here in Shanghai. You have this shipment in front of you. You have the claim. You believe the claim is not correct. Therefore, you could go to the exporter, follow proper protocol, order the exporter to make sure the claim is legitimate. This is special case. You are not doing this all the time.

Advanced rulings. Obviously, customs, companies do not like to dispute too much. If it does happen, within the FTA there is a chance for the company to seek the advanced ruling. I think in China the moment may be not so common to get the advanced ruling on origin issue. But in the future it might be common.

Disputes. Disputes arrive time to time. How to resolve disputes? When there is a dispute, it comes as a very political issue. Let's say the products come from Pakistan, if you deny the claim for preferential origin, you are making it more difficult for companies in Pakistan to export to China using the FTA. So the company will complain to Pakistan government. Pakistan government will come talk to China government trying to solve the issue. So it's very important to know that once you are trying to enforce the law, and do a good job, when you have a dispute with a company who is making the claim, that can escalate to be a government – government political issue.

To summarize on part II, we talk a lot about triangular invoicing. When you receive document, it's very common that you see invoice from Switzerland exporters, and Form A issued from Malaysia government. How to match the two? Maybe some different company names, good description should be the same. Maybe the values of the goods are different. There will be some discrepancies in documentations. These discrepancies need to be addressed. Also there could be discrepancies in HS code. Normally a certificate of origin will state the HS code of the product. The HS code maybe not match the HS code in "JIN KOU BAO GUAN DAN" (speak in Chinese) here in China. Maybe the first 6 to 8 digits of HS code are the same, and just the 9th or 10th digit do not match. Will you accept? Will you reject? This is a practical issue.

Labeling is a different issue. We haven't discussed on that. You could support products made in Singapore, for labeling purpose in the store, but that does not mean that the country of origin is Singapore. Taking Whiskey as an example, due to the blending and bottling, you label the product in the retail store as "made in Singapore" . But only the origin rule may be not qualified as a Singapore origin. Labeling doesn't mean origin.

Application. From Customs' point of view, you need to ask yourself, what is the sufficient processing? Where is the product made? Whether the processing is complex? You must have the certificate of origin.

China has already implemented several FTAs. Certificates of origin will be moving around everywhere.

Articles in this part are notes of lectures given by Damon Paling, a partner of PricewaterhouseCoopers World trade Management Services (Shanghai) Co., Limited, finished by the officers of Shanghai Customs District according to the sound recording, confirmed authorization by Demon Paling.

第三编

国际海关最佳实践

韩国海关 UNI－PASS 电子通关系统

（摘自韩国海关 UNI－PASS 通关系统介绍手册）

（浦东机场海关　李婷婷　办公室外事办　庄硕　译）

一、韩国海关 UNI－PASS 信息协会（CUPIA）

（一）简介

1. 基本情况

CUPIA 是由韩国海关建立的支持海关现代化建设的非营利性专业机构。

2. CUPIA 的设立

CUPIA 是韩国海关建立的非营利性机构，旨在将 UNI－PASS 系统介绍给外国海关和相关管理当局。

3. 组织结构

CUPIA 由前任或现任韩国海关官员和 IT 专家组成，共有 50 位成员。

——韩国海关官员及韩国海关和贸易发展研究所官员被派遣到海关 UNI－PASS 信息协会。

4. 主要服务内容

向外国海关提供业务流程和法律框架重新设计方面的咨询；

向外国海关提供信息技术方面的咨询；

为韩国海关提供研发、咨询、运作和维护方面的支持；

UNI－PASS 系统的运作和维护。

（二）主要服务项目

CUPIA 和相关管理当局在海关现代化建设方面开展合作。

1. 咨询

提供海关现代化/计算机化/自动化的机构流程再造和互联网服务供应商方面的咨询；

提供信息战略规划、项目审计等方面的信息技术咨询；

风险管理和监督。

2. 可行性研究

为外国海关进行海关现代化建设提供可行性研究。

3. 研发

海关数据模型研发及标准化；

关于 UCR 的机构流程再造和互联网服务提供商。（UCR 代表国际货物唯一追踪号码 Unique Consignment Reference number）

4. 系统开发

应用电子海关系统；

支持采购进程和系统开发审计；

风险管理。

5. 运作和管理

UNI - PASS 系统的运作和维护；

韩国海关的客户呼叫服务中心。

（三）主要项目（包括未来将开展的项目）

CUPIA 向各国提供 UNI - PASS 系统的专有技术和经验。

1. 实施 UNI - PASS 系统的国家

包括：多米尼加共和国海关、蒙古国海关。

——海关现代化项目的机构流程再造和互联网服务供应商；

——UNI - PASS 系统的应用。

2. 提供信息技术咨询和可行性研究的国家

包括：尼泊尔海关、肯尼亚海关、坦桑尼亚海关、危地马拉海关、阿塞拜疆海关、哈萨克斯坦海关、越南海关。

——向外国海关行政管理系统提供信息技术咨询；

——开展海关现代化/计算机化项目的可行性研究。

二、海关信息系统的发展历史

（一）1974 年－1992 年计算机的简单应用

——贸易统计（1974）；

——简单的在线空运货物数据。

（二）1992 年－1998 年电子数据交换（EDI）通关自动化

通关自动化 6 年计划（1992－1998）：海关手续 100% 计算机化，实现对货物从抵达到放行的高效、准确监管。

——进出口通关系统（1994－1996）；

——关税退税系统（1997）；

——进出口货物系统（1997－1998）。

（三）1998 年－2003 年信息管理便利化，对决策进程进行辅助

调查、监管、审计手续计算机化，采取应用程序接口技术便利信息使用。

——执法系统（1999）；

——旅客信息系统（2000）；

——后续审计系统（2001）；

——知识管理系统（2002）；

——海关数据库（简称 CDW，2003）。

（四）2003 年－2005 年互联网通关门户

基于互联网广泛应用和信息技术发展的互联网通关系统，为客户带来便利的同时提高系统的能力。

——互联网税则归类系统（2004）；

——互联网民事请求系统（2004）；

——互联网出口通关系统（2004）；

——互联网进口通关系统（2005）。

（五）2006年-2010年实现无所不在的海关

无形的海关无所不在，它创造着价值，随时随地提供服务。

——为通关和物流提供一站式服务；

——不间断的国际供应链，有助于供应链管理；

——智能化的风险管理；

——实时的个性化信息服务（CRM）。

面对国际贸易量的快速增加，韩国海关一直着力开发电子数据交换（EDI）系统，努力提高海关效率。

1992年，韩国海关提出了电子数据交换（EDI）通关自动化6年计划，以建立快捷准确的通关系统为目标，并在1998年成功实现了进出口通关100%计算机化。1999年，建立了执法信息系统，防止对便利通关手续的滥用，有效应对非法贸易活动。

2001年，韩国海关制订了信息管理系统3年发展计划，知识管理系统和海关数据库相继建立，通过管理知识的实时运用和系统化风险管理，提高效率和通关实绩。

2005年，韩国海关建立了“单一窗口”，提供一站式通关服务，包括8个政府规定的验核机构的参与，使得贸易商只需一次提交申报数据就能够最多完成10项政府规定的验核要求（例如，食品检验）。

同时，韩国海关整合电子数据交换（EDI）进程和互联网申报系统，开展互联网通关服务。综上所述，韩国海关正朝着实现海关“无所不在”的目标大步前进。

三、电子通关系统的新名称——UNI-PASS

UNI-PASS，是电子通关系统的品牌名称，指的是与海关监管相关的7个系统，这7个系统彼此关联，在进出口电子通关方面发挥核心功能。这7个系统是出口通关系统、进口通关系统、关税征收系统、进/出口货物管理系统、关税退税系统和“单一窗口”通关系统，这些系统在协调一致的基础上，在进出口电子通关方面发挥着核心作用。电子通关系统是最先进的海关信息化产品，它应用最新的信息技术，通过与客户开展积极合作，主动应对全球贸易环境的变化。

UNI－PASS，是电子通关系统的品牌名称，它具有多重的意义。它在进出口通关、关税支付、退税、验核规定的确认等方面提供统一标准的一站式服务。它提供全球化标准供世界各国广泛使用。它拥有独具特色的货物跟踪服务，通过这项服务客户能够获得实时的货物处理信息，在世界各国海关中首屈一指。“Pass”表示迅速的通关服务。这个名称亦代表着与客户间无所不在的联系、不间断的货物流动、交互的系统，以及客户参与的重要性，从而不断发展和完善系统。

四、韩国海关的代表品牌——UNI－PASS 电子通关系统

品牌核心：自由、愉快的海关通关服务。

品牌前景：成为韩国创建的世界通用的一流的电子通关系统。

品牌任务：随时随地、方便快捷的一站式通关服务。

品牌价值：成为韩国创建的、全球通用的海关通关模式，为客户节省时间、节约成本。

五、互联网通关门户

随着互联网的广泛应用，许多商业领域（如金融、物流）与互联网相连接，韩国海关在现有的电子数据交换（EDI）系统中增加先进的功能，建立方便、经济的互联网通关门户。

通过互联网通关门户，客户可以在家里、办公室、生产场所或其他任何地方通过连接网络办理海关手续，清除了以往电子数据交换（EDI）系统的地域障碍。

六、单一窗口

韩国海关建立了“单一窗口”，提供了办理所有通关手续的“一站式”服务平台，贸易商只需向海关提交一次电子数据，即能够完成申报并完成政府规定的验核要求。

所要求提交的数据项目已经标准化，可以满足海关和相关规定验核机构的共同要求。海关和相关机构对提交的数据实现共享，减少了数据重复申报所耗费的时间，从而促进了整体效率的提高。

七、出口通关系统

出口通关系统利用海关网络与贸易商、报关行、承运人和其他相关贸易机构等进行连接，向其提供申报和结果通知等方面的“无纸通关”服务。

该系统由出口通关系统、出口通关信息服务和统计数据等组成。出口通关系统包括接受申报、审查、查验和修改等服务。监管方的菜单包括批准、审查和查验的标准管理和筛选分配以及状态查询的服务。

该系统和进口通关系统、货物管理系统以及关税退税系统相连接，以实现相互之间的功能互补。

八、进口通关系统

进口通关系统利用海关网络与贸易商、报关行、承运人和其他相关贸易机构等相连接，向其提供申报和结果通知等方面的“无纸通关”服务。

该系统由进口申报和审查、进口货物选择查验、商标保护、手册通关和数据维护等服务组成。

该系统连接银行和验核机构，客户能够在线支付关税，也可以像在出口通关系统中那样，以电子方式提交验核申请。

九、货物管理系统

货物管理系统旨在结合进出口通关系统，监管物流全过程，包括货物运抵、卸载、运输、入境、通关及放行。该系统通过毛重监管系统下快速便捷的电子单证方式办理货物通关手续（如：舱单汇总/递交，监管运输通知，运入/运出通知）。

来自不同航空公司、船公司和货代公司的总运单和分运单信息被自动归并到舱单汇总系统，并向海关发送。这为物流企业和海关都提供了便利和效率。

十、客户导向型物流信息系统

客户导向型物流信息系统是以网络为基础，以客户为本的物流信息系统，其目的在于提升海关管理的质量和效率。它可为贸易商追踪查询每一票进口货物的实时货物处理信息，减少时间成本，确保货物即时派送。

客户导向型物流信息系统为进口商提供货物过去的、当前的和未来的处理情况，自动计算货物进口手续一般用时和标准偏差。

客户导向型物流信息系统利用现有货物管理系统和进口通关系统的时间测算功能对货物进行从运抵到放行的全程追踪。

十一、退税系统

海关退税是指特定情况下的部分或全额关税退还。

海关退税系统连接海关业务链中的贸易商、报关公司、金融机构。该系统根据计算机内的申报和关税缴纳记录验核退税请求，然后才把退还的税款汇入申请人的银行账户。

十二、旅客预检信息系统

旅客预检信息系统以打造高效的旅客识别系统为目标而开发，既能避免对旅客的不必要查验，又能提高对高风险旅客的识别精确度。

该系统根据航空公司在航班抵达前提供的电子数据和出入境管理机构提供的入境旅客信息，选择出高风险旅客，设置查验。该系统能精确地识别出高风险旅客，从而确保守法旅客快速通关。

十三、事后审计系统

事后审计系统进一步核查已经批准的申报和退税，以查明是否存在低价申报、关税税率适用错误，或者不当退税的情况。

该系统包括校验选择和退税选择，二者各有单独的选择标准。

十四、执行信息系统

执行信息系统主要用于有效预防滥用简化的通关程序进行不正当的非法贸易活动。

海关使用银行、出入境管理机构提供的外部数据的同时，对计算机系统中的内部数据进行维护，以此实现对监控名单上的进出口商进行严密监管。

十五、走私预警系统

近年来，走私活动日益智能化、国际化，走私量也相当惊人，引发了各国对传统应对措施中信息采集、分析和反应能力方面的质疑。走私预警系统用于对走私活动进行预测，提前防范，预防走私。

十六、海关数据库

海关数据库是一个综合数据库，通过汇集 1000 条不同种类的内部数据以及各种外部信息帮助进行有效信息分析，并且对数据进行组织，以加快分析速度。

特定海关业务环节（如：通关，稽查）所需数据被提取、整合，存储于每个业务环节的数据中心。为了进行便捷和多维分析，数据中心的数据以三维立体形式存储。该系统同时提供“用户界面”，以确保数据安全，分析快速，以及数据提供符合每个业务环节的特定需要。

十七、UNI－PASS 的优势

（一）大大缩短通关时间

进口通关时间由 20 世纪 90 年代初的超过 2 天缩减到 1.5 小时，出口通关时间由超过 1 天缩减为不到 2 分钟。

（二）减少物流成本

简化的单证和程序实现了物流便利通畅，每年可节约物流成本 38 亿美元，提升了企业生产力和国家竞争力。

（三）随时随地的一站式通关服务

客户可以通过计算机网络提交所需资料及申报，查询处理情况，而不用亲自跑到海关现场。此外，验核要求、审批、缴税、退税和税单签发程序都通过联通各验核机构和银行的计算机网络处理，不需要跑到海关办公地点办理。

注：本文摘自韩国海关 UNI－PASS 通关系统介绍手册，由韩国海关提供。

UNI - PASS Korean Customs Service

(Obtained from Korea Customs Service Manual of UNI - PASS System)
(Translated by Li Tingting, Pudong International Airport Customs House and Zhuang Shuo, Foreing Affairs Office of General Office)

1. Korea Customs UNI - PASS Information Association (CUPIA)

(1) Introduction of CUPIA

CUPIA is a non - profit, specialized organization in supporting customs modernization established by Korea Customs Service.

i. Establishment

- Non - profit Organization established by Korea Customs Service (KCS) to introduce UNI - PASS to foreign customs and relevant authorities.

ii. Organization

- 50 members formed by ex/current KCS officers and IT experts.
- Korea Custom officers and Korea Customs and Trade Development Institute officers are currently dispatched to CUPIA.

iii. Major Services

- Consulting on foreign customs business process & legal framework redesigning.
- Consulting on Information Technology for foreign customs.
- R&D, Consulting, Operation and Maintenance for Korea Customs Service.

- Operation and Maintenance of UNI – PASS System.

(2) Main Services

CUPIA performs in cooperation with relevant authorities in Customs modernization.

i. Consulting

- BPR and ISP for Customs Modernization/ Computerization/ Automatization.
- IT consulting such as Information Strategy Planning, Project Audit, and etc.
- Risk Management and supervision.

ii. Feasibility Study

- Conduct Feasibility Study on customs modernization for foreign customs authorities.

iii. R&D

- Customs Data Model R&D and Standardization.
- BPR/ISP for UCR (business process reengineering, Internet Service Provider, Unique Consignment Reference number)

iv. System Development

- Implementing e – Customs Systems
- Support for procurement process and system development audit
- Risk Management

v. Operation & Management

- Operation and Maintenance of UNI – PASS
- Client service call center of Korea Customs Service

(3) Major Projects (including future projects)

CUPIA provides various countries with know – how and experience of UNI –

PASS.

Implementation: Dominican Republic Customs, Mongolia Customs

- BPR/ISP performance for Customs Modernization Project
- Implementation of UNI – PASS

IT Consulting & Feasibility Study: Nepal Customs, Kenya Customs, Tanzania Customs, Guatemala Customs, Azerbaijan Customs, Kazakhstan Customs, Vietnam Customs

- IT consulting for foreign Customs Administration System
- Feasibility Studies for Customs Modernization/ Computerization Project.

2. History of Customs Information System

(1) 1974 – 1992 Simple use of computer

– Trade statistics (1974)

– Simple online data on air cargo

(2) 1992 – 1998 EDI clearance automation

6 – year plan for clearance automation (1992 – 1998):

100% computerized Customs procedures, efficient and accurate cargo control from arrival to release.

– Ex/Import clearance system (1994 – 1996)

– Duty drawback system (1997)

– Ex/Import cargo system (1997 – 1998)

(3) 1998 – 2003 Facilitating information management, supporting decision – making process

Computerization of investigation, surveillance, audit procedures, and APIS facilitated use of information.

– Enforcement system (1999)

– Passenger information system (2000)
– Post – Audit System (2001)
– Knowledge Management System (KMS, 2002)
– Customs Data Warehouse (CDW, 2003)

(4) 2003 – 2005 Internet Clearance Portal

Internet clearance system based on the universal use of the internet and IT development: raising convenience of clients and system capabilities.
– Internet Classification system (2004)
– Internet civil claims system (2004)
– Internet export clearance system (2004)
– Internet import clearance system (2005)

(5) 2006 – 2010 Realizing ubiquitous Customs

Invisible, value – generating u – Customs: providing Customs service anytime/anywhere
– One – stop service for clearance and logistics
– Non – stop global supply chain helping SCM
– Intelligent risk management
– Real – time, tailored information service

In the face of the rapid increase in the international trade volume, Korea Customs Service embarked on the development of EDI (Electronic Data Interchange) system in an effort to bring greater efficiency in the Customs administration.

In 1992, KCS came up with the "6 – year Plan for EDI Clearance Automation" aiming to establish a swift and accurate clearance system, and succeeded in 100% computerization of import and export clearance in 1998. In 1999, the enforcement information system was installed as a means to effectively deal with illegitimate trade activities that misuse the simplified clearance procedures.

With the 3 – year plan for development of information management system drawn up in 2001, Knowledge Management System and Customs Data Warehouse have been created to improve efficiency and productivity by enabling real – time use of administrative knowledge and systematic risk management.

In 2005, KCS completed the establishment of Single Window, a one – stop shop for all clearance services, in participation of eight requirement verification agencies, so that traders can obtain as many as ten government requirements (e. g. food inspection) with one – time submission of declaration data.

Meanwhile, KCS launched the internet clearance service by combining the EDI process with the internet declaration system. With that, Korea Customs Service is making great strides towards the realization of the ubiquitous Customs.

3. A New Name for e – Clearance System, UNI – PASS

UNI – PASS, the brand name of the e – clearance system, refers to seven systems among those related to customs administration that perform core functions of export/import e – Clearance on a consistent basis, namely: export clearance system, import clearance system, duty collection system, export/ import cargo management system, duty drawback system, and the clearance Single Window. The e – clearance system, the most advanced product of customs informatization, has been developed through vibrant cooperation with customs clients to actively respond to changes in global trade environment by leveraging the latest information technologies.

UNI – PASS, the brand name of the e – clearance system, take multiple meanings. It provides unified service for export/ import clearance, duty payment, duty drawback, and requirement confirmation all at one stop. It has adopted global standards for universal use by all countries around the world. It has a unique feature of cargo tracking service, where the client can access real – time cargo processing information, a service provided nowhere else in the world. "Pass" expresses the speediness of clearance. The name also embeds the meaning of ubiquitous connection by clients, non – stop cargo flow, interfaceable system, and the importance of client participation for its development and improvement.

4. Representative Brand of KCS

Korea Customs e – Clearance System: UNI – PASS

Brand Core

- Free and Enjoyable Customs Clearance.

Brand Vision

- Global Top e – Clearance system made by Korea & used by the world.

Brand Mission

- One – stop clearance service easily accessible anytime & anywhere.

Brand Value

- A customs clearance model born in Korea and used by the world, saving time and cost for clients.

5. Internet Clearance Portal

- With the universal use of the internet, and a number of areas of business (e. g. finance, logistics) wired to the world wide web, KCS established the convenient and cost – effective Internet Clearance Portal by adding advanced functions to the existing EDI system.
- Customs procedures can be carried out at home, at the office, on the production site, or at any other places with the internet connection through the Internet Clearance Portal which overcomes the geographical barriers of the past EDI system.

6. Single Window

- The Single Window provides a platform for one – stop service for all clearance procedures, so that traders can submit declaration and acquire government requirements with one – time electronic submission of data to the Customs.

• The data items to be submitted have been standardized for the common use by Customs and requirement verification agencies. The time for entering overlapping data items repeatedly is saved, while the data sharing boosts overall efficiency.

7. Export Clearance System

• The export clearance system provides paperless environment for declaration and result notification by connecting traders, Customs brokers, carriers, and trade – related agencies in the Customs network.

• The system consists of export clearance system, export clearance information service, and statistical data. Inside the export clearance system are: receipt of declaration, screening, inspection, and modification. Supervisors' menu includes approval, criteria management and case allotment for screening and inspection, and status inquiry.

• The system is connected with import clearance system, cargo management system, and duty drawback system providing one another with complementary functions.

8. Import Clearance System

• The import clearance system provides paperless environment for declaration and result notification by connecting traders, Customs brokers, carriers, and trade – related agencies in the Customs network.

• The system consists of import declaration and screening, imported cargo selectivity (C/S), trademark protection, carnet clearance, and data maintenance.

With banks and verification agencies connected in the system, duty can be paid through the internet and requirement verification requests are submitted electronically like in the export clearance system.

9. Cargo Management System

• The cargo management system is to monitor the flow of cargo throughout all phases of cargo movement: arrival, unloading, transportation, entry, clearance, and release, in connection with im/export clearance systems. The system processes cargo clearance procedures (e. g. manifest consolidation/submission, bonded transportation notice, carry in/out notice) by fast and convenient electronic documentation under the gross weight monitoring system.

• Both Master and House Manifests from different air/shipping lines and forwarders are automatically consolidated in the MFCS (Manifest Consolidation System) and sent to the Customs. This serves for the convenience and efficiency of logistics companies as well as the Customs.

10. Client Oriented Logistics Information System (CLIS)

• CLIS is the web – based client oriented logistics information system aimed at improving quality and efficiency of Customs Administration. It provides cargo tracking information of every imported cargo to trade community with real – time information on cargo processing to reduce time and ensure just – in – time cargo delivery.

• CLIS informs importers of cargo processing status of the past, present and future, and calculates automatically the average time consumed for import cargo processing and standard deviation.

• CLIS tracks imported cargos from arrival to release, utilizing time – measuring functions of existing CMS and ICS.

11. Duty Drawback System

• Customs duty drawback means a refund of paid import duty in part or in full when certain conditions are met.

• The duty drawback system connects traders, Customs brokers, financial institutions in the Customs network. P/L drawback request is examined based on the declaration and duty payment record stored in the computer system, before the refund is remitted to the bank account of the requesting person.

12. Advance Passenger Information System (APIS)

• APIS has been developed as an efficient passenger targeting system in order to avoid unnecessary inspection while raising accuracy in identifying high – risk passengers.

• High – risk passengers are selected for inspection based on the electronic data submitted by airlines prior to arrival and the inbound passenger information provided by the immigration authority. The system accurately identifies high – risk passengers while ensuring speedier clearance for law – abiding passengers.

13. Post – audit System

• The post – audit system is to further examine declarations and drawbacks that are already approved, in order to find out any cases of undervalued declaration, false application of tariff rate, or inadequate drawback.

• The system consists of Review Selectivity (R/S) and Drawback Selectivity (D/S), each of which has unique selection criteria.

14. Enforcement Information System

- The enforcement information system has been developed to effectively prevent illicit and unlawful trade activities that misuse the simplified features of clearance procedures.
- Customs keeps close tabs on importers and exporters on the watch list, and maintains internal database in the computer system, while utilizing external data provided by banks, immigration authority, etc.

15. Smuggling Alert System (SAS)

- Recently the world has witnessed smuggling businesses increasingly intelligent and international with remarkable magnitude, that raised questions about the capabilities of conventional counter measures: information collection, analysis, and reaction. SAS has been developed to predict future smuggling activities to halt them in a preemptive manner.
- Major items, smuggling patterns of each item, and affecting factors are identified and analyzed using CDW, SPSS, and other statistical tools in order to investigate the statistical co-relation between the factors and smuggling activities. With that, different levels of smuggling risks are established which make possible to deter smuggling preemptively by issuing immediate alerts when smuggling movement is detected.

16. Customs Data Warehouse (CDW)

- Customs Data Warehouse is a comprehensive database that helps efficient information analysis by consolidating 1, 000 different types of internal data with various external information, and organizing the data in a way to expedite analysis activities.

• Data required for a specific domain of Customs work (e. g. clearance, investigation) are extracted and consolidated to be stored in the DM (Data Mart) of each domain. The DM data is stored in the three – dimensional "cube" form for convenient and multi – dimensional analysis. The system also provides the "user view" which ensures data protection, faster analysis, and provision of data tailored to each domain.

17. Benefits of UNI – PASS

(1) Substantial drop in clearance time

Import clearance time has been reduced to 1. 5 hours down from over 2 days in the early 1990s, while export clearance time dropped from over 1 day to less than 2 minutes.

(2) Reduction of logistical cost

Smooth logistics flow facilitated by simplified documentation and procedures have led to the annual saving of 3. 8 billion USD logistical cost, raising productivity of businesses and national competitiveness.

(3) One – stop clearance service anytime and anywhere

Clients can submit a declaration with other required documents and inquire into the processing status through the computer network without having to visit Customs office in person. In addition, procedures for requirement verification request, approval, tax payment, drawback, and tax bill issuance are all processed without the need to visit the Customs office through the computer network that connects verification agencies and banks.

Article obtained from Korea Customs Service Manual of UNI – PASS System, courtesy of Korea Customs.

协调的边境管理——加拿大协调的边境管理

（摘自《世界海关组织新闻》2009 年 6 月 总第 59 期）

（浦东机场海关　夏虹　译）

加拿大向贸易和旅客开放近 9000 公里长的边境，在支持经济繁荣的同时，确保加拿大高度有效的边境管理。为了实现这一目标，5 年来，加拿大政府采取了协调的边境管理模式。

加拿大模式将进出境货物和人员流动的所有主要管理方进行集中，形成单一组织机构，即加拿大边境服务署。加拿大边境服务署汇集了过去分散在三个组织中的几个重要功能和职能：加拿大海关和税务总署中的海关业务；加拿大公民和移民署的情报、拦截和执法业务；以及加拿大食品检验局所负责的进口检验业务等。同时，加拿大边境服务署也是加拿大安全一揽子计划的一部分。加拿大安全一揽子计划始于 2003 年，其目的为确保所有联邦部门和机构协调运作，负责保护国家安全、应急管理、执法及更正、犯罪预防和边境服务的职责。

过去 5 年来，加拿大边境服务署已发展成为一个综合性的边境管理机构，在一个高度复杂的环境中，提供着有效进出境管理方案和服务。加拿大边境事务署负责处理通过国内外 1200 个服务站的每年近 1 亿人次、4000 亿加元贸易量的事务。通过审慎的资源管理并不断寻求机遇，加拿大边境服务署提供了广泛的人员与货物进出境的方案，以达到提高工作效益和降低成本的目的。

2008 年 12 月 12 日，加拿大边境服务署举行了五周年庆典。肯定取得的成绩，并开始构想将来的边境整合方案。“边境一体化是从边境管理角度，统一多机构管理中的各项责任、地点，服务和人员的边境管理模式。”加拿大边境事务署主席斯蒂芬·里格比说。“为了实现这一目标，加拿大边境服务署的改革议程将集中于推动边境概念外延，提高风险管理能力，强化该机构的公众服务导向，加强我们与合作伙伴间的关系，努力实现资源优化配置。”里格比先生补充道。

一、风险管理

现代化边境管理的关键原则在于有能力识别、评估并尽可能在源头减轻加拿大面临的风险。作为风险管理战略的一部分，加拿大边境服务署将继续推动边境管理活动与自然的边境的分离。只有最适宜在边境开展的管理活动将继续进行。

二、客户服务

加拿大边境事务署将通过设立透明的服务标准，再次建立起一个新的、以服务为导向的战略发展重点。这将使客户对事务署的服务有明确的期望，通过可预见的服务水平，来进一步促进国际贸易流通。同时，加拿大边境事务署认识到，每一个官员均对该机构履行其职责发挥着重要作用。同世界上其他国家的海关组织一样，加拿大边境事务署的官员们不断提醒自己要面对现实，提高警惕，谨慎从事。除此以外，边境事务署实施了以诚信和专业标准为主的战略，确保员工不论何时，真实面对他们的个人行为和活动，坚持最高操守标准和专业精神。高度诚信要求将反映在所有的加拿大边境服务方案和系统中。

作为改进服务导向重点工作的一部分，加拿大边境事务署正在发起和协调一项代表联邦 10 个部门和机构的“单一窗口”行动。这是一项针对以商业主体为首要服务对象的项目。该计划将通过创建单一电子接口，优化所有先进商业贸易数据收集，为企业提供满足进出口监管要求的信息。这也有利于增加贸易团体的竞争力，减少延误，提高货物通关效率，缩短放行时间。

三、战略伙伴关系

在协调的边境管理模式下，与伙伴合作极其重要。由于历史渊源，地源上的邻近，共同的边境，以及长期的贸易和经济关系，加拿大和美国之间有牢固的双边关系。“我们日益融洽，并且深信不疑，我们将继续携手合作，共享知识，确保我们的人民安全，防范与边境相关的风险，同时便利货物和人员合法进出境，”里格比先生说。

战略伙伴不仅限于美国。我们正在重新定义和深化与其他伙伴的合作。集装箱安全倡议，我们与美国海关互助协定以及相互承认安排等，将为减少延误和重复作业作出贡献。此外，我们正在研究如何进一步使我们信任的贸易伙伴和旅客们获益，同时扩大授信范围，确保为他们提供实实在在的利益。

该机构的主要业务成效指标包括：最佳的现代管理；强有力的核心政策能力；在该领域方案的持续执行能力；在财政约束条件下，以合理环境资源分配为目标，创新使用技术。

四、结论

总之，加拿大边境服务署已建立起坚实的基础，并取得了巨大进步。在前所未有的加强安全的环境下，该机构整合了以往三个机构。今天，加拿大边境服务署提供了多种创新方案，不仅确保加拿大边境安全，同时便利合法贸易和旅行。“该机构不断革新的一体化边境管理，将不断推进加拿大边境服务署逐渐接近我们实现可持续发展的目标，”斯蒂芬·里格比总结道。

注：本文原文发表于2009年6月版《世界海关组织新闻》杂志，由世界海关组织提供（www. wcoomd. org）。

Integrated Border Management in Canada

(Extracted from "*WCO News*", June 2009, No. 59)
(Translated by Xia Hong, Pudong International Airport Customs House)

Keeping Canada's nearly 9, 000 kilometers – long border open to travel and trade in order to support economic prosperity while protecting Canadians requires highly effective management of border operations. To attain this goal, five years ago the Government of Canada adopted an integrated border management model.

Canada's model brought together all the major players involved in managing the movement of goods and people into Canada to form one organization, the Canada Border Services Agency (CBSA). The CBSA combined several key functions previously spread among three organizations: the Customs programme from the Canada Customs and Revenue Agency; the Intelligence, Interdiction and Enforcement programme from Citizenship and Immigration Canada; and the Import Inspection at Ports of Entry programme from the Canadian Food Inspection Agency. At the same time, the CBSA became part of the Public Safety Canada portfolio that was created in 2003 to ensure coordination across all federal departments and agencies responsible for national security, emergency management, law enforcement, corrections, crime prevention and border services.

Over the past five years, the CBSA has evolved into an integrated border management agency, delivering its programmes and services in a highly complex environment. The CBSA is responsible for processing close to 100 million people and 400 billion Canadian Dollars in trade each year at approximately 1, 200 points of service across Canada and some international locations. Within this context, and by prudently managing resources and continually seeking opportunities to improve operational and cost efficiencies, the Agency delivers a wide range of programmes and services for people and goods.

On December 12, 2008, the CBSA celebrated its fifth anniversary. Achievements were recognized and a renewed vision of border integrity was launched for the future. "Border integrity is a view of border management that unifies the administration of multiple responsibilities, locations, services and people across the Agency," said CBSA President Stephen Rigby. "To achieve this, the CBSA's change agenda will focus on improving our capacity to manage risk by pushing the border out, enhancing the Agency's public service orientation, strengthening our partnerships and allocating our resources in an optimal fashion," Mr. Rigby added.

1. Risk Management

A key tenet of modern border management is to identify, assess and mitigate risks to Canada as close to their source as possible. As part of its risk management strategy, the CBSA will continue to move border management activity away from the physical border. Only those activities best performed at the border will be carried out there.

2. Client Service

The CBSA will place a renewed focus on service orientation through the development of transparent service standards. This will enable clear service expectations for clients and facilitate the flow of trade through predictable service levels. The CBSA recognizes that every single employee plays an important role in helping the Agency fulfill its mandate. As with every Customs organization in the world, CBSA employees are constantly exposed to realities that call for vigilance and caution. The CBSA has embarked on an Integrity and Professional Standards

Strategy to ensure that employees reflect and uphold the highest standards of integrity and professionalism in their personal conduct and activities on and off duty. This same high level of integrity will be reflected in all CBSA programmes and systems.

As part of its focus on improved service orientation, the CBSA is coordinating a 'single window' initiative on behalf of ten federal departments and agencies. This is a key priority for commercial stakeholders. The initiative will streamline the collection of advance commercial trade data by creating a single electronic interface for businesses to submit information to meet import and export regulatory requirements. It will also benefit the trade community by increasing competitiveness, reducing delays and improving the clearance and release times of goods.

3. Partnerships

It is impossible to overstate the importance of cooperation with partners in the integrated border management model. Historical ties, proximity, a shared border and long – standing trade and economic relations have forged a strong bilateral relationship between Canada and the United States. "Our rapport grows stronger each year and I feel certain that the depth of our cooperation will remain unchanged. We will continue to work together and share knowledge to ensure our populations are safe and secure from border – related risks and to facilitate the legitimate transit of goods and people crossing our shared border," said Mr. Rigby.

Strategic partners are not limited to the United States. We are redefining and deepening our cooperation with other partners too. The Container Security Initiative, our Customs Mutual Assistance Agreements as well as our mutual recognition arrangement with the United States are contributing to reduce delays and duplications. Additionally, we will be looking for ways to further expand the benefits and membership of our trusted trader and travelers programmes and ensure they provide tangible benefits.

The Agency's key business results enablers include: optimal modern management; strong policy capacity at the core; consistent programme delivery in the field; and innovative use of technologies will focus our resource allocation in an environment of fiscal constraint.

4. Conclusion

Overall, the CBSA has a solid foundation on which to build and enormous progress has been made. The Agency has integrated three legacy organizations amid an unprecedented intensification of the security environment. Today the CBSA delivers many innovative programmes to secure Canada's border while allowing the flow of legitimate trade and travel. "The Agency's integrated border management, enhanced by our change agenda, will move the CBSA towards the sustainable achievement of our goals," concluded Stephen Rigby.

Article published in the June 2009 edition of the WCO News magazine, courtesy of the World Customs Organization - www.wcoomd.org.

协调的边境管理——欧盟协调的边境管理

（摘自《世界海关组织新闻》2009年6月 总第59期）

（浦东机场海关　夏虹　整理翻译）

2007年6月，世界海关组织理事会同意欧洲联盟加入世界海关组织。虽然并非正式成员，欧盟的目标是把自己用40年发展关税联盟的独特经验，推广为在全球范围内的海关行动战略。

一、欧盟协调边境管理简介

欧盟虽然属于同一关境，但其27个成员国均拥有独立且独特的国家行政模式。欧盟所谓协调的边境管理，即一些成员国选择通过建立本国的边境机构来横向协调；一些成员国通过机构间签订正式协议的方式来协调彼此行为；还有一些完全依赖非正式的协调安排。因此，协调边境管理的具体情况，包括国家单一窗口的发展应用，仍然牢牢掌握在欧盟成员国自己的手中。然而，为了真正实现单一行政管理在这些国家的发展，欧盟采用在欧盟范围内统一指导监测的方式，以确保工作协调，衔接顺畅。

本着以上提出的精神，我想在更广泛的欧洲范围内，提出一些概念性的、与发展协调边境管理有关的想法，与大家一起分享一些关于在整个欧盟范围内实现协调边境管理特征的想法，告诉大家将在2009年7月1日开始在欧盟开展的革命性的海关边境管理，同时添加了一些个人意见和可能在全球适用的结论。

二、协调

无可否认，在战略合作与协调该如何定义，如何达成一致意见并付诸实践方面，欧盟已开展了大量的工作，具有相当长时间的经验。在这方面，我相信，欧盟的历史是一种优势，可以用来作为基准。经过50多年的不懈努力，可以说大多数欧洲人对一体化合作和协调都略知一二。在共同立法的基础上，努力实现共同的目标和方向，欧洲一直是，并将始终是一个相当独特的协调边境管理的测试实验室。这肯定是我们发展的优势。

三、欧盟边境

然而，欧洲一体化经验的另一面是，在不同政策领域，欧盟边境的发展似乎并不协调。具有讽刺意味是，由于历史和政治的原因，虽然欧洲大陆一体化消除了一个又一个障碍，最终实现人员、货物、服务和资金在其边境内自由流通，但其外部边境问题却日益复杂。

由成员国海关法规定义的欧盟海关关境，即通常意义上的“欧盟边境”，然而，由于历史原因，海关关区的大小不完全等同实际欧盟领土的大小。比如适用于人员流动的边境，如加入申根公约地区的边境，包括25个欧洲国家和3个非欧盟国家（冰岛，挪威和瑞士），但不包括5个欧盟成员国，它们选择退出（爱尔兰和英国）或执行过渡期（保加利亚、塞浦路斯和罗马尼亚）。

实际上，这意味着欧共体成员国将根据不同的法规运用不同的管理方式管理各自的边境。正如大多数欧洲机场物流情况所清楚地表明的，由于各自所处地理位置的限制，在实践中，对于什么是“协调”，不同地点必然设置不一样的参数；这当然需要高度的创造性和务实性，来定义边境管理的协调方式。机场的例子也说明当讨论边境协调管理时，我们为何需要考虑运输方式的概念——一种适用于海上交通的协调边境管理措施或办法不一定适用于陆地边境，反之亦然。

四、管理

那么，究竟我们的边境“管理”意味着什么？我们又期望得到些什么？欧共体的海关和移民立法对此分别定义为“控制”和“边境控制”——但这些与广义上的“管理”边境都相去甚远。事实上，“管理边境”的内容将随着管理部门所要完成任务和扮演角色的不同而有所区别。运输部门（如港口和机场管理部门）、边防部队、海关和刑事调查人员将从事不同的边境管理活动。

但是，广义上，在跨越边境的各个时刻，边境管理可以认为包括以下类型的活动：提前信息收集（从业界和其他地方）；风险评估与确保相关跨境的货物、人员、动物、交通工具的真实与守法；为确保安全现场处理和控制人员和货物流动；和在货物到达后和查验要求已经得到满足的前提下，办理有关海关出入境报关手续。

每个管理元素可以被分解、分析和分别定义——以通关为目的的协调信息收集可能意味着向电子海关单一窗口网站提交资料，却没有必要亲自前往海关。而协调管制措施，则需要管理部门之间组织架构与行动上更好地现场协作。

五、角色和责任

为了区别部门间各自的角色和作用，非常有必要研究边境管理的过程中相关的时间表，明确每个部门与哪个时间点有关，从而确定各自的角色。从海关清关观点来讲有 3 个时间要点：到达前阶段、货物申报阶段以及清关阶段。

通过将各部门放入各自的介入时间，无论关系到货物、乘客或交通工具，其各自的角色则更加明显。例如，运输管理部门主要涉及抵达前收集和传播信息。它们是第一个获取到达信息的，无论到达的是什么，都可以向其他部门传播信息，以起到有价值的协调功能。

目前，在欧洲，从海关角度理解的协调边境管理，始于商品申报和海关清关阶段。这是海关一直以来获取信息和宏观掌控的最佳领域，并且是建立协调机制的最佳时机，例如单一窗口提交申请资料等。

六、不断推进改革

这是我所描述的协调边境管理在欧洲的日益体现。2009 年 7 月 1 日，有关欧盟海关编码的“安全修正案”正式实施，欧盟海关将开始收集所有进出欧盟的商品抵达前和出发前的电子资料。从协调边境管理与海关的角度来看，这意味着海关将视野从传统的清关领域扩大到抵达前的领域。在包括海关执行风险分析方面等许多方面，这都将是革命性的。

然而，正如现今发生的巨大变化，我们仍应小心谨慎地随环境确定我们的角色，没有任何先验理由说明海关应起到抵达前协调边境管理的核心作用。随着项目进入总结声明阶段，为了满足程序和信息技术需求，到达前阶段仍然没有囊括在海关立法中，而是由外部的，如国际海事组织便利委员会或国际航空运输协会记录在案。因此，实质上，关于“海关”单一窗口的讨论仍将局限在传统的海关业务领域内，在这个传统领域，海关无疑是最佳的接收所有商品过境信息的唯一权威机构。

同时，随着跨境人员流动和交通工具的发展，最终将实现所有的系统在抵达前阶段的相互连接，我们可以顺应这样的形势做出更多的努力。例如，有关人员和/或交通安排的信息互补，可能对准确评估货物的风险状况至关重要。

七、因地制宜

在欧洲，显然我们至少有必要反思与边境管理有关的角色和责任。利益相关国家和区域，需要就如何改进协调边境管理开展更多的对话。很清楚的是，我们需要因地制宜，协调的边境管理需要一整套的解决办法，而不是单一的跨越所有不同国家和运输模式的简单模式。信息技术将是未来的重要推动者，但它不应该被看做实现协调边境管理的唯一因素。

八、收益

最后，我想和大家分享关于协调边境管理的一个非常普遍的问题：协调边境管理在使用中，其核心概念经常被每一个权力机构冠以一系列不同的定义。不必用华丽的辞藻给它们定义，我建议暂时把定义问题放在一边，而提出以下问题：边境协调管理可以给所有利益相关者提供什么收益和好处？以及如何才能获得这些好处？这就是我向欧盟海关和其他欧洲相关部门呼吁和提倡的关键。

作为世界海关组织不可或缺的组成部分，欧盟现在有这样的一个独特的机会，能与大家一起分享经验，并在全球范围内寻求最佳做法。我深信，全球对话将是我们更好地发展协调边境管理模式和方法的关键，这也将是我们成功的关键。

注：本文原文发表于2009年6月版《世界海关组织新闻》杂志，由世界海关组织提供（www. wcoomd. org）。

Border Management in the European Union

(Extracted from "*WCO News*", June 2009, No. 59)

(Translated by Xia Hong, Pudong International Airport Customs House)

In June 2007 the WCO Council agreed to the request of the European Communities to join the WCO. While not yet a full member, the EC aims to bring its own unique experience of 40 years of developing a Customs Union to the table of strategic discussions on developing Customs activity at global level.

1. Coordinated border management in Europe

Although a single Customs area, the 27 Member States (MS) of the European Union (EU) all have independent and unique national administrative models. In terms of coordinated border management (CBM), this means that some MS have chosen to 'coordinate' horizontally by establishing national border agencies; Some have separate authorities that coordinate their activities on the basis of formal agreements; still others rely on completely informal coordination arrangements. Thus, the details of CBM, including the development of national Single Window applications, are still very much in the hands of EU MS. However, in order to truly act as a single administration, these national developments are monitored and guided at EU level to ensure harmonized approaches and interfaces.

In that vein, I would like to offer some 'arms - length' thoughts on the broader European landscape relating to the development of coordinated border management (CBM). I would like to share a few thoughts about the peculiarities of CBM in the EU in general, about the revolution that European Customs border management is about to undergo on 1st July 2009, and add some prescriptive views and potentially globally applicable conclusions.

2. Coordination

Undeniably, the EU has had a lot of practice and a long history of defining, agreeing and implementing strategies of integration and coordination. In this respect, I believe that the European Union's history is a strength and can be used as a benchmark. With over 50 years of hands – on experience, Europeans arguably know a thing or two about integration and coordination. Working towards shared aims and objectives on the basis of common legislation, Europe has been and remains quite a unique test laboratory for coordinated border management. This is certainly our strength.

3. EU borders

The flip side of the coin of the European integration experience, however, is that the EU's borders have developed in a seemingly uncoordinated way across policy areas. Although the result of historical and political reasons, it could understandably be considered vaguely ironic that while the European continent has integrated and removed obstacle after obstacle to the free circulation of people, goods, services and money within its borders, its external borders have developed into an increasingly complex set.

The borders of the EU Customs territory, as defined by community Customs legislation correspond to a great extent to the layman's understanding of ' EU borders ' . However, due to historical reasons, the Customs territory is not fully equivalent to those of the physical EU territory as such. More significantly still, the borders applicable to the movement of people, i. e. that of the Schengen Area, include 25 European countries, including three non – EU countries (Iceland, Norway and Switzerland) and exclude five EU members either through opt – out (Ireland and the UK) or transitional periods for implementation (Bulgaria, Cyprus and Romania).

In practice this means that different authorities acting on the basis of different EC legislation are preoccupied with the management of different borders. As the logistics of most European airports easily illustrates, being physically restrained to different locations sets particular parameters on what 'coordination' can mean in practice, and certainly requires a high level of creativity and pragmatism in defining a coordinated approach to border management. The example of airports is also a case in point as to why, when discussing CBM, we need to consider the concept by mode of transport – a CBM approach for maritime traffic will not necessarily be applicable for land borders, and vice versa.

4. Management

So what exactly do we mean and expect from the term border 'management'? EC Customs and immigration legislation respectively define 'control' and 'border controls' – yet there is very little in the prescriptive sense about wider 'management' of borders. In fact, the content of 'managing borders' will differ depending on the role and tasks of the authority in question. Transport authorities (e. g. port and airport authorities), border guards, Customs officials and criminal investigators will engage in different activities with respect to border management.

In a broad sense, however, border management could be thought to encompass the following types of activity at various moments in the process of crossing the border: ex ante collection of information (from the trade and elsewhere); assessment of risks associated with ensuring correct and compliant cross – border movement of goods, persons, animals, modes of transport; processing and controlling of the movement on the spot for security/safety purposes; and processing a Customs declaration for Customs clearance purposes, after the arrival of the goods and checks ex post that the requirements have been fulfilled.

Each of these management elements can be dissected, analyzed and prescribed separately – coordinated information collection for clearance purposes could imply an electronic Customs Single Window portal for submitting data to authorities who never need meet each other physically, whereas coordinated controls would necessitate more organizational and operational collaboration between authorities on the spot.

5. Roles and responsibilities

In distinguishing among authorities and their respective roles, it is useful to examine the timeline associated with the border management process, identify at which point each actor is concerned, and consequently establish what their respective roles are. From a Customs clearance perspective there are three main points in time: the pre – arrival phase; the arrival phase when goods are presented; and the clearance phase.

By placing authorities in the timeframe of their intervention, whether it is related to goods, passengers, or modes of transport, their respective roles become more apparent; for example, transport authorities are mainly involved in pre – arrival and the collection and dissemination of information. They are the first ones to receive information on whatever is arriving, and can provide a valuable coordination function by disseminating that information to other authorities.

Currently in Europe, coordinated border management as we understand it from the Customs perspective starts at the presentation of goods and is most relevant to the clearance phase. This is the traditional area where customs have the best access to information and the broadest overview, and are best placed to put into place coordination mechanisms such as Single Window data submission applications.

6. The revolution ahead

This is where my descriptive of CBM in Europe turns increasingly reflective. On 1 July 2009, the so - called ‘security amendment’ of the EU Customs code will be implemented as Customs begin the collection of electronic pre - arrival and predeparture information on all goods entering and exiting the EU. From the CBM/ Customs perspective, this means that Customs will expand its horizons from its traditional operating sphere of clearance to that of the pre - arrival sphere. In many ways, including in terms of risk analysis carried out by Customs, this will be revolutionary.

Yet, as great a change as this represents, we should be careful about interpreting these new circumstances into new roles——there is no a prior reason why Customs should take a central role with respect to coordination of pre - arrival border management. With the exception of the entry summary declaration, the pre - arrival phase is still not sufficiently covered by customs legislation aiming at procedural and IT requirements while extensively documented for instance by the IMOFAL or IATA. Thus, concretely, discussions about the scope of the ‘Customs’ Single Window will still remain within the traditional area of Customs operations, where Customs undoubtedly is the best placed as the sole authority receiving information on all goods crossing the border.

At the same time, efforts might be made to follow the development in the other two areas of cross - border movement of persons and means of transport to be able to ultimately interconnect all systems already at the pre - arrival stage. The complementary information about people and/or transport movements might for instance prove to be crucial for an accurate assessment of the risk profile of cargo.

7. One size does not fit all

In Europe it is clear that there is a need to at least rethink the roles and responsibilities associated with border management – much dialogue will be needed among stakeholders at national and regional level on how coordination of border management can be improved. What is clear is that no one size will fit all——CBM needs to remain a set of solutions, not a single model across countries and modes of transport. IT will be an important enabler for the future, but it should not be seen as the single factor of success of better CBM.

8. Let's start with the benefits

A final but quite fundamental thought that I wish to share on coordinated border management is a very general one: coördinated border management, in all its uses, is often qualified as a series of different conceptual definitions in which every authority involved tends to imagine itself at the centre of the concept. In the absence of wise words to consolidate these definitions, I would propose to leave the issue of definitions aside and ask the following question: what benefits can coordinated border management provide to all stakeholders, and how best can we achieve these benefits? Certainly this is the approach I would advocate for EU Customs administrations and their European counterpart authorities.

As an integral part of the WCO family, the EC has a unique opportunity to share experiences, and look for best practices globally. I am convinced that in developing models and methods for better coordinated border management, this global dialogue will be a key contributor to our success.

Article published in the June 2009 edition of the WCO News magazine, courtesy of the World Customs Organization – www. wcoomd. org.

书目介绍

“关务通” 品牌图书

书名	作者	定价	书号	出版时间
关务通 · 监管通关系列				
1.**《监管通关政策实用指导手册》**	“关务通 · 监管通关系列”编委会	78.00 元	978-7-80165-907-1	2012 年 10 月第 1 版
2.**《通关实务操作与技巧**——货物、运输工具篇》	“关务通 · 监管通关系列”编委会	48.00 元	978-7-80165-909-5	2012 年 10 月第 1 版
3.**《通关实务操作与技巧**——进出境物品篇》	“关务通 · 监管通关系列”编委会	26.00 元	978-7-80165-905-7	2012 年 10 月第 1 版
4.**《通关疑难解惑 720 例》**	“关务通 · 监管通关系列”编委会	48.00 元	978-7-80165-903-3	2012 年 10 月第 1 版
关务通 · 电子口岸系列				
1.**《电子口岸实用功能》**	“关务通 · 电子口岸系列”编委会	32.00 元	978-7-80165-904-0	2012 年 11 月第 1 版
2.**《电子口岸实务操作与技巧**——通关篇》	“关务通 · 电子口岸系列”编委会	55.00 元	978-7-80165-906-4	2012 年 11 月第 1 版
3.**《电子口岸实务操作与技巧**——加贸篇》	“关务通 · 电子口岸系列”编委会	55.00 元	978-7-80165-908-8	2012 年 11 月第 1 版
4.**《电子口岸疑难解惑 400 例》**	“关务通 · 电子口岸系列”编委会	38.00 元	978-7-80165-910-1	2012 年 11 月第 1 版
关务通 · 双语系列				
《国际海关新视野》	上海海关	60.00 元	978-7-80165-918-7	2012 年 12 月第 1 版

待出系列

书名	作者
关务通 · 加贸系列	
1.**《加工贸易实务操作与技巧》**	“关务通 · 加贸系列”编委会
2.**《海关特殊监管区域和保税监管场所实务操作与技巧》**	“关务通 · 加贸系列”编委会
3.**《加工贸易疑难解惑 280 例》**	“关务通 · 加贸系列”编委会
关务通 · 稽查系列	
《小王在海关稽查的日子——企业如何配合海关稽查》	“关务通 · 稽查系列”编委会
关务通 · 企管系列	
《AA 类企业关务秘笈》	“关务通 · 企管系列”编委会